Q.K. Posey

Robertson L. Whiteside

Doctrinal Discourses

By

ROBERTSON L. WHITESIDE

1955

Published by

Inys Whiteside

Denton, Texas

Table of Contents

Table of Contents

(Continued)

To MAMMA RUTH
A consecrated Christian
An ever loving and faithful wife
A devoted mother.

Introduction

My papa, Robertson L. Whiteside, was born in 1869 in the hill country of middle Tennessee, a country made poor by the "Un-Civil" war. His early formal schooling was two or three subscription schools of two or three months' duration. Those were the days of the "three R's". Any one, however, who had "rasselled" with the Blue Backed Speller, McGuffie's Readers, and Ray's Arithmetic had laid a pretty good foundation for learning.

Here in his words are "some reminiscences": "I grew up on Swan Creek in Hickman county, Tennessee, near the line between Hickman and Lewis. Just how it came about I never did know, but there were a few —very few—members of the church in the community. They built a meeting house when I was a small boy, and called it Salem. As I remember the main force that kept that church alive and growing was the teaching and exhorting—and example—of that good man Houston Harder. In the small group were some good singers, which helped much. But no gospel preacher, if I remember correctly, held a series of meetings in that community till after the meeting house was built. In spite of bitter and unreasoning opposition the number of believers gradually increased. At the age of eighteen I was baptized in Swan creek by Brown Godwin. I was born into a fight. About half a mile up the creek was an old Methodist church; beyond that, perhaps a mile and a half, was a Cumberland Presbyterian church; a mile or two beyond that was another Methodist church. Down the other way, less than a quarter of a mile from Salem, was a Primitive Baptist church; across country, on a small tributary of Swan was a sort of hi-bred Baptist church. They washed feet like the Primitives, and called mourners and shouted like the Missionaries of that day. The Primitives never called mourners. If you were one of the elect, God called you in his own good time; and there was nothing anybody could do about it. About three or four miles down the creek was another Cumberland Presbyterian church; below them another Methodist church. It was farthest away of any of them, but close enough to do some long-distance fighting. I think about the time I came on the stage of action, these churches reached their climax of bitterness in their fight against us. One old lady said: "The Campbellites are worse than the devil. The Bible says, 'Resist the devil, and he will flee from you;' but you resist a Campbellite, and he'll flee right at you." So we had to fight or give up. I did not know much about the Bible; but I got a small stiff-back Bible; and worked out a system of chain-reference. In my study I was not hampered by any of these helps in Bible study, nor sermon-outline books. I remember distinctly problems I worked out as I rode a mule across the long ridge between Swan and Cathey's creek."

After papa decided that preaching the gospel was all that would satisfy, he spent some time under Bro. Freed in "West Tennessee Christian College" (Now Freed-Hardeman). The first year of "Nashville Bible School" (Now David Lipscomb College), he was one of the twenty or thirty boys there. Later in the 90's he spent two more years in Nashville Bible School.

By this time he had married, moved to Texas where he farmed for a living but preached anywhere and everywhere opportunity presented itself, because, like the apostle Paul, he felt "Woe is me if I preach not the gospel." Then because he felt he needed to go to school some more he moved with his wife and two small children back to Nashville. After he moved back to Texas from Nashville he continued as before, farming and preaching (in school houses, brush arbors, Baptist meeting houses, Methodist meeting houses any where a door was opened to him). He did not have to have a sign "Church of Christ" up in front of the place where he preached, there was no doubt in the minds of the hearers about what they were hearing.

He was ever a student, knew all the religious trends and in which direction they were headed. He knew what the gospel of Christ is and what it is not.

"In his early manhood brother Whiteside came under the influence of David Lipscomb and J. A. Harding. Bro. Lipscomb was his ideal as a teacher. He encouraged independent thinking and close study of the word of God as a guide. Bro. Whiteside was an independent thinker and a close student all his life. He came as near getting everything out of a passage of Scripture that the Holy Spirit put into it, and then stopping, as any man I ever knew. He was anxious to go every step as far as "that which is written" and just as anxious not to go one step farther. That was his idea of keeping the faith. He departs at a time when he is sorely needed."—Cled E. Wallace— G. G. January 18, 1951.

Publisher's Preface

Because so many of papa's preacher friends and others of the church insisted that his writings over the years be made available to the reading public, this book is published. The articles herein, some lifted from various religious journals (some no longer in existence) and some manuscripts unpublished, cover a period of time from the 1890's to late in the year 1950. It seemed logical to me to arrange the articles in a somewhat chronological order, and this in general is the way they appear. Where there was duplication of ideas or associated ideas the earlier material was combined with or placed with the latter.

For their courtesy in allowing me to use material from their papers, I wish to express my deepest gratitude to the present managements of: *Gospel Advocate, Gospel Guardian,* and *Firm Foundation.* Articles were also lifted from these papers no longer in publication: *Bible Banner, Christian Preacher, Texas Preacher, The Way.*

To the many who have encouraged me in this undertaking, I express my appreciation. Especially do my thanks go to Brethren C. R. Nichol, Claude B. Holcomb, and W. B. Barton, without whose help in editing and arranging the material this book would not have been possible.

In gathering and classifying material I found quite a bit of writing on the Pre-Millennial heresy, which at first I had intended to include in this publication. However, because of the volume of writing on this, I thought best to publish it in a small book to itself. This book will go to press this year. Announcement of time will be made later.

The Church of God

A study of the word used by the Holy Spirit to designate this institution will help us to understand more fully what it is and to see more clearly its boundary lines. It has helped me.

The Greek word is *ekklesia*. This word occurs in classic Greek. With the Greeks it had no religious significance. It means "the called-out," and was applied to any kind of a crowd or assembly of people. It is used a few times in this sense in the New Testament. In Acts, 19th chapter, we have an account of the confusion resulting from Paul's preaching in Ephesus. A raging mob cried, "Great is Diana of the Ephesians." "Some, therefore, cried one thing and some another: for the assembly (ekklesia) was confused." (V. 32). Here it is applied to a howling mob. In the speech of the town clerk, he refers to "a lawful assembly (ekklesia) or court." After his speech "he dismissed the assembly (ekklesia). Here again it applies to the mob. These references will help us to understand Stephen's use of the word in Acts 7:38, referring to the congregation of Israel in the wilderness. They were literally "called out" of Egypt, and any writer of classic Greek might have legitimately used this word (ekklesia) in referring to them.

But why should the Savior use this word to designate his followers? It is believed, of course, that he used it because it expressed exactly the meaning he wished to convey. Are his followers "called out" of anything? Jesus says:

*If ye were of the world the world would love
its own: but because ye are not of the world, but
I have chosen you out of the world, therefore the
world hateth you."* John 15:19.

They were called out from the world, not physically,
but spiritually and morally. In this sense are they
the called out. Hence the use of the word ekklesia in
referring to them. Christ's followers form a class
to themselves, differing from everything else. They
are in the world, but not of the world. They must
keep themselves unspotted from the world. (James
1:27). "Be ye separate." They have been translated
out of darkness into the kingdom of Christ. (Col.
1:13.) There are two classes in the world, viz., those
in the kingdom of Christ and those in the kingdom
of darkness, the saved and the unsaved. Every one
who has obeyed the Savior's invitation to come to
him has crossed the line that separates the kingdom
of darkness from the kingdom of light. He has been
called out of darkness into light, and is therefore one
of the "called out." He is therefore a part, a member, of the church, the ekklesia. He is then a member of the only church God ever designed that people
should be members of.

If, dear reader, you have been called out of darkness into light, I beseech you to live in harmony with
that fact. "Be not unequally yoked together with un-
believers." (2 Cor. 6:14). "Keep yourself unspotted
from the world." (James 1:27).

*And have no fellowship with the unfruitful
works of darkness, but rather reprove them."*
Eph. 5:11.

Imitate Paul:

But God forbid that I should glory save in the cross of our Lord Jesus Christ, by whom the world is crucified unto me and I unto the world. Gal. 6:14.

Be not conformed to this world, but be ye transformed. Rom. 12:2.

Abhor that which is evil; cleave to that which is good. Rom. 12:9.

That unceasing warfare that these passages demand has not been kept up against the world. The church in many places has ceased fighting and has undertaken the job of entertaining the world by music and dancing, kissing bees, fairs, suppers, etc. It would be a ridiculous sight for one army to stop in the thickest of the fight to entertain the enemy by music and dancing. This is just what the church has done in many places. In some places there has been a courtship going on between the church and the world until the marriage has been completed. Satan has skillfully managed the courting and now performs the ceremony. The church has prepared the marriage feast, and together they are making merry, while demons of darkness are dancing to the music of professed Christians. The whole company is drunk on the wine of Babylon.

Anvil Sparks:

If the entire church would work as hard for the Lord as a faction will work to carry its point, nothing could stop its progress.

The Work of the Church

Who guides and controls the work of the church? "And he is the head of the body, the church" (Col. 1:18; see also Eph. 1:22,23). The church is the body of Christ, over which he is head. The head guides and controls the body; the body is subject to the head. Christ guides and controls the church; it is subject to him. The church is a kingdom, an absolute monarchy. Christ is king, has all authority (Matt. 28:18), and must reign till he has conquered all enemies (1 Cor. 15:25).

In New Testament times, the will of Christ as revealed by his chosen representatives was the church's only guide. The New Testament is his revealed will to us.

The New Testament gives us an account of the work done by the church under the direction of inspired men. What is the work of the church? I believe it is comprehended in the three following divisions: First, edifying, or building up, itself; second, relieving the wants of the poor and needy; third, preaching the gospel to people who are not Christians. Let us notice these divisions in their order:

1. It is designed to edify itself, to develop its members in the divine life.

From whom all the body, fitly framed and knit together through that which every joint supplieth, according to the working in due measure of each several part, maketh increase of the body unto the building up of itself in love. Eph. 4:16; see also 1 Cor. 14:4,5,12,17,26.

The church is built up by the proper development of each member. The elders should strive to lead each member into activity in the Christian life. There can be no growth in grace without exercise.

2. The church is a benevolent institution. The needs of each member were supplied (Acts 2:44-45; 4:34-35). The poor widows were cared for in the Jerusalem church (Acts 6:1-6). The disciples at Antioch sent aid to the famine stricken at Jerusalem. (Acts 11:27-30). The churches in Macedonia and Achaia made another contribution for the poor saints at Jerusalem. (Rom. 15:25-31, 2 Cor. 8). Paul instructed Timothy concerning the support of widows, (1 Tim. 5:3-16).

3. The church is a missionary institution; the church sent direct to the missionary. Read carefully 2 Cor. 11:7-9 and Phil. 4:14-18.

Such, in brief, is the work of the church. But human institutions have robbed the church of its work. There are societies for doing every work God intended the church to do. But an objector says: "If they do the work God intends shall be done, they surely do a good work." Yes, the works aimed to be done by these societies are good works. "What objections, then, can you have?" It is God's wisdom that these works shall be done by the church. He planted it for that very purpose, and he who seeks to do them another way sets his wisdom against the wisdom of God. He who goes contrary to God's wisdom cannot succeed. These institutions may grow and prosper for awhile, but "every plant which my father hath not planted shall be rooted up." It is admitted by all that the church should do the work referred to, but society advocates say the church fails to do its duty and we must get up something that will do the work. That is, God undertook to do this work through the church but failed. We will beat him; we will organize societies that will succeed. That is the spirit of it. That is exalting human wisdom above God's wisdom and man's works above God's works. Vain foolish man! Brethren, that is the boldest sort of presumption.

Brother W. H. Timmons compared the societies to mobs. The comparison is true. Every man in a mob knows the government should punish criminals. But sometimes the authorities fail to enforce the laws as they should, and this furnishes a pretext for a mob. When the authorities fail to punish criminals, some get up something that will. This is the only plea for a mob, and it is the only excuse for the existence of a society or institution of any kind to do the work of the church. Men in a mob might say, "If we are doing what should be done, why object to the mob? This puts the mob and the society on the same footing; the principle is the same.

In robbing the church of its work, you rob God of his glory. Eph. 3:10-21.

Anvil Sparks:

A gospel feast is better for the church than a religious spree.

In churches, as in nations, peace at any price generally results in war at any cost.

Making the world safe for democracy may be the proper thing, but no church was ever made safe by democracy.

The Church As A Body

"For even as we have many members in one body, and all the members have not the same office, so we who are many are one body in Christ, and severally members one of another" (Rom. 12:4,5). "For as the body is one and hath many members, and all the members of the body, being many, are one body; so also is Christ" (1 Cor. 12:12).

Here the church is represented as a body, is compared to a human body. In thinking of a body, the following divisions and relations suggest themselves; the head, the body; the members of the body, the relation of members to each other, and to the head. These divisions and relations are found in the church.

1. Jesus is head of the body. God made him head, "when he raised him from the dead, and made him to sit at his right hand in the heavenly places, far above all rule and authority and power, and dominion and every name that is named not only in this world, but also in that which is to come; and he put all things in subjection under his feet, and gave him to be head over all things to the church, which is his body, the fulness of him that filleth all in all." (Eph. 1:20-23). "And he is the head of the body, the church: who is the beginning, the first born from the dead; that in all things he might have the pre-eminence" (Col. 1:18). The head is guide to the body and the source of wisdom. It is the law making power. It controls the movements and actions of the body. Hence the authority of Jesus in the church is absolute. His au-

thority is above all other authority, and from it there is no appeal. He alone has the right to make laws for the church. We have no right, therefore, singly or collectively, to legislate for the church, or to try to regulate by our authority men's duties in religion. To do so is to assume prerogatives that belong to Christ. It is approaching dangerously near the presumptuous sin. Yet men aspire to rule. Jesus met with this spirit in his own followers. "And there was also a strife among them, over which of them should be accounted the greatest. And he said unto them, the kings of the Gentiles exercise lordship over them; and they that exercise authority upon them are called benefactors. But ye shall not be so; but he that is greatest among you, let him be as the younger; and he that is chief as he that doth serve" (Luke 22:24-26). No member of the body is to exercise authority over another; but all alike are to submit to the Head, even Christ.

Why should I assume authority over my brother? Am I wiser than he? Has God delegated me the right to rule my brother, to say what he shall believe or not believe, do or not do? Hence I cannot be a part of a body of men no matter what it is called, whose object is to make laws for the body of Christ. Neither are we under obligations to submit to those who do. Yea, we are under obligations not to submit to them. All man-made creeds, disciplines, etc., are man's laws. In taking Jesus as our Lord we pledge ourselves not to submit to any of them.

Read the 4th and 5th chapters of Acts. Peter and John were commanded not to preach any more in the name of Christ. What did they say? What would you have said? Suppose that a conference were to inform a circuit rider that he must cease to preach a certain doctrine, what would he do? What should he do? Peter and John said, "We ought to obey God rather than men." They allowed no body of men to dictate to them what to preach. Will you? Do you know of any one that does?

2. The body over which Christ is head is the church. "And gave him to be head over all things to the church which is his body" (Eph. 1:22). "And he is the head of the body, the church" (Col. 1:18). Paul suffered "for his body's sake, which is the church." (Col. 1:24). The church of Christ is the spiritual body of Christ.

3. There is one body, one church. "For even as we have many members in one body, and all the members have not the same office, so we, who are many, are one body in Christ, and severally members one of another" (Rom. 12:4,5). "But now they are many members, but one body" (1 Cor. 12:20). God calls us in one body (Col. 3:15).

4. Jesus loves and nourishes his body and will save it. He loved his fleshly body, but gave it for his spiritual body. "Husbands, love your wives, even as Christ also loved the church, and gave himself up for it" (Eph. 5:25). "For no man ever hated his own flesh; but nourisheth and cherisheth it, even as Christ also the church; because we are members of his body" (verses 29,30). "'For the husband is the head of the wife, as Christ also is the head of the church, being himself the savior of the body" (verse 23).

Jesus loves you with a tender love if you are a member of his body.

5. There is a close relation existing between all the members of the body. "And whether one member suffer, all the members suffer with it; or one member be honored, all the members rejoice with it" (1 Cor. 12:25,26). There is union and harmony in the body. Diversities of offices there are, yet a oneness of design and purpose—a wonderful harmony of action. "If one member suffers, all the members suffer with it." If your arm is broken the whole body sympathizes; the other members shield it. Just so if any member of our body becomes diseased, everything possible is done to restore it to health. But when all efforts in its behalf fail, and the life of the body is in danger because of the member, we resort to amputation. Then, delays are dangerous; so should it be in the body of Christ. Everything possible should be done to restore to health a diseased member. But when all efforts fail, and he continues to grow worse, and the way of truth is evil spoken of because of him, we should not hesitate to withdraw from him.

6. A close relation exists between each member and the head. Wound a member, and the brain knows it immediately. Are we so closely related to Christ? On his way to Damascus, on a mission of persecution, Saul of Tarsus heard the voice saying, "Saul, Saul, why persecutest thou me?" "I am Jesus of Nazareth, whom thou persecutest." How was Saul persecuting Jesus, now crowned King of kings and Lord of lords? By persecuting his body, of course. If you injure

my body, you injure me. Jesus will say to those on his right hand at the last day, "Come, ye blessed of my Father, inherit the kingdom prepared for you from the foundation of the world: for I was an hungred, and ye gave me meat; I was thirsty, and ye gave me drink; I was a stranger, and ye took me in; naked, and ye clothed me; I was sick, and ye visited me; I was in prison, and ye came unto me. Then shall the righteous answer him, saying, Lord, when saw we thee an hungred and fed thee, or thirsty and gave thee drink . . . . ?" The King shall answer: "Inasmuch as ye have done it unto one of the least of these, my brethren, ye have done it unto me." (Matt. 25:31-46).

Brethren, here is a golden opportunity. If Christ were on earth, we would gladly do anything we could for him. There are needy disciples. Will you not give them relief? This will be ministering to Christ. Do you refuse to associate with a brother because he is poor or ignorant? Think of this text of Scripture, "Ye have done it unto me." I know of congregations where once love reigned supreme and the body was a unit, but the seeds of discord were sown—poisons were administered to the body. Wreck and ruin followed. Some were driven out. Jesus says, "Inasmuch as ye did it to the least of these, my brethren, ye did it to me."

When, with things unauthorized, you drive out a member, you drive Christ out. There are hundreds of congregations out of which he has been driven. Are they churches of Christ now? How can they be, since he has been driven out of them? I do not want to be a member of such a body—a church out of which Christ has been driven—for it cannot be the body of Christ.

Anvil Sparks:

Some "additions to the church" are not "conversions to the Lord".

Some one said to a church, "Nothing is so small but that you can have trouble over it if you want to, and no trouble is so large but that it can be settled if you want to."

Some men use the church to further their own interests; others use themselves for the glory of the church.

We may become so busy trying to build up the Lord's church that we forget he has any right or authority in it.

You may flatter people into a mutual admiration society, but only the pure gospel will bring them into the kingdom.

A church is losing its grip on the gospel when it puts more stress on "a good mixer" than it does on a good preacher. Beware of the serpent — he was a good mixer.

A good mixer sometimes mixes up a terrible mess.

A knowing look does not necessarily indicate a knowing mind.

Brass is a poor substitute for brains, but, if polished, it is more shiny.

If Absalom were living today, he would be in great demand, for he was the best mixer in the kingdom.

When one who loves to flatter meets one who loves to be flattered, you have the proper combination — the slobberer and his bib.

There is a difference between encouraging people for their good and flattering them for your gain.

The elders should not lord it over the church; neither should the church lord it over the elders. I have seen it practiced both ways.

Work In the Vineyard

Matt. 20:1-16:

1. Hired and Sent into the Vineyard.—The agreement was reached before they entered the vineyard. "When he had agreed with the laborers for a penny a day, he sent them into his vineyard." "Didst not thou agree with me for a penny?" They had freedom of will; they could work or be idle. There was no iron-clad decree compelling or restraining them. "Why stand ye here all the day idle?" "Because no man hath hired us." "Go ye also into the vineyard." No one remained idle because he was one of the non-elect. Jesus says the kingdom of heaven is like this. No one, then, is compelled to enter the vineyard of the Lord and work or to remain outside in idleness. Whether we enter or not is determined by the exercise of our own free will. "Whosoever will." There is no reward for outside service. A person inquires: "Can I not work without entering the church?" Certainly you can. But for whom do you labor? In whose vineyard? Suppose you contract with a man to work for you, and when you direct him to the work, he replies: "Can I not work here as well as in your field?" Certainly he could. For that matter, he could work himself to death; but would you be under obligations to pay him for his work? The question, then, is not, "Are you working?" but, "For whom do you labor, and in whose vineyard?" There are, so to speak, but two vineyards in which to labor. You are working for God or Satan. If you are not in the church of God, you are not working for him.

2. Hired Laborers.—All are expected to work. There is no room for idlers. Strive earnestly to please the Lord of the vineyard. Be a faithful servant. Let that be the chief aim of your life. "This one thing I do." "Seek ye first the kingdom of God, and his righteousness." "Faith, if it hath not works, is dead." (See James 2:14-26). He did not hire any bosses. The church needs no bosses. He did not hire any one to lay plans for others to carry out. He made all the plans necessary and sent laborers into the vineyard to work. Now suppose a scene in that vineyard at about three o'clock in the afternoon, and the lord of the vineyard enters to see how the work is progressing. Some are ceaselessly, but quietly, toiling at their task. Under a beautiful shade tree in the midst of the vineyard is a group of men apparently engaged in some important business. The lord of the vineyard approaches unobserved to within hearing distance. One is addressing the crowd. He listens, and catches the following words: "It behooves us to be up and doing. Look at those who will not confer with us and help us in this most important work; they are 'anti' everything and opposed to all progress. Look at the thorns, thistles, and weeds; they are fast taking the vineyard. The vines need pruning. The work must be done, and we must employ some one to do it. We have the men ready at any time to go to work, but we are sadly in need of funds. Shall the work go undone and sufficient workers lie idle just for lack of money? It must never be. I now call for contributions and pledges to support some to do this work." Here the curtain falls; and while we are wondering what the lord of the vineyard

did with those men, another scene is presented to us. It is the church in its present condition. Are not the two scenes very much alike? Behold the countless numbers who are quietly toiling for the Master. See the salaried officers of usurping societies, and listen to their speeches similar to that in the first scene. A question comes to us: What is to be the final outcome of these things? The curtain of death falls and the next scene is the great judgment day. Here our question is answered. Jesus comes, "in flaming fire taking vengeance on them that know not God, and that obey not the gospel of our Lord Jesus Christ: who shall be punished with everlasting destruction from the presence of the Lord, and from the glory of his power." (2 Thess. 1:8,9). The laborer must do the work assigned him and as he was directed. He was not responsible for results. Honest work according to the orders of the Lord of the vineyard was the extent of his responsibility. Here alone was he responsible for failure. Some in the Lord's vineyard do a great deal of needless worrying over results. Be thoughtful and diligent in carrying out orders. Rejoice when that is done. Fret not about results; that is no part of your business. In fear do his commandments; that is your whole duty. If people would not worry over results, there would not be so many changes made in the Lord's ways to have better results. Here many good people depart from the right ways of the Lord. There are, of course, a great many people who care nothing about religion, save for the entertainment they get out of it. These pervert the right ways of the Lord for the entertainment they get out of the changed order.

There are others who go with the crowd. I do not speak of these. These classes, in the main, have not departed from the Lord, for they have never been with him. I refer to those who desire to see the cause of God prosper, but worry about results till they, in ignorant zeal, adopt questionable methods to have better results. I care not how much a person may be noted for soundness in faith, I fear for him when I hear him begin to complain about results. He has taken the first step in departing from God and his word. Some others are great workers, but are so self-important they make poor servants. Their pride will not suffer them to submit to authority. Yet they toil unceasingly. But for whom do they labor? For self? For God as he directs? Think seriously. Here we make many blunders. Because a man is a great worker and has big results in protracted meetings his services are sought but is he humbly working as the Master directs? The Lord of the vineyard wanted the laborer to work as he directed. So do you if you hire a man. He might work hard and at the same time ruin things. Aside from the Bible, we are ignorant of work in the Lord's vineyard. Hence some of the greatest workers in religion today are doing the most harm.

3. No Encouragement to Procrastinate.—Some went at the eleventh hour, but all went at the first opportunity. "Why stand ye here all the day idle?" "Because no man hath hired us." Can you live in sin till old age and then give that excuse? Not in a land of Bibles. Do not delay; enter today.

The College Question

By experience, observation, and study I have learned some things about the Bible-college question. It appears to me that both those who favor and those who oppose Bible colleges have said and done some foolish and hurtful things, and that by neither side have the colleges been fairly represented. This has grown out of the fact that the real function of schools and colleges has not always been clearly defined and stated. Those who oppose them seem to regard them as church institutions, owned and controlled by the church, and those who favor them have generally written as if that were a fact.

But is that the issue? Is it possible for the churches in Texas, in Arkansas, or in Tennessee, to own or operate a college? If so, how? If not, why so much loose talk about building colleges for the church of Christ, turning over to the church of Christ one already built, securing another college for the church of Christ, etc.? I know of no such colleges and deprecate such talk. As a member of the church of God, I have no property rights in any school, nor do I have any control over any. I unhesitatingly affirm that the church of God in Texas cannot own colleges, nor property of any sort; neither has it any way of appointing agents to control such property. A chartered Bible college (and all should be chartered) owns its own property and manages its own affairs. It is owned by no church and no church controls it. The fact that the charter provides that the trustees must be members of churches of Christ does not make it a church school any more than the fact that they must be citizens of the United States makes it a government school.

But it is argued that these schools do the work God intended the church to do. Here again we stumble in the dark. It is impossible for me to think of them as supplanting the church, or as, in any way, doing the work God intended the church to do. A little reflection, a little common sense, will help to clear up matters. It is the duty of parents, so far as they are able, to provide all needed things for their children, including such education and discipline as will best prepare them for usefulness in life. This includes teaching the Bible, as well as other necessary branches of learning. But parents are not usually prepared to give their children all needed education and training, and must send them to school or neglect a parental duty. Then the college or school, for the time being, as the agent of the parents, gives as best it can, the needed education and discipline; and, as such, it is the duty of the school to teach the Bible faithfully to the students in its care. The function of schools is parental, not ecclesiastical. When parents feed, clothe, and teach their children the Bible and other useful things, no one thinks they are usurping the work of the church. When parents transfer, in part, these parental duties to a college, why should any one of sense think that the college, in accepting such trust, is doing the work of the church? It is manifest to any thinking person that the school is not doing the work of the church, but the work of parents—work that the parents were unable to do.

When, therefore, a school or college for a time takes, in part, the place of parents in the life of the child, as well as its other needs. If it does not teach the Bible, it fails in an important parental duty. Let the schools and colleges realize that they are foster parents to every student committed to their care, and then as faithful parents proceed to give the student the needed care and training. And remember: Educating children is not church work, but parental; and schools are not church agencies, but parental agencies.

Anvil Sparks:

It is hard to find a Scriptural way to do an unscriptural thing.

You have also observed that a meddlesome preacher can keep up as much trouble in a church as a tyrannical elder.

All the available evidence goes to show that the reverse of evolution is true. For instance, we have all seen men making monkeys of themselves, but no one ever saw a monkey making a man of himself.

Darwinism teaches the survival of the fit; the gospel teaches the revival of the unfit.

Evolutionists claim that our tonsile are the remnants of the gills of our fish ancestors. Well, I knew all the time that there was something fishy about evolution.

It may not amount to much, but it is my opinion that the man who sprang from an ape should not have landed in a professor's chair.

Science has no missing links.

The great question, "If a man die shall he live again?" has no interest for the infidel — nor the ox.

When the monkey advocates get through figuring on where they came from, perhaps they will put in some time figuring on where they are going.

Churches and Colleges

Shall churches contribute to the support of "Christian colleges" by cash on hand, by pledges, or by including some college in their "budgets"? That is the question. What is your answer?

Men are frequently unconsciously influenced in their thinking by their own interests. All agree that colleges and schools are human institutions and no man can make me believe that churches are dependent upon colleges for their existence. Colleges can be useful, or they can be a curse. A big endowment fund looks attractive to the worldly minded schemers; and such men can make great pretentions to soundness of faith and practice. Vultures will gather wherever there is money.

As an individual I can give or not give to a college —that is strictly my own personal affair; but there is something wrong with a man's thinking when he thinks a church is at liberty to do the same thing. If I am a member of a church that has made a pledge to a college, or has the college in its budget, I am forced to contribute to the college, or refuse to contribute anything on the Lord's days. Also it might be that the college the church is supporting might be such that I could not support it. Besides, I cannot see that any group of elders has any right to pledge members to support any college.

Many years ago the Foreign Missionary Society of the Christian Church began to tell each church how much it should give for missions. After that plan got going full-blast, I had a talk about it with

A. D. Rogers. He, of course, favored the plan; but said no church was bound to give the amount designated—that churches could give or not give, just as they pleased. (That sounds very much like what has been said about churches giving to colleges—give or not give just as they please). I made reply to A. D. about as follows: There are different ways to force people to do things—they can be surrounded by such conditions and circumstances that they have no choice but to fall in line or be counted out. Human organizations become more and more centralized and powerful. If one of your preachers fails to encourage the church where he preaches to send in its assessment, he will incur the displeasure of the higher-up, and will soon have no place to preach. He will have to toe the mark, or be counted out. And A. D. has lived to see that I was right. Some time ago a prominent preacher said that, if a church has a preacher that opposed including some Christian college in its budget, that church should get another preacher. If all colleges develop that attitude, their students will go out with the same spirit. If that spirit is not checked, the colleges will become the rulers of the churches and preachers.

Even now a lot is being said about "college trained preachers." A man who will not preach unless he can be "college trained" is not fit to preach, no matter how much college training he has. And I do not like to hear it said the churches are dependent on Christian colleges for preachers. That puts colleges above churches, or does it make colleges the foundation of churches?

Settling Doctrinal Questions By Popular Vote

Things new to me keep coming up. When I was twenty years of age, I heard a Cumberland Presbyterian preacher in debate refer to the fifteenth chapter of Acts to prove the scripturalness of the General Assembly of the Cumberland Presbyterian Church. Some years ago I attended the Mason-White debate in Dallas, Texas, and heard Brother Mason use this same scripture to prove their right to hold conventions. Just recently I heard this same scripture put to a new use—namely, to prove the right of a church to settle a question of doctrine by popular vote. This seems to be a convenient chapter. Will the reader please stop here and carefully read that chapter?

The last preacher referred to was accused of preaching unsound doctrine in that he had preached that the blood of martyrs is the seed of the kingdom, and had challenged any one to show where the Bible says that the word of God is the seed of the kingdom. In a meeting called to consider the matter, the preacher took the position that the whole church should by popular vote settle the matter of his soundness. A visiting preacher argued against such procedure and raised this question: "If a preacher should preach that sprinkling is baptism would you leave it to a popular vote to determine his soundness? Where would such a course end?" In reply, the accused preacher brought up the proceedings of the meeting outlined in the fifteenth chapter of Acts, and argued that the whole church at Jerusalem settled the question of circumcision that was then agitating the churches, which were composed of both Jews and Gentiles. It was later pointed out to him that the decision was inspired, for the document sent out says: "For it seemed good to the Holy Spirit, and to us," etc. (Verse 28.) To this the preacher replied: "It seemed good to the Holy Spirit just as it seems good to the Holy Spirit now when we come to conclusions in harmony with the Scriptures." To hear a Christian preacher argue that a church may by popular vote settle a matter of doctrine is astonishing enough, but to hear him try to prove his point by the proceedings of that meeting is amazing beyond measure. If there is another gospel preacher who would take such a position, I would like to hear from him.

What are the facts concerning this meeting? What gave rise to it? How was the matter under consideration settled? In all the churches composed of Jews and Gentiles the question of circumcision was for a while a disturbing question. A certain class of Jews from Jerusalem was very determined to bind the law of Moses on all Gentile converts. "And certain men came down from Judea and taught the brethren, saying, Except ye be circumcised after the custom of Moses, ye cannot be saved." (Acts 15:1.) This was at Antioch in Syria. "The fact that these men came from Judea, where the gospel was first preached, and where the original apostles had been the teachers, gave their utterances much authority with the Antioch brethren; so it is not necessary to suppose that they claimed express authority from the apostles for their teaching, though it is possible they did . . . . The phraseology employed shows what is brought out expressly farther on (Verse 5), that they insisted on circumcision 'after the custom of Moses,' because they held that all the baptized, whether Jews or Gentiles, must keep the law of Moses in order to final salvation. . . . Paul, who had long ago received by direct revelation from Christ a correct knowledge of the gospel which he preached (Gal. 1:11,12), knew perfectly that this teaching was erroneous, and Barnabas had learned the same from him, if not from some other source: so the two united with all their might in opposing the Judean teachers. . . . Paul and Barnabas did not succeed in silencing their opponents, but they so conducted the discussion as to bring about a fortunate decision of a provisional character." (McGarvey.)

"And when Paul and Barnabas had no small dissension and questioning with them, the brethren appointed that Paul and Barnabas, and certain other of them, should go up to Jerusalem unto the apostles and elders about this question." (Verse 2). These Judaizers did not recognize the authority of Paul as an apostle; if so, his word would have settled the matter. And had it been proper for a church, by popular vote, to settle matters of doctrine disturbing it, why did not the church at Antioch take a vote to see which set of teachers was teaching sound doctrine? Why send them to Jerusalem at all? The question was not disturbing the Jerusalem church, but only those churches composed of Jews and Gentiles, or of Gentiles only. If the church at Jerusalem had the right to determine by popular vote what other churches should believe and practice, would not another church have the right to reverse by popular vote the decision of the Jerusalem church, and thus bind circumcision on all? Is not such an idea absurd in the extreme? Is it not absurd that a Christian preacher should argue that the Jerusalem church, by agreement and without the aid of direct inspiration, should settle a great question for all churches for all time?

When Paul and his company reached Jerusalem, "they were received of the church and the apostles and the elders, and they rehearsed all things that God had done with them." (Verse 4.) It seems that they did not mention the question of circumcision, leaving that for the Judaizers to bring up. "But there rose up certain of the sect of the Pharisees who believed, saying, It is needful to circumcise them, and to charge them to keep the law of Moses." (Verse 5.) After the Pharisees had stated their position, the assembly, so it seems, adjourned. Perhaps so much time had been consumed that they had no time at this meeting to go further into the matter. Another meeting was held. "And the apostles and the elders were gathered together to consider of this matter." (Verse 6.) At both meetings the church was present. (See verses 4, 22.) "There was, however, between these two public meetings a private meeting of Paul and Barnabas with the three apostles who were then in the city." (See Gal. 2:1-10.) Paul sought this interview with the old apostles that he might know, before proceeding further, how they stood on the question; for he knew that if he found them on the side of the Pharisees, their influence would outweigh his, and his life work would be destroyed by his converts among the Gentiles being brought under the bondage of the law, and his work would be in vain. But the other apostles approved Paul's course, and indicated their approval by giving to Paul and Barnabas the right hand of fellowship. Concerning this, McGarvey remarks: "With this information as to the perfect understanding and agreement between the inspired apostles before us, we can plainly see that the second public meeting of the whole church was called, not for the purpose of bringing about an agreement between the apostles, but for the purpose of enabling the apostles to bring the whole church into agreement with themselves. In this light we must study the proceedings, or we shall totally misconstrue them."

In this second meeting the Judaizers were allowed to fully argue their case before any reply was made. "Then, when they had completely emptied themselves, the apostles, one by one, and in a succession apparently prearranged, gave utterance to the facts and judgments which compelled assent." The speeches of these inspired men overcame all opposition, so that the whole church concurred in selecting men to send to Antioch with Paul and Barnabas. A document was prepared, which these men carried with them and which is referred to in Acts 16:4 as the "decrees which had been ordained by the apostles and elders that were at Jerusalem." It is absurd in the extreme to think Luke would have referred to this document as "decrees" had it embodied only the conclusions of a body of uninspired men; neither, in that case, could he have said that these "decrees" had been ordained by the apostles and elders. Besides, if these "decrees" were only the uninspired conclusions of the church at Jerusalem, what right did they have to impose them on other churches, and why should other churches be under obligations to regard them? McGarvey says of this document: "It makes a formal claim of inspiration by the words, 'it seemed good to the Holy Spirit, and to us.' No uninspired men could dare to use such language; and this circumstance differentiates it from all the decrees and deliverances from that day to this. . . . Furthermore, it decided, on the authority of inspired men who directed its decisions, a question of doctrine affecting the salvation of souls; and this no set of men except the apostles have ever had the right to do. In no sense, then, can its action be pleaded as a precedent for the existence of any ecclesiastical court whatever outside of the individual congregation, or for the purpose of settling by authority any question of doctrine."

"It seemed good to the Holy Spirit, and to us, to lay upon you no greater burden than these necessary things." What right did the Jerusalem church as a body of uninspired men have to lay any burdens upon any other church? They did not do it. The document sent out was inspired by the Holy Spirit; as such, it was binding on all churches in all countries and for all time.

A Good Mixer

So often the announcement runs about as follows: "We are anxious to secure a preacher. He must be a good mixer, and . . . " But no matter about the rest. Anything else is of secondary importance, whether the call comes from Bat Creek or from Progressive Hollow. No others need apply.

What is a good mixer? Can't define the term? No matter; every one knows a good mixer when he sees him in action. A person may be courteous and in every sense a gentleman without being a "good mixer."

The Bible gives us an account of one good mixer, only that is not what the historian calls him. This man, the son of the favorite king of Israel, had led a rather wayward life. He was selfish, devoid of sympathy for others, and without interest in their welfare. He killed his brother Amnon, and fled to Geshur, where he remained in exile three years. David finally brought him back. Now this man Absalom was more than a good mixer; for "in all Israel there was none to be so much praised as Absalom for his beauty: from the sole of his foot even to the crown of his head there was no blemish in him." (2 Sam. 14:25.)

Absalom had a big selfish purpose to accomplish. He set his heart on dethroning God's anointed king, his own father, that he might obtain the kingdom for himself, even if he must murder his own father to accomplish his purpose. But he could never do this without first winning the people. He knew the

value and utility of being a good mixer. He formu-
lated a plan. "And Absalom rose up early, and stood
beside the way of the gate: and it was so, that when
any man that had a controversy came to the king
for judgment, then Absalom called unto him, and
said, Of what city art thou? And he said, Thy servant is of one of the tribes of Israel. And Absalom
said unto him, See, thy matters are good and right;
but there is no man deputed of the king to hear thee.
Absalom said moreover, O that I were made judge
in the land, that every man which hath any suit or
cause might come unto me, and I would do him justice! And it was so, that when any man came nigh
to him to do him obeisance, he put forth his hand,
and took him, and kissed him. And on this manner
did Absalom to all Israel that came to the king for
judgment: so Absalom stole the hearts of the men
of Israel." (2 Sam. 15:1-6).

Of course he kept his purposes in the dark, while
by the arts of flattery and deceit he was working
himself into the good graces of the people. He made
them believe he was so kind, so sympathetic, so unselfish—such a good man! When they came to believe him to be the best man in the kingdom, they were
then ready to support him in a move to gain the
throne, even if God's king and his own father must
be murdered to accomplish the purpose. Thus Absalom, the finest-looking man in the kingdom, was
also the best mixer in Israel, and—the basest scoun-
drel!

But is it not strange that a man could be so selfish
and base, and yet be the most idolized man in the

kingdom? It is not strange that he practiced the arts of flattery and became a good mixer. That was a part of the game, without which he could have made no headway. But the people love to be flattered, and they love a good mixer; and Absalom knew it. In that line he was an artist. I never read a call for a good mixer without thinking of Absalom; and if he were living, I would recommend him for the place. And would he not make a great showing as a modern pastor, or "located minister?" He was such a fine-looking man, so entertaining, seemingly so unselfishly interested in every one's welfare, that he would have captured the whole town or city. And had he discovered that the elders were growing suspicious of him, how easily he could have stirred up his enthusiastic supporters, deposed the old elders, and appointed some who would retain him as their preacher and be thoroughly submissive to him.

Be courteous, of course—truly, genuinely, sincerely courteous. If a man loves God and man, neither bigotry, impudence, selfwill, nor any of the other unbecoming traits of character will find a place in his heart. He will be considerate and forbearing, gentle and forgiving, kind and sympathetic, toward all, rich and poor. But genuine love will prompt one, when occasion demands, to do a thing that, under ordinary circumstances, would not seem courteous. To rescue a child from immediate danger may require you to snatch him in a way that under ordinary conditions would seem extremely rude. And to rescue a man from sin may require you to rebuke him in such way as to destroy your reputation for being a good mixer; but genuine love, true courtesy, requires it. A physician will not flatter one concerning his prospects for a long life and good health, when he knows that a serious operation is the only means of prolonging his life; only a quack would console him into the idea that he needed only mild treatment.

Some people are naturally more demonstrative than others. Extreme friendliness seems to be a part of their nature. It is not strained and professional. They have the fluidity of spirit that mixes in easily with others; and, for that reason, they cannot be leaders. A good mixer mixes easily and gracefully with his surroundings, and catches the spirit of the crowd. How can one possessing such fluidity of spirit have sufficient boldness and concentration of spirit to lead others? He is more likely to be affected by them. As Brother D. Lipscomb said: "A good mixer is easily mixed." You would have to change human nature for it to be otherwise. But it is certainly no sin to be naturally a good mixer, though this trait so highly prized by some may really be a liability instead of an asset. Neither is it wrong to cultivate a friendly, sympathetic disposition. In fact love for man creates sympathy and a desire to be helpful. If genuine love masters a man, he will be kind and courteous to all, neither fawning on the rich nor patronizing toward the poor, recognizing that all are God's creatures upon whom is engraven or may be engraven the image of the divine nature. This is true courtesy.

But let us not forget that courtesy may be put on

as a cloak. There is such a thing as professional courtesy. What may be genuine fruit in one may be merely artificial trimmings in another. And here is the danger. The preacher who is a good mixer is in demand. Seeing this, a young preacher may cultivate it as an ornament, as a means of making a success in his calling. Hence, he flatters that he may please, and seems interested when he is not, because both contribute to his success. He shakes hands with everybody in his own meetings; but when he attends another's meeting, he does not. Thus he makes courtesy a professional matter. Such a course is rotting to character and makes one the basest of hypocrites.

Flattery, an essential trait of the professional good mixer, is insincere praise, and is a product of selfishness. No one ever flattered another for the other's benefit, but for his own. Hence, David classes the flatterer among his enemies. (See Ps. 5:8,9). And no wonder for the flatterer seeks to use others for his own selfish ends. I like true courtesy; but when a new acquaintance is too sweet to me, I wonder what he is priming me up for.

Flattery is an evil, a great sin, and is severely condemned in the Bible. And yet a young preacher said: "People like flattery and being bragged on, and I am going to give it to them." All such should read and ponder the following: "Help, Jehovah; for the godly man ceaseth; for the faithful fail from among the children of men. They speak falsehood every one with his neighbor: with flattering lip, and with a double heart, do they speak. Jehovah will cut off all flattering lips, the tongue that speaketh great things." (Ps. 12:1-3.) "A flattering mouth work-eth ruin." (Prov. 26:28.) "And in his place shall stand up a contemptible person, to whom they had not given the honor of the kingdom: but he shall come in time of security, and shall obtain the kingdom by flatteries." (Dan. 11:21.) "And such as do wickedly against the covenant shall he pervert by flatteries; but the people that do know their God shall be strong, and do exploits." (Verse 32.) Rather than be a contemptible flatterer, let us follow the example of Paul: "For neither at any time were we found using words of flattery, as ye know nor a cloak of covetousness." (1 Thess. 2:5.)

Anvil Sparks:

A slogan is one thing; a principle of action is quite another. A slogan is a rallying cry, and relates to parties and classes. It harks back to the days of Scotish clans. "Where the Bible speaks we speak; where the Bible is silent we are silent" was adopted by the Campbells as a guiding principle in their religious life. As a party slogan it would be subject to much criticism; as a principle to guide a person in his religious teaching it measures up to Scriptural requirements.

Some people's weakness is the strongest thing about them.

No, Adam did not hear the serpent's lie, nor did he believe it and obey it, as preachers have so often said. Adam was not deceived."

Two wrongs never make a right, but two "rights" always make a wrong.

Knowing the Doctrine

Doctrine is teaching. It used to be common for denominational preachers to preach what they called "doctrinal sermons." On such occasions they preached on controverted points, or on points wherein their churches differed from others. Had they examined the Bible more closely, they would have discovered that any sermon with teaching in it is a doctrinal sermon, no matter what might be the nature of the teaching. "But speak thou the things which befit the sound doctrine: that aged men be temperate, grave, sober-minded, sound in faith, in love, in patience: that aged women likewise be reverent in demeanor, not slanderers, not enslaved to much wine, teachers of that which is good," etc. (Tit. 2:1-3.) Notice what a wide range sound doctrine covers—temperance, gravity, faith, love, patience, etc. To say that a sermon is a doctrinal sermon is to say that it is a teaching sermon; and why should a person try to preach any other sort?

It will be noticed, too, that Paul exhorted Titus to confine himself to "sound doctrine." And he exhorted Timothy: "Hold the pattern of sound words which thou hast heard from me, in faith and love which is in Christ Jesus." (2 Tim. 1:13.) To stay with the revealed will of God is to hold the pattern of sound words. My heart is fully set on doing that very thing.

To indoctrinate a person is to fill him with teaching; and is not that the great need of the hour? Not simply teaching, but sound *teaching*. To stir the emotions and the will without imparting knowledge is to make an ignorant zealot, or a religious fanatic. To have zeal without knowledge is to be lost. Ignorance will not save. "My people are destroyed for lack of knowledge." (Hos. 4:6.) Of his own nation Paul said: "For I bear them witness that they have a zeal for God, but not according to knowledge. For being ignorant of God's righteousness, and seeking to establish their own, they did not subject themselves to the righteousness of God." (Rom. 10:2,3.) No one can subject himself to God's righteousness while ignorant of it. False teaching leaves the mind in a state of ignorance. There are two classes of ignorant people—namely, those who have never learned anything and those who have filled their minds with false teaching. The sad part of it is, many people do not want to know, and many others fill themselves with false teaching, thinking it is the truth. Paul speaks of some who are "ever learning, and never able to come to the knowledge of the truth." (2 Tim. 3:7.) It is midnight darkness in the soul of one who has not been enlightened by the word of God, no matter what his pretensions or professions may be. "The opening of thy words giveth light; it giveth understanding unto the simple." (Psalms 119:130.) A passing acquaintance with the Bible is not sufficient. "Let the word of Christ dwell in you richly." (Col. 3:16.) It is the duty of every child of God to strive earnestly to arrive at a point where he can teach others; but we fall short of this God-appointed goal, even as they did in Paul's day. "For when by reason of the time ye ought to be teachers, ye have need that some one teach you the rudiments of the first principles of the oracles of God; and are become such as have need of milk, and not of solid food." (Heb. 5:12.)

But seeking to fill ourselves with the knowledge of God, what rules of interpretation shall we follow? That is a point of interest to some. I could give a system of rules that have been recommended, but to the average reader most of them are rather difficult of application. The best guide I know of in Bible study is *common sense and an earnest desire to know the will of God*. In the absence of either of these, there is little hope that one will gain accurate information, no matter how many rules of interpretation he may adopt.

It is comforting to know that a great host of people read the Bible with a sincere desire to learn the will of God. They love to meditate on its commands, its promises, the people it mentions, the story of Jesus, and the glorious prospects it holds out before them. They feel as David when he prayed: "Open thou mine eyes, that I may behold wondrous things out of thy law." (Ps. 119:18.) And with David they can truthfully say: "O how love I thy law! It is my meditation all the day." (Ps. 119:97.) And such characters are the salt of the earth.

Another class read the Bible merely to be informed, just as they read other literature. They admire its beautiful language rather than its glorious truths. With them the Bible is literature. Well, it is the greatest literature ever written; but it is a pity that those who admire its literature fail so often to see anything else in it. But if a person reads it merely for its literature, he is foredoomed to see nothing else in it. The Bible does not yield up its precious truth to the one who is not searching for it.

But some read the Bible for the sake of argument. To them it is merely an arsenal from which to draw munitions of war. What they learn they use as a club with which to beat the other fellow over the head, or as a keen blade with which to skin the opponent. They, savagelike, delight in seeing the other fellow squirm and writhe as they cudgel and scalp him. They delight in making wounds, but they heal none. Jeremiah's question has never occurred to them: "Is there no balm in Gilead? is there no physician there?" Does a person like that know the Bible? He does not so much as know what it is for. The Bible does not yield up its truth to one who will abuse it.

It has been said that any man can find his doctrine in the Bible. That is another way of saying that we can find in the Bible what we want to find, and there is more truth in that statement than we are accustomed to think. In that respect there is no other book like it. In what spirit do you approach the Bible? That determines what you will find in it. "And the word of Jehovah came to me, saying, Son of man these men have taken their idols into their heart, and put the stumblingblock of their iniquity before their face: should I be inquired of at all by them? Therefore speak unto them, and say unto them, Thus saith the Lord Jehovah: Every man of the house of Israel that taketh his idols into his heart, and putteth the stumblingblock of his iniquity before his face, and

cometh to the prophet; I Jehovah will answer him
therein according to the multitude of his idols."
(Ezek. 14:2-4). God answers people according to
the desire of their hearts. Read carefully the case
of Balaam. (See Num. 22-24.) When God saw that
Balaam's heart was fully set on going to curse Israel
for reward, he said: "If the men are come to call
thee, rise up, and go with them." "And God's anger
was kindled because he went." Jesus spoke in parables on certain occasions, because the Pharisees were
so base in heart that they would have abused him
and the truth had he spoken the truth in plain language. And Paul says concerning some who received
not the love of the truth that they might be saved:
"And for this cause God sendeth them a working of
error, that they should believe a lie: that they all
might be judged who believe not the truth, but had
pleasure in unrighteousness." (2 Thess. 2:11,12.) The
Bible is so skillfully arranged to that end that any
man can go the way he wants to go, and flatter himself that he has an excuse for going. But if a man
sincerely loves the truth, he will find it; but God's
truth is too precious to be intrusted to those who will
abuse and misuse it.

Anvil Sparks:

Sometime ago, a preacher wrote a scathing article
about some writers who criticise others without calling
names. He called such writers bush-whakers and a lot
of other hard names. But he unwittingly condemned
himself and put himself in the class with those he criticized for he did not call the names of those writers he
so severely condemned. Happy is the man who condemns
not himself when he condemns others.

Obedience

Every American citizen does many things that the government of England requires; but he is not obeying the laws of England. He has no thought of such a thing. Every man of any moral worth does many things that God requires, but he may be doing so because his own judgment and the circumstances of his life indicate that it is best to so live. If so, he is not obeying God. To obey any authority is to do what that authority requires, and because it requires it. To obey God is to submit willingly and wholeheartedly to his authority. It is taking God at his word and doing what he says; it is bringing your will and ways into harmony with his will and ways. His word must become the controlling force in your life. God is waging war to that end: "Casting down imaginations, and every high thing that is exalted against the knowledge of God, and bringing every thought into captivity to the obedience of Christ." (2 Cor. 10:5.) God demands a complete and unconditional surrender. That does not mean that he will require no conditions, but it means that you are not allowed to name the terms upon which you will surrender. About all some people do is raise the flag of truce and begin to parley about whether they have to do this or that, and some openly declare that they will not do certain things. In such cases there is no surrender to God, and the war continues.

God gave man will power. "Will" is force, and, like all other forces, it must be controlled, or it will do harm. About the first quality noticeable in a baby, aside from instinct, is its kicking against restraints. That is not an indication of inherent perversity; it is merely an unrestrained will asserting itself. By many bumps, bruises, and burns the child learns restraint, which is another way of saying that it learns some lessons of obedience. If he did not early learn these lessons, he would soon destroy himself. Life is made up of obedience, or burns and bruises. Parents owe it to their children to teach them obedience. Much of the crime of today is a result of the failure of parents and teachers to see that the children intrusted to them learn obedience. If they do not learn obedience in the home and in the school, they are not likely to respect authority anywhere. Paul says of Jesus: "Though he were a Son, yet learned he obedience by the things which he suffered." (Heb. 5:8.) Every human being must learn obedience, or he will be a criminal against the laws of God and of man. With a lot of bunk about allowing the child to develop self-expression, we have failed to realize that he also needs to develop self-repression. The most valuable lesson any one can learn is obedience.

As a citizen, do you obey the laws that you approve, and disobey those you do not like? That is not obedience at all; it is anarchy. Is the Bible a book of authority with you, or merely a book of advice? We get lots of advice from people, and follow it if it suits us. Is that the way you treat the Bible? Do you treat its commands as nothing more than well-meant advice? If so, you have not learned the first thing about obedience. What moves you to act in religion?

Perhaps we are not always able to know all the motives that lead us to do a certain thing. How, then, are we to determine whether we are obeying God, or merely following a course that our judgment dictates? It is well for us that our loyalty be tested. For that reason God has always had a way of testing his servants and professed servants. In the very nature of a test, it must be something that reason would not suggest, nor see any connection between the thing commanded and the result promised. The tree of the knowledge of good and evil was a test for Adam and Eve. God said: "Thou shalt not eat of it." From every standpoint, human reason would suggest that eating it was the proper thing to do. The only thing that restrained them was their respect for the authority of God, and that was not strong enough to stand the test. Contrary to all human experience and reason, Naaman was commanded to dip seven times in the Jordan for the cure of his leprosy. That was a severe test for the proud Naaman, and he came very near not standing the test. A Methodist preacher said: "What good can immersion do the human soul?" Because human reason cannot see how immersion will do the soul any good, it is for that reason a severe test of man's spirit of obedience; and many do not stand the test. Many go so far as to say: "If I have to be baptized in order to be saved, I will never be saved." That expression reveals all the rebellion that a heart can possibly hold.

It would be an easy matter for any sinner to see clearly what to do to be saved, if he would give heed to what God has told sinners to do; but so many will not do that. They listen to blind guides as they darken counsel in their philosophizing about God's side of the question. If the sinner could realize that God has prepared a plan of salvation perfectly adapted to man's needs, and that he has revealed that plan in language that the sinner can understand, and that he is now calling on the sinner to act, he would have little difficulty in understanding what God is telling him to do. In the absence of blind guides, the sinner would have no trouble in understanding such passages as these: "He that believeth and is baptized shall be saved." "And Peter said unto them, Repent ye, and be baptized every one of you in the name of Jesus Christ unto the remission of your sins."

When the apostles and other inspired men told inquiring sinners what to do to be saved, the sinner did not stop to puzzle over God's part in the matter, but promptly did what he was told to do. "Then they that received his word were baptized." They had not been blinded by being told that man could do nothing and that salvation was wholly a matter of grace. Let the theologians, and also thoughtful people, ponder the following statement of the matter: There are two sides in the sinner's salvation—namely, God's side and man's side. On God's part, or side, man's salvation is wholly a matter of grace; on man's part, or side, man's salvation is wholly a matter of works. I will not enlarge on these statements, but will leave them for the reader to ponder over.

It has been said that God can save a sinner any way and anywhere he wants to. I think that it is true; but I do not know how nor where he wants to save a sinner, only as he tells me. If God can save the sinner any way and anywhere, then he can save him in the act of being baptized. If he has expressed himself on that point, then the matter is settled. God has plainly expressed himself: "He that believeth and is baptized shall be saved." If God wants to save a sinner in that way, who am I that I should object?

Because we preach the plan of salvation as it is laid down in the New Testament, it is sometimes said that we try to limit God to one way of saving people. That charge grows out of a mistaken view of the whole matter. It seems rather to me that God has limited us, and in limiting us to one way he has made it possible for us to know exactly what to do. If there had been no definite plan of salvation revealed, and the matter had been left to our own guesses and speculations, how could any one be sure he was right—how could we be certain that we were pleasing God? It is to man's advantage that he has been limited to one way plainly revealed. A brief study of God's method of dealing with man will help us to understand his limiting business. In matters of life and death, God has at all times been very definite and specific in telling man what to do. Instead of that being a hardship on man, it has been a great blessing.

The following Scriptures warrant us in going to the Old Testament for examples and illustrations as to God's method of dealing with man: "For whatsoever things were written aforetime were written for our learning, that through patience and through comfort of the scriptures we might have hope." (Rom.

15:4.) "Now these things happened unto them by
way of example; and they were written for our admonition, upon whom the ends of the ages are come."
(1 Cor. 10:11.) We shall refer to a few of these
examples to illustrate the principle now under consideration.

When God sent a flood upon the earth to destroy
the wicked, he saved Noah and his family. The way
he saved Noah is well known. So far as I know God
might have saved Noah in any one of a million more
ways. God was not limited; but when God selected
one way and told Noah what that way was, then Noah
was limited to that one way. God was not limited,
but Noah was. That was a blessing to Noah, for he
knew exactly what to do.

On one occasion in their wilderness journeying,
the Israelites raised a disturbance about their food
and drink. (See Num. 21:4-9.) "And Jehovah sent
fiery serpents among the people, and they bit the
people; and much people of Israel died." This
brought the people to their senses. "And the people
came to Moses, and said, We have sinned, because we
have spoken against Jehovah, and against thee; pray
unto Jehovah, that he take away the serpents from
us." No one will be so foolish as to say that the Lord
was so limited in power and resources that he could
relieve the situation in only one way. No; he could
have relieved the situation in any one of a thousand
more ways; but when he selected the one way—
namely, their looking at a serpent of brass made by
Moses and erected upon a standard—the people were
limited to that one way. It was look and live, or re-

fuse and die. God was not limited, but they were; and it was a great blessing to them that the way to be healed was thus limited and made plain, for then there was no doubt as to what to do.

The healing of Naaman, as recorded in 2 Kings 5:1-14, is another plain illustration of the principle we are now considering. He was the great commander of the armies of the king of Syria, but he was a leper. From a captive maiden brought from the land of Israel, Naaman learned that there was a possibility of a cure in the land of Israel. In his search for this healing, he finally stood before the door of the house of the prophet Elisha. "And Elisha sent a messenger unto him, saying, Go and wash in the Jordan seven times, and thy flesh shall come again to thee, and thou shalt be clean." Who would dare say that Jehovah was limited to that one way, so much so that he could not have selected some other way? But when he announced this one way, Naaman was limited to that way; and Naaman did not like to be thus limited. Like some people of today, he thought some other way would do as well, or even better. "Are not Abanah and Pharpar, the rivers of Damascus, better than all the waters of Israel? May I not wash in them, and be clean?" Now, that is the way he felt about it, and likely at that moment he would not have given his feelings for all the prophet said; and had it not been for the common sense of his servants he would have returned a leper. He had turned away from the prophet in a rage, when the servant brought him to his senses by saying: "My father, if the prophet had bid thee do some great thing, wouldest thou not have done it? How much rather then, when he saith to thee, Wash, and be clean?" Then Naaman decided to bring his feelings and thoughts into submission to Jehovah, and follow the one way to which Jehovah had limited him. "Then he went down, and dipped himself seven times in the Jordan, according to the saying of the man of God; and his flesh came again like unto the flesh of a little child, and he was clean." Jehovah was not limited, but Naaman was.

In the New Testament God has announced the conditions upon which he proposes to save the sinner. "He that believeth and is baptized shall be saved." "Repent ye, and be baptized every one of you in the name of Jesus Christ unto the remission of your sins." The same plan is set forth in many other passages. I think no one will say that God was so limited that he could not have selected other ways; but when he announces this one way, then the sinner is limited to that one way. God was not limited, but he has limited the sinner. And in so limiting us he has conferred a great blessing on us, for in so doing he has enabled us to know exactly what to do.

Anvil Sparks:

A preacher frequently needs encouragement, but never flattery. If the sermon lifts you a little higher, or helps you to better understand some knotty problem, or enables you to see new beauty in things divine, tell the preacher so. To learn that he is helping others encourages him to press on.

To boast of blue blood indicates senile pride and snobbery; the possession of red blood means energy and action; the results of the blood of Christ is humility and self-forgetfulness.

The Body An Instrument

There is an inward man and there is an outward man. "Though our outward man is decaying, yet our inward man is renewed day by day." (2 Cor. 4:16.) Our spirits can communicate with each other only through the instrumentality of our bodies. The inward man is the responsible part of man. God makes the inward man responsible for the actions of the body. "Present your bodies a living sacrifice, Holy." (Rom. 12:1.) "Let not sin therefore reign in your mortal body, that ye should obey the lusts thereof: neither present your members unto sin as instruments of unrighteousness; but present yourselves unto God, as alive from the dead, and your members as instruments of righteousness unto God." (Rom. 6:12, 13.) The hand that murders a man is not responsible for the bloody deed; it is merely an instrument. And so of the tongue when it slanders.

Some religionists contend that the spirit of a regenerate man never sins—that the sins committed by a child of God are sins of the body, in which the spirit has no part. This effort at argument is made in the interest of the doctrine of the impossibility of apostasy. Just how the spirit can remain pure and guiltless while the body murders and engages in debauchery has never been satisfactorily explained. Such an idea is repugnant to common sense and contrary to the teaching of the Bible. The doctrine implies that the spirit, full of love for the enemy, seeks to do him good, while the body, full of hate, murders him; that the spirit, pure and holy, can seek the conversion and salvation of a person, while the body, full of lust, seduces and accomplishes the moral ruin of the same person. If a man who believes such did not show decided traces of sanity along other lines, we would believe that he should be locked in a padded cell where he could do neither himself nor another any harm.

The spirit is the responsible part of man. It is that which lifts him above the animal and makes him a responsible being. Just how the spirit of a sinner is responsible for what he does and the spirit of a Christian is not responsible for what he does is beyond comprehension. But suppose we admit, for argument's sake, that every sin committed by a child of God originates in the appetites and passions of the flesh, that by no means frees the spirit from responsibility and guilt. The flesh may lust, but the purpose and plan to gratify that passion are formed in the heart. It seems as clear as daylight to me that God makes the spirit responsible for what the body does. Read again Rom. 6:12: "Let not sin therefore reign in your mortal bodies, that ye should obey the lusts thereof." Here Paul addresses the intelligent, responsible part of man, some part of man distinct from the body is made responsible for what the body does. That, of course, is the spirit of man. To that spirit he gives a charge over the body: "Let not sin therefore reign in your mortal body." If, then, the spirit allows sin to reign in the body, the spirit disobeys God, and, therefore sins. The language shows plainly that when the spirit yields and allows the body to sin, the spirit is obeying the lusts of the body instead of God. Can any one think for a moment that the spirit which obeys the lusts of the flesh instead of God can be guiltless? In this same chapter (Rom. 6:16). Paul says to these same brethren: "Know ye not, that to whom ye present yourselves as servants unto obedience, his servants ye are whom ye obey; whether of sin unto death, or of obedience unto righteousness?"

The desire for certain things may grow out of the fleshly propensities, but the purpose to gratify that desire is formed in the heart. Hence, Jesus said: "Every one that looketh on a woman to lust after her hath committed adultery already with her in his heart." (Matt. 5:28.) The sin of the heart comes first. If the Bible said nothing on this point, any thoughtful person would recognize this truth. But hear Jesus further: "For out of the heart come forth evil thoughts, murders, adulteries, fornications, thefts, false witness, railings: these are the things which defile the man." (Matt. 15:19,20.) "For from within, out of the heart of men, evil thoughts proceed, fornications, thefts, murders, adulteries, covetings, wickedness, deceit, lasciviousness, an evil eye, railing, pride, foolishness; all these evil things proceed from within, and defile the man." (Mark 7:21-23.) That settles it. Every conceivable sort of sin comes from the heart—from the inward man. Add to the foregoing what is said in James 2:1-4: "My brethren . . . do ye not make distinctions among yourselves, and become judges with evil thoughts?" Does the body or the spirit do the thinking? Settle this in your mind, and you will have no trouble in determining whether the spirit sins.

Adam was a son of God (Luke 3:38), and yet he sinned and fell. The Baptists bear witness to the fact that his spirit sinned. But, contrary to their plea that the spirit of a child of God cannot sin, these advocates of the impossibility of apostasy argue that Adam's body and spirit became totally depraved by his sin, and that this depravity of body and spirit passed to all his posterity. And thus these advocates of the impossibility of apostasy, these who claim that the spirit of a child of God cannot sin base their doctrine of the depravity of the body and spirit on this assumed universal apostasy. Can anything be more contradictory?

The body is the instrument through which the spirit acts either for good or bad. Only through the body may the spirit while tabernacling here manifest itself. The members of the body are not responsible, but they may be used by the spirit as instruments of either sin or righteousness. "For as ye presented your members as servants to uncleanness and to iniquity unto iniquity, even so now present your members as servants to righteousness unto sanctification." (Rom. 6:19.) Herein is the spirit's responsibility; and in the way it uses these members of the body is seen either its glory or its shame; and this use determines the spirit's standing with God. Hence, Paul affirms: "For if ye live after the flesh, ye must die; but if by the Spirit ye put to death the deeds of the body, ye shall live." (Rom. 8:13.) It would be needless to say to a thoughtful person that Paul does not here refer to the death of the body, for that will die, no matter how you live. Nor does he affirm that the spirit of an alien sinner will die if he walks after the flesh, for the spirit of the alien sinner is already dead. He here speaks of the spirit of the child of God: that will die if it allows the flesh to dominate.

"Flee fornication. Every sin that a man doeth is without the body; but he that committeth fornication sinneth against his own body." (1 Cor. 6:18.) This is a striking passage when allowed to speak in its own language, though few passages have been more abused. It teaches that the body is not the responsible agent in sin—"Every sin that a man doeth is without the body." "Without the body," "exterior to the body," "beyond the body." See the lexicons of the Greek adverb "ektos," here used with the force of a preposition. Look at the different translations. I am writing this away from my books and cannot quote from them. I heard a good brother quote Paul thus: "Every sin that a man doeth is without the body but the sin of fornication." I was amazed. Paul said no such thing. Read again what Paul said. Paul's doctrine is that, while every sin that we commit comes from the spirit and not the body, as Jesus also taught, there are some sins (and here he mentions specifically the sin of fornication) that are against the body —that is, they are hurtful to the body. While all sins defile the spirit, there are some sins that hurt the body. The body is not the responsible part of man in sin, but such sins as fornication, drunkenness, etc., are hurtful to the body.

Hence, it is clearly seen that the doctrine that the spirit of a regenerate man never sins, though the body does, is directly in opposition to the plain teach-

ings of the word of God. The doctrine itself becomes
an excuse for sin and gives comfort to a person who
sins. Any doctrine that excuses sin or gives a man
any feeling of comfort while he indulges in sin is of
the devil.

"I beseech you therefore, brethren, by the mercies
of God, to present your bodies a living sacrifice, holy,
acceptable to God, which is your spiritual service."
(Rom. 12.1.) Instead of "spiritual" the King James
Version has "reasonable." But the word "reasonable" has been greatly abused. It is true that the
word frequently means *fair, equitable,* as when we
speak of a reasonable price; but that is not its meaning here. Certainly Paul did not pass judgment on
God's requirements and recommend them to the
brethren on the grounds that he considered them fair
and equitable. The word "spiritual" comes closer
to Paul's meaning; at least, it is freer from the possibility of being misunderstood. Hence, to present
our bodies a living sacrifice is a spiritual service, or
worship. It is spiritual because every act of acceptable obedience comes from the heart, or spirit. We
obey from the heart (Rom. 6:17), and every transformation in conduct comes from renewing the mind
(Rom. 12:2.) The spirit serves through the instrumentality of the body.

One frequently hears and reads such expressions
as "external ordinances" and "carnal ordinances."
It is easy to see to what such writers and speakers
refer, but it is hard to know just what they mean by
"external" and "carnal" when applied to anything
pertaining to Christianity. As every act of obedience
must come from the heart, there can be no such thing

as an "eternal" or "carnal" ordinance in the religion of Christ. When I was a young man, I heard a preacher raise the question: "How can baptism do the soul any good? For the water does not touch the soul." Immediately other questions occurred to me: "How can the Lord's Supper do the soul any good? Do the bread and wine touch the soul? Where does he think the soul is anyway?" I grant now that that was not such an elegant line of thought, but the questions occurred to me then as a complete answer to the preacher's question. If these preachers think that a service is external or fleshly because the body is engaged in it, then everything about service to God is external and fleshly; for there is not one command of God that a person can obey without the use of the body in some way. If we sing or pray, we use the members of our body in expressing our praises or our desires. Of course, if the heart is not in what we do, it is a fleshly performance, and if it is a fleshly performance, it is also a hypocritical performance. We cannot minister to the sick or help the needy without the use of our bodies, and yet that is a spiritual service, as all will admit. However, if our heart is not in what we do, it also is a fleshly performance, and, therefore, hypocritical. Baptism also would be a mere fleshly performance if our heart were not in the act. When a baby is sprinkled for baptism, so far as that baby is concerned, it is wholly a fleshly performance; for if it has any mind about it at all, it protests against the performance. But the baptism of a person who is sincerely trying to bring his life into harmony with God's will is a spiritual service in the highest degree. Think on these things.

The Greatest War

The greatest of all wars is the war between right and wrong. It is greatest in point of numbers engaged and involved. Every responsible person is on one side or the other. There are no neutrals; neither can there be any. Jesus settled that when he said: "He that is not for me is against me." If you are not fighting for the right, your very example, no matter what your desires may be, is helping the wrong. Even the helpless infant suffers as a result of sin in the world. This is the greatest war, if measured only in dollars and cents. Think of all the government machinery engaged in protecting the good citizens and in apprehending, trying and punishing the criminals. To that must be added the loss of good citizens murdered and also the vast amount of property criminally destroyed; also we must add the cost of every lock, every safety-deposit vault, etc. And, above all, it is greatest because of what is involved. Some wars decide the destiny of nations; your part in this war will decide the destiny of your soul.

This is a war of conquest—the conquest of hearts. You may surrender to either side. God is leading the forces of righteousness; the devil, the forces of evil. So far as you are concerned, you decide the issue. "Know ye not, that to whom ye present yourselves as servants unto obedience, his servants ye are whom ye obey; whether of sin unto death, or of obedience unto righteousness?" (Rom. 6:16.) The devil has gained a point every time he induces you to do wrong, and he has gained a victory when he induces a person to make no effort to obey God. Be sure that he is using everything possible to keep people from obeying God. He uses religious theories with great effect, such as universalism, unconditional salvation, "one way is as good as another," and so on through the whole catalogue of false theories.

Let this statement find permanent lodgment in your heart: Anything, whether it be doctrine preached from the pulpit, or business affairs, or social relations, or anything else, that keeps you from doing God's will or makes you feel at all comfortable in disobedience, is of the devil.

But people who earnestly desire to do right will not be led astray. "Blessed are they that hunger and thirst after righteousness: for they shall be filled." (Matt. 5:6.) This means that they will attain to what they desire. Every one who sincerely and earnestly desires to do right will find the right. That promise of Jesus is as plain and definite as: "He that believeth and is baptized shall be saved." I cannot doubt either promise. Hence, I believe that every honest person comes to know the truth.

But many people who are honest with their fellow men are not honest with God. What is honesty? It is to render to the other person everything that rightfully belongs to him. If I take or withhold from my neighbor that which rightfully belongs to him, I am not honest with him. If I am indifferent about my obligations to him, I am not honest with him. If I withhold from God that which rightfully belongs to him or am careless or indifferent about my obligations to him, I am not honest with him. I owe it to

God, as I do to my fellow man, to treat his word fairly. Also, I have been bought with a price; by right I belong to God. Honesty requires that I deliver to him in full that which belongs to him, to be used by him as he pleases. To act on the principle that one way is as good as another is dishonest. In busines affairs we have certain standards of values, weights, and measures. To deviate from these carelessly or intentionally is dishonest. God's word is the standard by which our conduct is to be regulated. By it we are evaluated, weighed, and measured. Let us be honest with him in making a determined effort to abide by that standard. The devil is a skillful warrior; be not deceived.

Anvil Sparks:

The well-rounded character is square in his dealings.

A confessed missing link in any theory proves it to be a guess.

Keeping a cool head may prevent your rushing into a place where you will get cold feet.

Any preacher likes to have friends, but when friendship degenerates into worship trouble begins.

No man is a safe teacher or preacher if he is seeking a reputation. The desire for Man's applause utterly unfits one for being a true believer. "How can ye believe who seek glory one of another?"

Wisdom never pretends to be wise; foolishness often does.

Excuses fool no one but the person who makes them.

Misunderstood

To misunderstand a person is to fail to understand his purposes and aims. We may know exactly what he is doing, but we fail to understand his reasons for so doing. Because of this we often criticize when we should praise, and thereby cause many heartaches. Children are sometimes misunderstood, and so are parents, and such misunderstanding may cause wounds that never heal. Offense is often taken where none is intended, because we do not understand. Serious troubles have come up in churches because no honest effort was made to understand one another. When we know that our own purposes are good and true, we do not like for others to misunderstand and criticize. To put all we have and are into an unselfish effort to do good, and then to be misunderstood and criticized, and sometimes abused, by our friends and those we would help, causes indescribable sorrow to any unselfish soul.

Both enemies and friends misunderstood Jesus, and for a time even his brothers and his mother. His enemies said he was a lawbreaker and a blasphemer and possessed of a demon. His friends said he was mentally unbalanced, crazy (Mark 3:21); and his brethren seemed to think so, too., "for even his brethren did not believe on him" (John 7:5). But little men cannot even understand great men; much less can the finite understand the Infinite. A few years ago a man wrote a book about Jesus, and the title of the book was, "The Man Nobody Knows." There is more in the title of his book than even its author would recognize. "No one knoweth the Son, save the Father," said Jesus. (Matt. 11:27.) Nothing less than Deity could fully understand Deity.

But these people could have known and recognized his mission and the purity of his life and motives. They, for a time at least, rejected the only key to the wonders of his life and works. They tried to account for him as a man. On these grounds no one can account for him. Had they seen in him God manifest in the flesh, all else could have been easily accounted for; for this great truth that he was the God-man is the only explanation of his marvelous life and works. The world's greatest tragedy is its failure to understand Jesus.

Anvil Sparks:

It is evident from the actions of some men that the Lord did not take the bone out of man's head to make woman.

A sermon should be well proportioned; its length should correspond with its width and depth. Some sermons are long at fifteen minutes.

Yes, there are people today who would die for Christ.

Liberalism as proclaimed today is just another name for indifference to truth.

Also it is evident that a man sometimes has warm enemies as well as warm friends.

If a man you regard as an enemy criticises you, profit by his criticism, instead of trying to show that he is also bad.

It seems that a man these days cannot hurl a bit of gospel truth in any direction without raising a howl. Well, a howl registers a hit!

Foundations

Every denomination has some doctrines peculiar to itself. These peculiar doctrines are the basis for its existence; upon them it was founded. Without these peculiar doctrines it would have had no excuse, no foundation, for its existence. Till recent years every denomination tried earnestly and persistently to justify its existence by a constant effort to prove the truthfulnes of its doctrines. Both preachers and laymen believed their doctrines, and wanted everybody else to believe them. Their doctrines were preached and debated publicly and privately. If you knew to what church a person belonged, you knew what he believed. But all that sort of thing is changed now. You cannot tell from the label what is on the inside. With few exceptions, the denominations make no decided effort to promulgate their doctrines. As a result, their members know very little about the doctrines of their church. When a church ceases to emphasize the doctrines upon which it was founded, it surrenders all the excuse it might have had for an existence.

We are gravely told that we all agree on the essentials, differing only on the nonessentials. But different churches are not built upon points of agreement, but on points of disagreement—on doctrines concerning which they differ. It amounts to this: Different denominations are built on doctrines that they confess are nonessentials. I raise this question: How can you build an essential church upon a nonessential foundation? If these doctrines about which they differ are nonessential, then a church that is built to propagate these doctrines has a nonessential mission—a nonessential church, built on a nonessential foundation, with a nonessential mission!

There are, of course, as many foundations as there are churches. Anything can be a foundation for a church, but there is only one foundation upon which a church of God can be built: "For other foundation can no man lay than that which is laid, which is Jesus Christ." (1 Cor. 3:11.) If Jesus be not the Christ, then there is no excuse for a church of Christ, any more than there would be for a church of Plato. But he is the Christ, and a church built upon him has a sure foundation. But factions—parties—sometimes arise even in churches built upon Christ, and the factious spirit sometimes leads to a formal separation. There are then two churches where there was one. Which group is the church of Christ at that place, or is either of them a church of Christ? That which gives rise to a faction or party is the foundation of that faction. A faction may be built on some theory, some speculation, or some method of working or worship. Any of these things may become a foundation for a new party. Without that particular thing the party would not have existed. Or the preacher may be the cause of a faction; if so, he is the foundation for that faction. That is self-evident; for had he not been there, there would have been no faction. And it occurs occasionally that democracy becomes the foundation for a new party in the church. A group want majority rule, and they will split the church in order to have it; and majority rule is the foundation for that group. Churches founded on such things cannot be churches of Christ. Have you been a party to a division in a church? What caused a party to spring up in the church? Such matters demand serious consideration, for a man can render no better service to the devil than to cause division in a church.

Anvil Sparks:

Some people have to be knocked down before they will "sit up and take notice."

It is not exactly accurate to speak of it as "the rule or ruin spirit"; for that kind of spirit usually rules and ruins.

Some people are a vital part of the church, and some are just stuck on much as children stick chewing-gum on the furniture.

The devil outside of a church can do it very little harm, but many a church has been wrecked and ruined by the devil inside of it.

It has never been proved that a monkey can make a man of himself, but we see it demonstrated every day that a man can make a monkey of himself.

Do not pull your ideas too green; for when later they have shriveled and wrinkled, you will be ashamed of them. Besides, matured fruit is more palatable and wholesome.

If man did come from the lower animals, and there is such a thing as reversion to original species, then we have incontestible evidence that some men came by way of the donkey family.

Love looks to the ultimate good, rather than the present pleasure, of the one loved.

"Speaking the truth in love" does not mean speaking it in such a vague way that no one will object to it.

When a preacher begins to study how to arrange his sermons so as to please the people he has "junked" his interest in heaven.

The Law A Tutor

"So that the law is become our tutor to bring us unto Christ, that we might be justified by faith. But now that faith is come, we are no longer under a tutor." (Gal. 3:24,25.)

Paul had shown that the law could not give life; neither could people be justified by the law. Why, then, was the law given? What purpose did it serve? Some of the Jewish converts to Christ were so devoted to the law of Moses that they contended that even Christians must keep the law or they could not be saved. Paul seeks to correct them by showing that by the law no one could be justified, and that the law was never intended to be of perpetual obligation, but that it served the purpose God had in view in giving it.

God intended that the law should be a tutor; literally, a pedagogue. Among the Greeks and the Romans, the pedagogue's work was rather primary teaching, training, guiding, leading. A little reflection will convince the thoughtful that the world needed some training, teaching, and discipline before Christ would mean much to them. What lessons, what training, what discipline, did the world need? We call attention to some needs that the law supplied. We should also bear in mind that the law, through the Israelites, mightily influenced the thoughtful in all civilized nations.

1. It was intended to firmly implant in the hearts of the people the idea of one God, thus destroying the corrupting influence of idol worship. "Thou shalt

have no other gods before me. Thou shalt not make
unto thee a graven image, nor any likeness of anything that is in heaven above, or that is in the earth
beneath, or that is in the water under the earth: thou
shalt not bow down thyself unto them, nor serve
them." (Ex. 20:3-6.) Men cannot, by studying nature, know how many beings engaged in making the
world, though they may know that it did not originate itself. The idea of one God is due to revelation.
So often the law sets forth the idea of one God, and
that beside him there is none other.

2. The human being needs the bracing conviction
that God is his Creator. "In the beginning God created the heavens and the earth." "And God created
man in his own image, in the image of God created
he him; male and female created he them." (Gen.
1:27.) "I have made the earth, and created man
upon it: I, even my hands, have stretched out the
heavens; and all their host have I commanded." (Isa.
45:12.) To realize that God is his Maker gives man
a feeling of personal responsibility to God. To know
that God created all men gives us a fellow feeling
for all men. It is not good for man to believe that
he is the result of a series of chance developments
from a tiny spark of life accidentally generated. The
person who eliminates God from creation and makes
man merely the climax of a series of animal developments has no basis for any feeling of responsibility
to God or man. The lower order of animals have no
ideas of morality, and the evolutionists have no basis
for any. Why should I have any more regard for
the life of one animal than another? Get the idea

firmly fixed in the average person's mind that he is no more than a sort of improved animal, and he is ready for any crime known to man. In my judgment, no other theory so promotes crime as does atheistic evolution. We need again to learn the lesson that God is our Creator.

3. Because God is the Creator of this world, he is its rightful ruler. The whole law of Moses impressed the idea that it is God who commands and that we must obey. "What thing soever I command you, that shall ye observe to do: thou shalt not add thereto, nor diminish from it."

4. By living under the law the Hebrew learned that God's way was best, and that "it is not in man that walketh to direct his steps." This he learned by seeing that he prospered when he obeyed God, and that disobedience brought disaster. He learned that in obeying God he was walking by God's wisdom, and that in disobeying him he was walking in the darkness of man's notions. The law was thus training him so that he could walk by faith, not by sight.

5. Thorough teaching in the matter of giving was prominent in the Jew's religion. They learned to sacrifice. The first-born of all animals and every tenth one born in their flocks and herds, whether good or bad, belonged to the Lord; also the first fruits of their fields and vineyards belonged to the Lord, and also a tenth of all that was produced. They did not give this—it was the Lord's to begin with. The half shekel paid into the tabernacle funds by every male over twenty years old seems to have been of perpetual obligation. Their sacrifices and offerings—their sin

offerings, trespass offerings, peace offerings, thank offerings, etc.—must have been of considerable value. They were required to attend yearly the three stated feasts, and they were not to attend these feasts empty-handed. "Every man shall give as he is able, according to the blessing of Jehovah thy God which he hath given thee." (Deut. 16:16,17.) No definite amount is here stipulated. The time devoted to their Sabbath days and years and to other holy days, together with the time required to attend their three yearly feasts, must have amounted to something like one-third of their time. They were required to help the poor and to take care of the stranger, and they were not allowed to charge the poor brother any interest on loans. When the kingdom was established, or, rather, when they made themselves a king, they had to pay a tenth to support the government. This tenth had nothing to do with the Lord's tenth. Now, can you figure up how much the Hebrew gave? But we can easily see that the person who says the Jews gave a tenth has made a very superficial study of what they gave. They did give a tenth, and much more.

6. The law developed in the people a consciousness of sin till sin weighed upon them as a burden. It was necessary that they come to realize their need of a Deliverer—One who could deliver them from the bondage of sin. Jesus as Savior can be of no benefit to one who does not feel his need of salvation from sin.

Jesus, therefore, came as soon as the people were ready for his coming. John the Baptist had come "to make ready for the Lord a people prepared for him." (Luke 1:17.) Or giving full value to the Greek participle, we have, "to make ready for the Lord a people having been prepared for him." The law ended at the cross; the pedagogue had served its purpose. "But now that faith is come, we are no longer under a tutor." (Gal. 3:25.) We have now been enrolled in the great school of Christ.

Anvil Sparks:

Every person should so cultivate his mind that when he takes off his hat there will still be some real value above his ears.

If the "professional debater" whose days, we are told, are past, is to be followed by the professional preacher, have we gained anything?

A paradox: God is never far from us, but we are sometimes very far from him.

The party spirit in a church murders God's truth and makes liars of its devotees.

Extremes meet: the farthest place on earth from where you are is right where you are.

Some wise men have made monkeys of themselves by trying to make apes of their ancestors.

No, beloved: I'll not get on your toes if you keep them where they belong — I am preaching to your head and heart.

If you could see beneath the surface, you might discover that the man who scolds the woman for using rouge has only painted himself up to look like a saint.

Some speakers electrify their hearers; others merely gas them.

The Gospel of Christ—God's Power to Save

Jesus commanded his apostles to "go . . . into all the world, and preach the gospel to every creature." Paul exhorted Timothy: "The things that thou hast heard of me among many witnesses, the same commit thou to faithful men, who shall be able to teach others also." (2 Tim. 2:2.) "Preach the word." "Let him that heareth say, come." An awful responsibility rests upon the preacher, and the curses of God rest upon him if he does not fully preach the gospel of God. All Christians should feel enough interest in the salvation of humanity to become, as far as they can, preachers of the gospel of Christ.

Preachers have the gospel to deliver. The gospel is not ours; it comes from the Supreme Being to his dependent creatures. The preacher is not responsible for the nature of this gospel, is not responsible for the effect it has on those to whom it is sent; he is responsible alone for its faithful deliverance. Why, then, will a preacher apologize to people for preaching the gospel to them? Neither is it becoming in him to insult and abuse those to whom he delivers it; he has no right to change it to suit his hearers. Such a course is stealing God's word from the people. "I am against the prophets, saith the Lord, that steal my words every one from his neighbor." (Jer. 23:30.)

Let us preach that which saves. Paul never thought of preaching any less than a full gospel. "So as much as in me is, I am ready to preach the gospel to you also that are in Rome. For I am not ashamed of the gospel: for it is the power of God unto salvation to

(74)

every one that believeth; to the Jew first, and also to the Greek. For therein is revealed a righteousness of God from faith unto faith." (Rom. 1:15-17.)

In trying to emphasize a point, we sometimes weaken it. One often hears speakers emphasize "the" in this passage—"*the* power; not *a* power; but *the* power." But it so happens that "the" is not in the Greek at this place. The strength of the passage may be better seen by reading it thus: "I am not ashamed of the gospel, for it is God's power for salvation." Lard so renders it; and so does the Cambridge Greek Testament for Schools and Colleges. So do others. I would not limit God's power; he is all-powerful. Paul's language differentiates his saving power from the other manifestations of his power. The gospel is not God's power for creating man, but for saving him. In creating man, he used his creative power; in saving man, he uses his saving power, and his saving power is the gospel. If a man is ever saved, God must save him; and if God saves a man, he will do it with saving power. Think of the many manifestations of God's power—creation, motion, gravity, cohesion, adhesion, magnetism, etc. —in the physical world. We call them "laws of nature," but they are simply various powers of God. But God does not use these physical powers to save man. But remember that each power has its own sphere of operation, its one end to serve, and you will never make the mistake of thinking that God will save a person any way except through his saving power. That power is the gospel. If we will not let him save us by the gospel, we are doomed.

Read our text again, and notice how the statements
are connected by the conjunction "for." Also read
the next verse after our text. Paul desires to preach
the gospel in Rome, "for" he is not ashamed of the
gospel; he is not ashamed of the gospel, "for" it is
God's power for salvation; it is God's power for salvation, "for" in it is revealed a righteousness of God
by faith; God's righteousness by faith is revealed,
"for" his wrath is revealed against all ungodliness
and unrighteousness of men.

There must be some connection made between
power and the thing to be moved. There is great
power in a locomotive, but it cannot move the train
of cars till proper connection is made. There is sufficient power in the gospel to move every sinner out
of sin into the blessings of salvation; but that power
moves no one till proper connections are made.
Preaching is the means of establishing that connection; it is God's way of bringing the sinner under the
influence of his saving power. For that reason Paul
was not ashamed to preach it. The gospel exerts no
power over the heathen who has never heard it, nor
over the infidel who will not hear it, and it exerts
but little power over him who looks for the power to
come some other way. It exerts a power over us
for good to the extent that we place ourselves under
the influence of its teaching. The cyclone has no
power over the man who is safely hidden away in his
storm cellar; but it would be foolish for him to come
out after the storm and confidently affirm that there
was no power in the cyclone, but no more foolish
than for a man who will not heed God's word to af-

firm that there is no converting power in it. Such a one talks fluently of the insufficiency of the word of God; and of course he is not conscious of any power it has. There is such a thing here as personal experience; and the man who takes the Bible as the full revelation of God's will, loves it, studies it, meditates upon it, and tries faithfully to fulfill its requirements in his life—such a man never says that the word has no power in it. He knows better (the Bible has taught him better); he has realized its power in the upbuilding of his own character; he has seen its transforming influence on the hearts and lives of his friends and neighbors. The power of the word is no longer a theory with him; it is a living reality. He never speaks slightingly of God's commands; neither does he refer to the Bible as the *mere* word of God. Sentiments such as the following are the ruling passions in his heart: "Thy word have I hid in mine heart, that I might not sin against thee . . . Open thou mine eyes, that I may behold wondrous things out of thy law. . . . Thy testimonies also are my delight and my counselors. . . . This is my comfort in my affliction: for thy word hath quickened me. . . . The law of thy mouth is better unto me than thousands of gold and silver. . . . O how love I thy law! It is my meditation all the day. . . . How sweet are thy words unto my taste! yea, sweeter than honey to my mouth!" (Ps. 119:11-103.) "More to be desired are they than gold, yea, than much fine gold: sweeter also than honey and the honeycomb. Moreover by them is thy servant warned: and in keeping of them there is great reward." (Ps. 19:10,11.)

The Gospel is God's power for salvation, for in it

is revealed God's righteousness, which is by faith, in order to faith. Perhaps no statement in the Bible is fuller of meaning or covers a wider range than does our text, for the whole plan of human redemption is included in it. It is not surprising that denominational commentators, who do not understand the plan of salvation, should differ as to the meaning of a passage of Scripture that sets forth, in a condensed form, the whole plan of salvation. Among them there is some confusion as to the meaning of the last sentence of our text. A study of the translations made by some commentators is helpful. Macknight: "For the righteousness of God by faith, is revealed in it, in order to faith." Lard: "For in it is revealed God's justification by belief in order to belief." Grubbs: "Therein is revealed a righteousness of God by faith in order to faith." Whatever this righteousness is, we attain to it by faith, not by works of law. And this plan of righteousness is revealed in the gospel in order to produce faith. "Even we believed on Christ Jesus, that we might be justified by faith in Christ, and not by the works of the law." (Gal. 2:16). Justification is a mighty motive to lead a condemned sinner to an active faith in Christ Jesus. This is one reason as to why the gospel is the power of God unto salvation—it leads the sinner out of sin into active faith in Jesus the Christ.

But what is the meaning of "righteousness of God," or "God's righteousness"? It cannot refer to God's personal holiness. That had been fully revealed in the law and the prophets, whereas the righteousness spoken of in our text is revealed in the gospel. A statement Paul makes concerning the Jews sheds light on the question: "For being ignorant of God's righteousness, and seeking to establish their own, they did not subject themselves to the righteousness of God." (Rom. 10:3.) They were not ignorant of the truth that God was a righteous Being, but they were ignorant of the plan of righteousness revealed in the gospel, and to it they did not subject themselves —that is, they did not obey the gospel.

There are two conceivable ways by which a person may be righteous—namely, (1) so to live as never to sin, or, (2) having sinned, to be forgiven—thoroughly cleansed from sin. We can think of the first way, but none of us ever live without sin. Some plan by which guilty men may become righteous is necessary, or all men are doomed. And that is the very reason the gospel plan of making guilty sinners righteous has been revealed. That is the force of Paul's "for" in Rom. 1:18—"For the wrath of God is revealed from heaven against all ungodliness and unrighteousness of men." Then he proceeds to show that all men, both Jew and Gentile, are sinners, and concludes the argument by restating the doctrine set forth in our text: "But now apart from the law a righteousness of God hath been manifested, being witnessed by the law and the prophets; even the righteousness of God through faith in Jesus Christ unto all them that believe; for there is no distinction; for all have sinned, and fall short of the glory of God." (Rom. 3:21-23.) This gospel plan by which sinners may attain to a state of righteousness is our only hope.

Some of the creeds teach that the saved man retains his former corruption, and is merely counted as righteous for Christ's sake—that is, he is clothed with Christ's personal righteousness as a means of covering his remaining corruption. If that is all the gospel does for the sinner, it is more of a sham than an efficient means of cleansing the sinner. But when a sorrowing sinner puts sin out of his heart and yields himself in humble obedience to God, and God then forgives him, there is not then one sin against him. He is as free as if he had never sinned; in God's sight he is righteous, for there is nothing held against him. Having been cleansed by the blood of Christ, he is as clean as if he had never been soiled by sin.

There are two ways for your handkerchief to be clean—namely, (1) never to become soiled, or, (2) having become soiled, to be washed clean again. When washed, it is as clean as if it had never been soiled, though the fabric may have been weakened by use. Just so may the person be clean. If he never sins, he is righteous by the perfection of his own works. If he sins, and we all have sinned, he may again become, by the power of the gospel, as clean as if he had never sinned, though his moral nature may have been weakened by abuse. And the personal righteousness of Christ is not bestowed upon him any more than is the cleanliness of the washerwoman bestowed upon the clothes she washes. The gospel of Christ is no make-believe arrangement; the blood of Jesus Christ cleanses us from all sin. Because there is revealed in the gospel this plan by which guilty sinners are made righteous, it is the power of God unto salvation. If it did not lead men out of sin and cleanse them from sin, thus putting them in a state of righteousness before God, it could not be God's power to save them.

"And now, brethren, I commend you to God, and to the word of his grace, which is able to build you up, and to give you an inheritance among all them which are sanctified." (Acts 20:32.) "Wherefore . . . receive with meekness the engrafted word, which is able to save your soul." (James 1:21.) The Apostles preached the gospel; they relied on it as God's appointed means of converting the world. Paul says: "God forbid that I should glory, save in the cross of our Lord Jesus Christ."

Anvil Sparks:

Not all educated people are intelligent.

Knowledge is useful only when it is directed by wisdom and an unselfish desire to help others.

While writing on the duty to love one another it might help wonderfully to make ourselves more lovable.

A man may be a great scholar and lack the essential elements that go to make up a great man.

I fear some people will not be satisfied in the next world unless the Lord lets them try their hand at making a better world than this.

When a man who has a little learning feels that he is not appreciated simply because others do not surrender up to him their right to think for themselves he soon becomes sour and useless.

Some men delight in making a line of monkey parantage, and some women's motherly instinct runs to poodles. These are great times, my countrymen.

Concerning Elders

Our thoughts and actions in business and politics influence our thoughts and actions in religious matters. The reason for this is plain. In every relationship in life, our thoughts and actions form and shape our character; and this character, in turn, manifests itself no matter where we are or what we are doing. Certain traits of character are developed in the manager of a group of men in big business. The politician who carries his point by scheming becomes a schemer in the church. And so it runs through all the various lines of activity and phases of character. The transforming power of the gospel is the only remedy, and this requires time and effort. But where a new convert plunges in to manage the affairs of the church the gospel has had no chance to work the needed change. Even with the older Christian there is constant need for watchfulness, lest the spirit of the world dominate him.

While Christians have mightily influenced the world, they, in turn, have been influenced by the world. Any student of church history knows this. In the age of tyranny religious people become tyrannical. Protesting against Rome, the reformers, such as Luther and Calvin, had some of Rome's characteristics. The Puritans, fleeing from religious intolerance and oppression, showed themselves also to be somewhat tyrannical. It all goes to show that it is hard for men with the purest and loftiest ideals to be entirely free from thoughts and ideals of the times. Other illustrations are at hand.

So-called liberalism, which began to be urged some time before the world war, was given a mighty impetus by that war, so that now one is supposed not to have very strong convictions on anything. Very few believe their creeds: even fundamentals are sacrificed so that infidels teach our children and occupy pulpits with little protest from any. Many churches, formerly loyal to the Lord, are being infected with this indifference to truth. It is a deadly contagion filling the air, and we are breathing it. The only remedy is constant innoculation with Bible truth.

The spirit of democracy, which has grown more or less luxuriantly on American soil for so long, has spread over the world as a result of the war. Democracy, the rule of the people, is the cry. Wilson's plea to make the world safe for democracy spread like wild-fire. Monarchies fell, kings took a hasty departure, and thrones crumbled. Democracy was in the air, and the people everywhere became infected. It became a habit of thought to such an extent that it found its way into some churches of Christ, and majority rule become the order of procedure. In these churches any man would, if he could muster up a majority vote, run rough-shod over God's overseers, or even depose the elders and appoint others. It is the spirit of the world over-riding the Spirit of God.

As an excuse, not a reason, for majority rule in the church we have the plea that elders are not infallible. No one, not even the most tyrannical of elders, claims that elders are infallible. For that matter courts are not infallible; but the wildest democracy ever known would not claim that, therefore, every decision of the courts should be passed on by a vote of the people to determine whether or not they would respect the decision. And yet no one claims that courts have the right to rule absolutely and arbitrarily, nor that they are under divine guidance in their judgments, but that courts are to be guided in their judgments by the laws and constitution of the land, and that it is possible for them to err in their understanding. But what sort of government would any people have if every dissatisfied man under the jurisdiction of the court should go out of his own responsibility and work up or try to work up a majority vote against the decision of the court. To carry his point he could make the same plea against the court that is made against the elders. And this canvassing and counting of votes being under no one's jurisdiction but his own, we can imagine how fair the returns would be. Besides, there is a serious sophistry in the whole pleadings. It seems to be implied that, although elders are fallible and their decisions not therefore binding, majorities are sufficiently beyond the possibility of error that the minority should always submit to the majority. Besides, when a majority is worked up by the activities of one man who lays all the plans and inaugurates every move, such majority represents the thoughts and purposes of only one man. Is that really a majority?

The Holy Spirit makes elders, or bishops, and the Holy Spirit makes Christians; but only when the Holy Spirit's teachings are followed. A man-made elder is no better than a man-made Christian. Disregarding the qualifications for elders laid down by the Holy Spirit and failing to recognize that there is a difference between choosing or selecting elders and appointing them churches sometimes have man-made elders as overseers. The present revival of interest in this matter both on the part of the preachers and on the part of the churches will result in good, if it leads to a closer adherence to the New Testament teaching on the subject.

"I recently held a meeting on Goose Creek with ten baptisms, organized a church, and appointed elders and deacons." Who, in the past, has not seen such announcements as this? Such zeal results in a set of man-made elders and deacons, for it takes time for God to make elders and deacons. Before a man can be God's elder he must learn God's will, develop a well-rounded Christian character, and prove his fitness for such duties, and then be selected in a Scriptural way. Besides, should there be some good men, qualified for the work, who had recently moved to Goose Creek, the members would not know enough about them nor about the qualifications of an elder to act intelligently in selecting them.

The selection of bishops for a church is a serious and solemn matter, for the future usefulness of the church, and perhaps its destiny, is involved. Besides, in proving, or testing men for the eldership, the church itself is undergoing a test; its actions in the matter show whether it is guided by the word of God or by ignorance and passion. The duty and responsibility of selecting elders belong to the congregation as a whole. No man or set of men should undertake to do the selecting for the church.

It is true Titus was to appoint elders, but choosing or selecting comes before appointing. For the preacher to do the selecting, besides being unscriptural, would virtually be clergy-rule, a thing most obnoxious to every free-born child of God. Besides, if the preacher should be selfish and ambitious, such a course would place the church at the mercy of a man who had no mercy where his own interests were involved.

It is laudable for a man to desire to be an elder, yet no man has a right to elect himself to that work. Neither is a man always a good judge of his own qualifications. Being an elder in one congregation does not make a man an elder wherever he may move. Each church must select its own elders; and for a man to claim to be an elder where he moves because he was an elder where he formerly lived is about the same as for a man to appoint himself.

Another plan fraught with much danger to the church is for the elders to select others to serve with them; for an ambitious eldership, if they felt that their present numbers or standing did not give them sufficient weight or prestige to carry out a cherished scheme, would call to their assistance those who sympathize with them, or would be controlled by them. It is needless to say that elders would not do such things—they are human, and such things have been done. Even the best of men are influenced by their predilections. Neither is it any better for the elders to confer and decide that they want a certain man to serve with them, and then announce, "We have selected Brother John Doe as an elder. If we have no objections, his selection stands approved." This is taking advantage of the church. A congregation thus taken by surprise is not prepared on the moment to present any objections, even if they should have them. There is also a natural timidity in doing so. Besides, in such a course the Scriptures have been disregarded, and the church has been robbed of a right that belongs to the whole congregation.

The examples and teaching of inspired men are our guide. Let us keep in mind that elders, deacons, and special messengers, are all servants of the churches. Even the apostles did not infringe on the right of churches to select their servants. When Paul was collecting contributions for the poor in Judea he had need of help. He sent Titus to Corinth, but the churches selected others to assist in the matter (2 Cor. 8:18-21.) The churches would naturally co-operate more readily if they selected their own ministers for the work; and for the churches to have a free hand in selecting their own servants freed Paul from the possibility that any one would accuse him of manipulating matters for his own advantage and pleasure. "For we take thought for things honorable, not only in the sight of the Lord, but also in the sight of men."

"Now, in these days when the number of the disciples was multiplying, there arose a murmuring of the Grecian Jews against the Hebrews, because their widows were neglected in the daily ministration. And the twelve called the multitude of the disciples unto them, and said, it is not fit that we should forsake the word of God, and serve tables. Look ye out therefore, brethren, from among you seven men of good report, full of the Spirit and of wisdom, whom we may appoint over this business. . . . and the saying pleased the whole multitude; and they chose Stephen, a man full of faith and of the Holy Spirit, and Philip, and Prochorus, and Nicanor, and Timon, and Parmenas, and Nicolaus, a proselyte of Antioch; whom they set before the apostles; and when they had prayed, they laid their hands on them." (Acts 6:1-6.) I heard a preacher say that the apostles selected these men. Nothing is further from the truth. The apostles laid down the required qualifications and called on the church to select the men. The Apostles had a part in appointing, but not in the choosing. While these seven men were not to serve as elders, thoughtful Bible students understand that this case gives us an example of the way the early churches, under the direction of inspired men, proceeded in selecting their servants.

The churches, then, choose their servants. But it might be urged that the preacher or the elders know more about who should serve as elders than the church does. Perhaps this is sometimes true. So did the apostles have more knowledge than the church at Jerusalem, but they put the burden of selecting the seven on the church. Either ignorance of the Scriptures or a boss spirit that ignores the Scriptures is at the bottom when one man or a set of men does the choosing for the church, and elders thus chosen are no more Spirit-made elders than if they were appointed by the Pope of Rome. And no self-respecting man can have much respect for the pretentions of men whose selection is the result of schemes or party spirit.

In selecting elders, every care should be exercised to select men possessing the required qualifications. Better have no elders than to disregard the word of the Lord in their selection. Man-made elders are worse than no elders. If a party spirit or selfish ambition dictates the selection the result is a body of man-made elders. Every precaution should be exercised to guard against a factional spirit, or a spirit of rivalry. To put forth opposing candidates to see which will get a majority of the votes is a sure road to trouble. Besides, there may be serious defects in the character of one or more of the proposed elders, which only a few in the congregation have any knowledge of. But to favor a man on partisan grounds, is to give the welfare of the church and the demands of the word of God no consideration.

Anvil Sparks:

God is not so much concerned about the fact that you sinned: but since you have sinned, what are you going to do about it?

"Baptized some of the leading citizens of the town." Why make special mention of the fact? Did you think they needed the gospel worse than the poor and obscure?

Ignorance is an opiate that lulls many a conscience to sleep.

Some people are so constituted that, to them, any restraint is tyranny.

Majority rule in the church was never resorted to as a means of helping the Lord's cause.

Elders and Majority Rule

The evidence that elders were intended to be a permanent feature in churches of Christ seems so clear as to admit of no doubt. It is not my purpose to argue this point at length. However, I call attention to two considerations, which, to my mind, settle the matter without further argument.

1. In every group of men there must be leaders, some one or more, to take the oversight, or there can be no order or system. That has always been true, as all men of experience and discernment must admit. It is as true of the church as of any other group of men. Certainly they are as much needed now as in the days of the apostles. Then they were called "elders" or "overseers." If men of age and experience now direct the affairs of a church, are they not elders and overseers? The whole contention on this point seems to me to be a war about words and names, a striving about words to no profit.

2. It is assumed by some that elders, or bishops, were made such by spiritual gifts, belonging, at least, to the class of inspired men. Is that so? God selected the men upon whom he bestowed spiritual gifts. "But all these worketh the one and the same Spirit, dividing to each one severally even as he will." (1 Cor. 12:11.) For that reason it was not necessary for the Lord to tell the church, or any member of it, what qualifications men must have in order to the reception and use of these spiritual gifts. Men did not appoint miracle workers, prophets, unknown-tongue speakers, etc. But men did select and appoint

elders, and for that reason we needed to know what sort of men to select. And so God gave full directions as to the necessary qualifications for elders. Develop this argument; it completely refutes the idea that elders were spiritually gifted men and passed away with the passing of spiritual gifts.

"Take heed unto your selves, and to all the flock, in which the Holy Spirit hath made you bishops, to feed the church of the Lord which he purchased with his own blood. I know that after my departure grievous wolves shall enter in among you, not sparing the flock; and from among your own selves shall men arise, speaking perverse things, to draw away the disciples after them. Wherefore watch ye." (Acts 20:28-31.) The word from which we have "bishop" is defined by Liddell and Scott as "an overseer, watcher, guardian." This definition harmonizes with the duties laid down by Paul in the foregoing quotation. As a guardian, the elder is to see that the flock is fed and cared for; as a watcher, he is to see that no enemy comes in and destroys the flock. The overseer is an inspector. Any one can see trouble after it develops. An elder, by close and constant inspection, should be able to detect the seeds of trouble without waiting till the ripened fruit appears. Not many people apostatize suddenly. A little watchfulness at the right time might save a soul. Neither does division in a church come suddenly. Complaints come that a preacher has run things over the elders and the more conservative members by majority rule. How did it happen? The elders employed a preacher and allowed him gradually to assume control. When he reaches a point where they can stand him no longer, they find that he is the ruler and they are the ruled. It is too late then to save the congregation from ruin.

The responsibility of the watchman is set forth in Ezek. 33:1-6. If the watchman does not sufficiently inform himself so as to be able to recognize an enemy, how is he to be of use as a watchman? The watchman on the walls must know the enemy when he sees him approaching. Any man who divides churches is an enemy. If we do not inform ourselves concerning such men, how can we obey Paul's injunction? "Now I beseech you, brethren, mark them that are causing the divisions and occasions of stumbling, contrary to the doctrine which ye have learned; and turn away from them. For they that are such serve not our Lord Jesus Christ, but their own belly; and by their smooth and fair speech they beguile the hearts of the innocent." (Rom. 16:17,18.) Because we have not informed ourselves concerning such men so as to avoid them, much harm has come to many good churches. Sometimes the watchers, instead of giving the alarm when such enemies appear, go out and invite them in, and practically turn matters over to them. Then, before the elders realize it, the enemy has spiked their guns and is in full charge. In a recent letter from a friend where the church was in trouble, I found a statement like this: "If we had investigated Brother Blank's record, we never would have had him here." Because of that failure, trouble has been stirred up that may never be settled. Instead of giving alarm at the approach of the enemy, they went out and hired him to come in, thinking he was a friend. The preacher who runs over the elders and divides a church is doubly a sinner, but the elders must share their part of the blame. They frequently wake up too late. But trouble may be expected when the command to watch is disregarded, and also when God's order both in nature and the Bible is disregarded, as it is when mere boys are given practical charge of a church. Also, Absaloms are too much in demand for the welfare of the kingdom.

The Bible tells us to submit to those who have the rule over us, but gives no hint that we are to submit to majority rule. In majority rule Paul would count no more than Mr. Care Less, who cusses, gets drunk sometimes, and goes fishing on Sunday. Generally there is no such thing as real majority rule, even when it is claimed. That is especially true when the party spirit runs high. A group rallies around a leader, and he dictates every move. He votes his followers. Instead of going through the farce of calling for the votes, the leader might as well say: "I control the votes of my two hundred followers, and I cast their votes so and so." When the preacher is the bone of contention, he naturally becomes the party leader. As he has more experience in public speaking and manipulating a body of people than the elders have, he has a decided advantage over them, even if they should care to resort to his tricks. And Paul says of such men that their god is their belly, and they will work all the harder for their bread and butter. As he votes all his followers, there is really only one voice raised on that side. All he needs to do is to tell how he stands and how many followers he has. That is all there is to such voting as that, and it is folly to call it "majority rule." And we are told that the ballot is a safeguard against the unfair rulings of the elders!

It is readily conceded that God's plan of church government is imperfectly carried out. The best men make mistakes. Elders have a heavy responsibility and a hard task. They are not infallible. They may, at times, deal unjustly with a preacher; but it is better that the preacher suffer wrong than to divide a church. If the preacher thinks it unfair for them to put him out, how does he figure that it is fair for him to put them out?

Whereto shall this voting lead? Where will it stop? It is contended, of course, that only matters of opinion shall be voted on; but who shall decide what are matters of opinion? The Methodists and some others have decided that the form of baptism is a mere matter of opinion. Some contend that your opposition to instrumental music in the worship is a matter of opinion. If you believe in voting, and your congregation decides by popular vote that these things are matters of opinion, what can you do about it?

But it is contended that every expression of a preference is a vote. If that is so, some men, when a political campaign is on, vote several times a day for months before election day! If that is voting, most of the votes are cast prior to the election and are never counted. But the claim is too absurd for serious consideration.

Opinion, Faith, Knowledge

Imagination, fancy, notion, and sentiment are all different sorts of opinions. We usually form opinions about everything with which our minds have to do, but no one should allow himself to form an opinion that is hurtful to his faith or that leads to any sort of wrongdoing. Even socially a man can make himself a nuisance by seeking to impose his opinions on others. Socially, an opinionated man is a bore; politically, he is a radical; religiously, he is a disturber of churches; in every way he is undesirable. When such a man makes a plea for the right of opinion, or for liberty of opinion, he is really making a plea for the right and liberty to force his opinions on others. If that were not his object, he would merely form his own opinions, keep them to himself, and go on about his business. I have never had to make a plea for liberty of opinion, and yet I am not conscious that any one ever tried to take that liberty from me. There is something suspicious about a man's designs when he makes an urgent plea for the liberty of opinion. It is almost a certainty that he is laying a foundation for forcing his opinions on others. Otherwise, why the plea?

To really believe in God is to take him into account in everything we do; it is to commit our whole life into his keeping. Many persons think they trust God when they are merely trusting their own feelings or some theory. Full faith, full confidence in God leads one to do unquestioningly what he commands. Faith does not sit down and *trust*; it gets up and follows.

The man who, for any reason, hesitates to obey God is lacking in faith. If you believe in God with all your heart, you will do his will with all your might. Disobedience is certain proof of a lack of faith.

There is a difference between faith and knowledge, but is the difference what we have sometimes been told? In the estimation of some people, there is no knowledge except experimental knowledge. With them, there is no knowledge except information we gain by personal contact through our five senses. They will not allow that we can acquire knowledge through evidence. They will not allow that we can acquire knowledge by reasoning from cause to effect or from effect to cause, or that we can gain any knowledge by putting certain facts together and drawing a conclusion. If a person holding that theory has not seen, smelled, heard, felt, or tasted a thing, he does not know it. He would not know what would happen to a man if he were placed on a ton of nitroglycerin and the nitroglycerin were exploded!

I am now pecking on a typewriter. I did not see any one make it; neither have I ever seen any one make a typewriter of any sort. Yet I know that this typewriter did not grow on a tree, and I know that it was not mined from the earth in its present finished condition. I know just as surely that it was made as if I had seen it done. In the same way, may we not know that some one made this vast machine which we call the universe? In the English language we call that maker God. And that is only one way in which we may know there is a Being whom we call God. But some one remarks: "If you know there is a Being whom you call God, where is your faith? Now, that question reveals how shallow our thinking sometimes is. We confuse persons with things. Your faith in the existence of a thing ceases when you come to know that the thing exists. But God is not a thing; he is a Person. You know that good neighbor of yours, and for that reason you have great faith in him; and the more you come to know God, the more faith you will have in him.

But we will let the Bible have a voice in settling this matter of knowing. May we know that God is? Moses said to Israel: "Know therefore that Jehovah thy God, he is God." (Deut. 7:9.) Job said: "I know that my Redeemer liveth." (Job 19:25.) And David sang: "Be still, and know that I am God." (Ps. 46:10.) In speaking of the New Covenant, Jehovah said through Jeremiah: "They shall all know me, from the least of them unto the greatest of them." (Jer. 31:34.) Paul applies this language to those who are in the New Covenant. (Heb. 8:11.) If, then, a person does not know Jehovah, he is not in the New Covenant. Hosea admonished Israel: "And let us know, let us follow on to know Jehovah." (Hos. 6:3.) Peter said: "Let all the house of Israel therefore know assuredly, that God hath made him both Lord and Christ, this Jesus whom ye crucified." (Acts 2:36.) But what is the penalty, if we do not know? Jesus will come again, "rendering vengeance to them that know not God, and to them that obey not the gospel of our Lord Jesus." (2 Thess. 1:8.) Paul said: "I know him whom I have believed." (2 Tim. 1:12.)

As to the Bible, what may we know? Well, we certainly can know what it says. But can we know that it is from God and not a human production? On this point Jesus speaks plainly: "If any man willeth to do his will, he shall know of the teaching, whether it is of God, or whether I speak from myself." (John 7:17.) This passage is often quoted to prove that if a person wants to know the truth, he can find it. That idea is true, and is abundantly taught in the Bible; but that is not the point Jesus was making. Jesus had just said to the Jews: "My teaching is not mine, but his that sent me." The Jews had raised this question: "How knoweth this man letters, having never learned?" They could not understand how he could have originated such teaching. He tells them that he did not originate his teaching, but that it was from God; and if they would put it to the test, they would find out that it was from God. If any man is determined to do the will of God, he will come to know whether the teaching is from God or originated here on earth. Is there anything strange about that? Is it not reasonable to conclude that by actual practice of the religion of Christ a person could decide definitely whether it is the greatest truth ever made known to man or the greatest fraud ever perpetrated on man? And then he ought to be able to say with Paul: "For we know that if the earthly house of our tabernacle be dissolved, we have a building from God, a house not made with hands, eternal in the heavens." (2 Cor. 5:1.)

"These things have I written unto you, that ye

may know that ye have eternal life, even unto you that believe on the name of the Son of God." (1 John 5:13.)

In an effort to show the distinction between opinion, faith, and knowledge, a speaker once used this method: "I hold something in my hand so that you do not see it, and ask you what it is. You say that it is a penny; that is opinion. I tell you that I hold a penny in my hand, and you, on that testimony, accept my statement as true; that is faith. I open my hand so that you can see what I hold in my hand, and you then say it is a penny; that is knowledge." But does that fairly represent these words? Does it give the correct idea as to what opinion, faith and knowledge are? It does not. The first person who said it was a penny merely expressed the thinnest sort of guess. He did not express an opinion, for he had nothing on which to base an opinion. Opinion, in common parlance, is an idea or notion arrived at by a process of deduction from facts or evidence not sufficient to produce a decided conviction or judgment. More evidence might upset the opinion, or it might develop it into faith.

It is often said that every man has a right to his own opinion; but even that is not always true, for no man has a God-given right to an opinion that hinders his prompt and faithful obedience to God. No man has a right to an opinion that disrupts the fellowship in the church or breeds rebellion against God. Too often a person thinks that his right of opinion gives him the right to force his opinion on others, or even to neglect obedience to a plain command of God. Yet opinion is not always hurtful. In fact, there is one example wherein it seems that opinion was really helpful. Jehovah commanded Abraham to offer Isaac as a burnt offering; yet Jehovah had promised Abraham that the promised blessing should be fulfilled through Isaac. Here it would seem that God's command and his promise were in conflict. If Abraham fulfilled the command, how could God fulfill his promise? Abraham did not doubt God's promise even if Isaac were offered up. Naturally his mind would work on this problem. He decided that, if he slew Isaac, God would immediately raise him up from the dead, "accounting that God is able to raise up, even from the dead; from whence he did also in a figure receive him back." (Heb. 11:19.) In his mind's eye, he saw Isaac coming back from the dead so that God's promise might be true. That was opinion. It did not hinder Abraham's obedience; in fact, did it not make the heart-rending ordeal a little lighter? Suppose Abraham's opinion had taken a different turn? Suppose he had said in his heart, "If I slay Isaac, God cannot fulfill his promise," his opinion would have headed in a dangerous direction. If your opinion has a tendency to lessen your faith or diminish your obedience, dismiss it as a pernicious thing.

"Faith" and "opinion" are frequently used rather loosely, the one for the other. Unless I am mistaken, the word "opinion" is found only three times in the American Standard Version, and only in the Book of Job, and there used only by Elihu. But as the Bible speaks in the language of human beings, we may reasonably expect to find the writers using words very much as we use them. In one place, at least, "faith" seems to be used somewhat loosely, as we sometimes use it. "The faith which thou hast, have thou to thyself before God." That is, keep it as a matter between you and God. This cannot refer to faith in God, for no one is to keep quiet about his gospel faith. It refers to the brother's idea as to the propriety of eating certain meats. "One man hath faith to eat all things; but he that is weak eateth herbs." Read Rom. 14 and you will see that "faith" means there about the same as the word "opinion." It is sometimes difficult to draw the line between an opinion and a weak faith.

Genuine faith is based on evidence that admits of no doubt; and to believe in a person means more than to believe that such a person exists. "He that cometh to God must believe that he is, and that he is a rewarder of them that seek after him." (Heb. 11:6.) In addition to accepting the truth that God is, we confidently trust him for the fulfillment of his promises. In all genuine faith there is, therefore the element of confidence and trust. We trust him to fulfill him promises, and we confide in his wisdom and goodness. It is true, as so often said, that Abel heard God's command and obeyed it, and therefore he made his offering by faith. But there was something back of all that. Why did he do what God said, and why did not Cain do what God said? Abel had confidence in God's wisdom and goodness; Cain had confidence in his own wisdom and way. Hence, Abel followed God's way; Cain followed his own way. Abel did what God commanded, because he had more confidence in God than in himself. A man does not believe as he should till he can truthfully say: "Lord, I know not the way; I am blind, helpless. Now, Lord, I put my hand in thine; lead thou the way, and I will follow. Not one time will I be so foolish as to try to have my own way, nor change one word of thine."

On one occasion Moses turned his confidence from God to self. The people were thirsty in their journey. God commanded Moses to assemble the people and to speak to the rock that it bring forth its water. Moses and Aaron assembled the people before the rock, but he did not speak to the rock, but to the people: "Hear now, ye rebels; shall we bring you forth water out of this rock?" "Shall we"—thus leaving God out of the transaction. Then God said to Moses and Aaron: "Because ye believed not in me," etc. Moses had no more doubt then of the existence of God than he had any other time; yet God says he and Aaron did not believe in him. They did not have sufficient confidence in God to do what he said, but followed their own way; and no man does that except through lack of faith in God.

An effort has been made to show a clear dividing line between faith and knowledge. Well, there is a difference between the two, but not the difference that some seem to think. It is thought by some that faith ends where knowledge begins. But does it? Is it not rather a fact that faith can be increased only by an increase of knowledge? It is also true that there can be no faith at all where there is no knowledge. It is also true that knowledge sometimes destroys faith, or even makes faith impossible. You say: "I have no faith in that man." Why? "Because I know him." And yet you have faith in some people because you know them. Will faith be lost in sight, as we have so often heard? Where does the Bible say anything like that? Have we not had this thing all wrong? Are we to think for a moment that the more we know God, the less we will believe in him? I cannot think so.

And is knowledge confined to our own personal experiences? A good brother illustrated his idea of the difference between faith and knowledge in this way: "I know there is a Dallas, Texas, for I have seen it; but I believe there is a New York City." But how did he know the city was Dallas when he saw it? Likely the conductor said, "All out for Dallas;" and he believed the conductor. But there are some things that we may as certainly know as if we had seen, heard, felt, tasted, and smelled. A little reflection will convince any one that he has some knowledge of things outside his own personal experiences. Proof of this lies all about us.

Anvil Sparks:

It is easier to be radical and extravagant in stating your opinion than it is to be cautious and reserved.

Evidently those who believe in voting the elders out when they do not suit the preacher are afraid to say so through the papers.

Flattery is an intoxicant, and is prohibited in God's word. The flatterer is therefore a bootlegger, peddling for his own gain.

Paul's Natural Man

"Now the natural man receiveth not the things of the Spirit of God: for they are foolishness unto him; and he cannot know them, because they are spiritually judged. But he that is spiritual judgeth all things, and he himself is judged of no man." (1 Cor. 2:14,15.)

Many theories have been advanced as to what Paul's "natural man" is. Before studying some of these theories, let us consider the term, "the things of the Spirit." In verse 9 Paul quotes the prophet to the effect that man, by his own unaided powers of seeing and hearing, had never been able to find out "the things which God had prepared for them that love him," but in the next verse he tells us that God had revealed them through his spirit. It was necessary that these things of the Spirit be revealed: for, as stated in verse 11, no one can know the things of God, save the spirit of God, any more than you can know the thoughts, emotions, and volitions of man. In both cases the things must be revealed, or we cannot know them. Hence, Paul states in the next verse that they had received "'the spirit which is from God; that we might know the things that were freely given to us of God." This Spirit had communicated to the apostles the things of God, the things which otherwise no one could know. "Which things we also speak." Then Paul calls these things "spiritual things." "The things of the Spirit of God," then, are those things which the Spirit has revealed through inspired men, the gospel of the Son of God.

And these are the things which the natural man cannot receive. Whatever or whoever Paul's "natural man" is, his case, as a natural man, is hopeless; for that sort of man cannot receive or know the gospel of Jesus Christ.

The advocates of hereditary total depravity assume that the "natural man" is the unconverted man, the unregenerate sinner; that the unconverted man cannot receive the gospel, and that he must be converted by a direct work of the Spirit to enable him to understand and obey the gospel. It seems not to bother them much that this theory frees the sinner from any responsibility and makes God responsible for the damnation of every soul lost in hell. But the theory is entirely foreign to Paul's argument. He was not seeking to show that sinners could do nothing without a direct operation of the Spirit, and to put such an idea into his conclusion when he had not so much as hinted at it in his argument is slandering Paul's logic. Besides the passage itself disproves the theory. The Greek word here translated *natural* occurs six times in the New Testament, and not one time does it mean inherent depravity. Examine carefully how it is used, and see for yourself. Of the body in death, Paul says, "It is sown a *natural* body; it is raised a spiritual body. If there is a *natural* body, there is also a spiritual body." (1 Cor. 15:44.) No one can say that a dead body is either moral or unmoral. A dead body has in it the elements of physical corruption, but not of moral corruption. It is just such a body as God created, and then gave it life. Sin therefore is not inherent in the body; it is not a part of the body nature. When

Adam and Eve were first created and placed in the Garden of Eden, they had all the human nature that they ever had, or that any has had since. From the way some people argue, it seems that they think Adam and Eve had no human nature about them till after they sinned. But notice his: "The first man Adam became a living soul. The last Adam became a life-giving spirit. Howbeit that is not first which is spiritual, but that which is *natural;* then that which is spiritual." (verses 45,46.) Hence when Adam and Eve were created, they were natural, but not sinful. They were able to know and to do what God said, and yet Adam was a *natural* man.

In James 3:15 the Greek word for natural is translated "sensual." "This wisdom is not a wisdom that cometh down from above, but is earthly, sensual, devilish." But James here does not even hint at the condition of an unconverted man, but a course of life that might spring up among the brethren. This you can easily see by reading the two preceding verses. "Who is wise and understanding among you? Let him show by his good life his works in meekness of wisdom. But if ye have bitter jealousy and faction in your heart, glory not and lie not against the truth." It is that sort of wisdom that is sensual (natural); that is the course of life he warned the brethren against.

Jude 19 has sensual for the same Greek word: "These are they who make separations, sensual, having not the Spirit." The words, "these are they," show clearly that Jude was speaking of people of a certain class, and not of all unconverted people. You can see the people he had in mind by reading the preceding verses. In none of these passages where the word occurs was the writer seeking to prove that the natural man is an unconverted man.

The references show that the word is used with different shades of meaning. In James and Jude the natural man is the one who lives a worldly, selfish life. In 1 Cor. 15:44 Paul applies the term to the dead body, and his use here certainly proves nothing concerning an unconverted man. In verse 46 the term applies to Adam as he was when created, and certainly not to inherit depravity.

It is argued by some that the natural man is the body, the physical man. The few who hold this theory contend that the physical man is animal, and in and of itself is without intelligence, emotion, or volition, and, therefore, cannot receive the gospel; only the spirit of man can do that. But that process of reasoning eliminates the body from the possibility of being the natural man; for Paul's "natural man" is capable of thinking and forming judgments. He has thought on the matter, and has rejected the gospel because he considers it foolishness. It is singular that the very argument made to prove that the natural man is the body proves conclusively that it is not the body. Besides, there is in this theory the false assumption that the body of a man is the only part of him that is natural to him; but is it not just as natural for a person to have a spirit as it is to have a body? And the theory misses the point entirely. Paul is not discussing the helplessness of man's body without his spirit: in no sense is he contrasting the body and the spirit of man.

But who is this "natural man" of 1 Cor. 2:14? In

seeking an answer to this question, we must not arrive at conclusions that contradict other plain statements of the Scriptures, or give the sinner any excuse for continuing in sin. The whole course of revelation shows that God holds man accountable for his conduct, and we must not put a construction on a passage of Scripture that will nullify that great and important truth. Beginning with chapter 1 verse 18, and continuing through the second and third chapters, Paul shows the inability of man by his own wisdom—his own power of research—to know God or what God has provided for them that love him. "Greeks seek after wisdom," and so do scientists and philosophers of today; but "the world through its wisdom knew not God," nor can it now so know him. But many have ruined for themselves the whole course of Paul's argument by using chapter 2, verse 9, to prove that God has not revealed the things which he has prepared for those who love him, but Paul was using that quotation from Isaiah as a part of his argument that man by his own unaided powers of research had never conceived in his heart the faintest idea concerning the things God has prepared for those that love him. If people did not do such scrappy reading, they would see how miserably that passage is perverted; for Paul immediately adds, "But unto us God revealed them through the Spirit." And then verse 13: "Which things we speak, not in words which man's wisdom teacheth, but which the Spirit teacheth." Search closely all that Paul is here saying, beginning with verse 18 of chapter 1, and you will not find one thing said about the condition of an unconverted man—no contrasting the condition of the unconverted man with the condition of the converted man. The contrast is between man's wisdom and God's wisdom—between man's discoveries and God's revelation in the gospel. Worldly wisdom learns many things about the material universe, but it cannot find out God nor the things God prepared for those that love him. Natural science and philosophy are useful, but have limitations. The gospel—God's wisdom—is foolishness to the one who thinks nature reveals all that can be known. He is the natural man—the man of nature—to him revelation by inspiration is foolishness. So long as he depends on nature as the only source of knowledge, he will not, he cannot, "receive the things of the Spirit, for they are foolishness unto him." The ultra modernist rejects all revelation as foolishness. The natural man rejects revelation, because, to him, it is foolishness. Any man therefore that rejects revelation as foolishness is a natural man, for that is what the natural man does. Can such a man be converted? Not so long as he holds that attitude toward the gospel as a revelation from God. He must realize his limitations, his poverty of spirit. "If any man thinketh that he knoweth anything, he knoweth not yet as he ought to know." (1 Cor. 8:2.) "Let no man deceive himself. If any man thinketh that he is wise among you in this world, let him become a fool, that he may become wise." (1 Cor. 3:18.) The one who receives the gospel must realize that to seek God through any other way is to grope in darkness. The world by its wisdom does not know God, and cannot know him. "For seeing that in the wisdom of God the world through its wisdom knew not God, it was

God's good pleasure through the foolishness of preaching (Greek, "thing preached"—margin) to save them that believe." (1 Cor. 1:21.) We must quit scoffing at the idea of revelation, realize the uselessness of trying to find God by our own wisdom, and come to the study of the Bible in the true spirit of honest inquiry, or we can never know the things "that are freely given to us of God."

Anvil Sparks:

When humility says, "Look at me," it ceases to be humility and becomes arrogant self-righteousness. Obtrusive humility is only a cloak worn to be seen of men.

It is sometimes hard to tell whether a man is full of enthusiasm or simply so full of egotism that he thinks nothing will be done right unless he looks after it.

There is a marked difference between swelling and growing; but the egotistical bombast thinks he has grown immensely, when he is only afflicted with the swell-head.

And we also conjure with the words "firmness" and "stubbornness". If I refuse to be turned from my course, it is firmness; if the other fellow does the same, it is stubbornness.

A crank is a useful thing if kept under proper control, but many a Ford owner knows how dangerous a crank is if the explosion comes too soon.

If the devil had any self-respect, he would not associate with some of his children.

Some preachers manipulate the people; others teach them.

If there are forty-nine ways of talking without saying anything, some people know all of them.

Some Old Doctrines Restated and Examined

The Doctrine of Hereditary Total Depravity
Examined

What any one believes about the theory of inherited sin will not change the condition of the child at birth. Why then discuss the theory? It is necessary to discuss it because of the hurtful doctrines and evil practices that grow out of it. Infant baptism would never have been practiced had it not been for this doctrine of inherited sin. At the beginning of the practice the child was baptized to save him from inherited corruption. It is also the basis for the doctrine of the direct work of the Spirit in conversion. It has the tendency to destroy a feeling of personal responsibility. The denominational preacher may not have much to say about this doctrine of inherited depravity, but it is the basis for everything he says about the salvation of sinners. These doctrines, made popular among early protestants by Calvin's teaching, were incorporated in many of the Creeds and Confessions of Faith. The Great Westminster confession was published in 1648. Of this confession Pro. W. J. McGlothlin, in Baptist Confessions of Faith says: "It was the product of much labor, and is certainly one of the noblest of all protestant confessions, if indeed it has a peer."

If I should state this doctrine in my own words and name the churches that hold to it, some people might think I was slandering good people. I shall therefore let them state it in their own words. I appeal to the creeds to which they subscribe and which they publish. As some of my readers may not have these creeds, I shall quote at length from them.

The Presbyterian Confession of Faith, Chapter 6:

I. Our first parents, being seduced by the subtility and temptation of Satan, sinned in eating the forbidden fruit. This their sin God was pleased, according to his wise and holy counsel, to permit, having purposed to order it to his own glory.

II. By this sin they fell from their original righteousness and communion with God, and so became dead in sin, and wholly defiled in all the faculties and parts of soul and body.

III. They being the root of all mankind, the guilt of this sin was imputed, and the same death in sin and corrupted nature conveyed to all their posterity, descending from them by ordinary generation.

IV. From this original corruption, whereby we are utterly indisposed, disabled, and made opposite to all good, and wholly inclined to all evil, do proceed all actual transgressions.

V. This corruption of nature, during this life, doth remain in those that are regenerated: and although it be through Christ pardoned and mortified, yet both itself and all the notions thereof, are truly and properly sin.

In the Larger Catechism of the Presbyterian Confession of Faith we have this:

Q. 25. **Wherein consisteth the sinfulness of that estate whereinto man fell?**

A. The sinfulness of that estate whereinto man fell, consisteth in the guilt of Adam's first sin, the want of that righteousness wherein he was created, and the corruption of his nature, whereby he is utterly indisposed, disabled, and made opposite unto all that is spiritually good, and wholly inclined to all evil, and that continually; which is commonly called original sin, and from which do proceed all actual transgressions.

Q. 26. How is original sin conveyed from our first parents unto their posterity?

A. Original sin is conveyed from our first parents unto their posterity by natural generation, so as that all that proceed from them in that way, are conceived and born in sin.

"This Westminster confession, altered to suit Baptist views of the church and its ordinances, was adopted in 1677 by "the elders and brethren of many congregations" in London and the country. In 1689 messengers from one hundred and seven churches in England and Wales met in London and approved this confession. In America the Baptist Association which assembled at Philadelphia, September 25, 1742, "ordered the printing of a new edition of this confession to be printed in America." Two articles were added: one, "concerning the singing of Psalms in the worship of God;" the other, "laying on of hands upon the baptized believers." In this country this confession is known as the Philadelphia Confession of Faith. These matters will serve as a background for some things I wish to say.

I have allowed the advocates of this hideous doctrine to state their doctrine fully; for many people, especially the younger, do not know that this doctrine is a fundamental doctrine with the Presbyterians and Baptists, and others. The doctrine that infants inherit the sin of Adam gave rise to the practice of infant baptism, or greatly augmented the practice. With Augustine it was the only way of saving infants. Both Calvin and Luther were greatly influenced by Augustine's doctrine and practice. Later most of the infant sprinklers revolted at the idea of the damnation of unbaptized infants, and shifted their defense of the practice to other grounds.

But other evils grew out of the doctrine of hereditary total depravity. Its advocates taught and do now teach, that an individual is so depraved by nature that he cannot, without a direct, enabling power of the Holy Spirit, obey the gospel of Christ. Being depraved, he is opposed to everything good, and continually inclined to all evil. He is therefore opposed to God and the gospel till he is regenerated. Being dead, he cannot do anything till he is made alive by a direct work of the Spirit. With such teachers every conversion is a miracle. The London Confession of Faith (Baptist) tells us that the sinner "is converted by no less power than that which raised Christ from the dead." The creeds also affirm that the inherent depravity remains with those that are saved, and "that the same power that converts to faith in Christ, the same power carries on the soul still through all duties, temptations, conflicts, sufferings, and continually whatever a Christian is, he is by grace, and constant renewed operation from God, without which he cannot perform any duty to God, or undergo any temptation from Satan, the world, or men." If that is so, it all amounts to unconditional election; it therefore makes no difference to a man whether he was elected or reprobated from all eternity or after he reached maturity. In either case he can do nothing about it until he is regenerated; and after he is regenerated he does not need to do anything, for he is then saved eternally. It is a paralyzing and God-dishonoring doctrine; it makes God responsible for the damnation of every unsaved man. The doctrine will not allow you to say, that man is responsible for he must be willing to be regenerated; for according to the doctrine he cannot even be willing to be regenerated. Do you think this statement is too strong? Then read what the Westminster Confession (Presbyterian) and the Second London Confession (Baptist) says: After the fall of man, "it pleased the Lord to make a covenant of grace wherein he freely offereth unto sinners, life and salvation by Jesus Christ, requiring of them faith in him; and promising to give unto all those that are ordained unto eternal life, his Holy Spirit, to make them willing, and able to believe." This quotation is from the Second London Confession: the punctuation differs a little from the Westminster Confession, and adds the word "eternal" before "life." And so God promised sinners his Holy Spirit to make them willing to be saved. Therefore according to these Presbyterian and Baptist confessions, an unregenerate sinner is not willing to be saved. And so, whether God regenerates this sinner or that one, it is purely a matter of unconditional election, whether the choice was made on the spot or before man was created.

In an effort to show the inefficiency of the gospel to convert, Mr. Rice, in Campbell-Rice Debate, argued that the more light a sinner had concerning God and his revelation the more he hated both. His conclusion: "It is, then, perfectly clear, that every individual must experience a radical change in his moral character before he ever will love God or embrace the gospel of Christ. But are the truths of revelation sufficient to effect this change? They are not." Again: "A dead man does not perform the acts which flow from life. He is first alive, and then he acts. Those who are spiritually dead, do not put forth the acts of spiritual life. They are first quickened, then they exercise true faith and love." Again, "Regeneration is the cause of which faith is an effect. The fact that an individual believes, is proof that he is regenerated." This is a paralyzing doctrine to all who accept it. If it were true, a sinner could not even want to be saved, for he would be opposed to all that is good and wholly inclined to all evil, and too dead to even want to be made alive.

It seems to me that these makers of creeds could not have used stronger words had they been describing the character of the devil. "Made opposite to all good, and wholly inclined to all evil." Not simply opposed to some good, but to "all good;" not simply inclined to do some evil things, but "all evil;" not simply inclined, but "wholly inclined," to all evil; not simply inclined to do evil sometimes, but "wholly inclined to all evil, and that continually." These are the results, as these creed makers see them, of what they are disposed to call "hereditary total depravity." When the advocates of this doctrine are brought face to face with these statements of the doctrine, they try to make a play on the word "total." They seem very anxious to soften the doctrine. They say that a person may be totally depraved and yet grow more wicked. They tell us the word *total* does not refer to the degree of depravity, but to all the faculties of man; man has some depravity scattered all through him, but he can get worse. That might do very well as an explanation, were it not for some explanatory terms used in the creeds, such as "utterly indisposed, disabled, and made opposite unto all that is spiritually good, and wholly inclined to all evil, and that continually." Certainly a sinner may go on sinning, but does he grow any worse than he is here pictured? And when these preachers argue the need for a direct operation on the sinner, do they not make him as helpless and as bad as total depravity—as a total degree of depravity could make him? In "Baptist Principles Reset," A. E. Dickinson, D. D., then Editor of Religious Herald, says, "The Baptist begins with asserting that every human being that is born into the world is dead in sin—conceived in sin, and born dead—and that nothing but the Almighty Spirit of God can infuse life into that dead soul." Recently I heard a "Fundamentalist" preacher say over the radio, "Some people wonder why a sinner can hear gospel sermons, and not be converted. The fact is, the sinner does not hear the gospel at all. He cannot hear it, for he is dead. When God regenerates him, and makes him alive, he then becomes a free moral agent." A few days later another of the same sort, but from another town, said, "The Scriptures are not for sinners, but for Christians." But that sort of teaching has been going on ever since the days of Luther and Calvin. It is in the Presbyterian and the Baptist confession of Faith in the same words: "Nevertheless we acknowledge the inward illumination of the Spirit of God for the saving understanding of such things as are revealed in the word." ". . . promising to give unto all those that are ordained unto life, his Holy Spirit, to make them willing and able to believe." If that is true, a sinner is not even willing to be saved till he is regenerated by this direct work of the

Spirit. If the sinner is opposed to all that is spiritually good and wholly inclined to all evil, he is not only not willing to be saved, but is actually opposed to being saved. Mr. Rice, in Campbell-Rice Debate, says of sinners, "They are unwilling to be taught the truths of revelation," p. 631. Then he argues on pages 633-634 that there is in every sinner an aversion to God and the gospel. That is only another way of saying, as his Confession of Faith says, that the heart of the sinner is opposed to all good, and wholly inclined to all evil. Hence, the sinner does not want to be interfered with. Their theory of the regeneration of such sinners by a direct impact of the Holy Spirit looks like an uneven wrestling match!

We are told that God created Adam in his own image; but by transgression Adam lost that image, and we lost it in him. It has been argued that if we still had that image, we would not need to be regenerated, and that the lost image is restored by regeneration. Now notice this: "Whoso sheddeth man's blood, by man shall his blood be shed: for in the image of God made he man." (Gen. 9:6.) If the sinner does not bear the image of God, then this prohibition against murder applies only to murder of a regenerate man, a man in whom the lost image has been restored! Of the tongue James says, "Therewith bless we the Lord and Father; and therewith curse we men, who are made after the likeness of God . . . My brethren, these things ought not so to be." (Jas. 3:9,10.) If the total depravity advocates are right, alien sinners are not made after the likeness of God, would it be all right to curse them?

It is interesting to note that this confession (Westminster), which has been "held as authoritative by all English speaking Presbyterians," says about God's decrees. "God from all eternity did by the most wise and holy counsel of his own will, freely and unchangeably ordain whatsoever comes to pass; yet so as thereby neither is God the author of sin, nor is violence offered to the will of the creatures, nor is the liberty or contingency of second causes taken away, but rather established." (Chapter 3, Article 1.) If you can understand that, you can go to the head of the class. In the "Larger Catechism," ratified and adopted by the Synod of New York and Philadelphia, held at Philadelphia, in May, 1788, we have this question and answer:

Q. 12. **What are the decrees of God?**

A. God's decrees are the wise, free, and holy acts of the counsel of his will, whereby, from all eternity, he hath, for his own glory, unchangeably foreordained whatsoever comes to pass in time, especially concerning angels and men.

If a man could bring himself to the point of really believing these pronouncements, he would not feel any responsibility for anything he did or failed to do. But the decrees are further stated: "By the decree of God, for the manifestation of his glory, some men and angels are predestinated unto everlasting life, and others foreordained to everlasting death. These angels and men, thus predestinated and foreordained, are particularly and unchangeably designed; and their number is so certain and definite that it cannot be either increased or diminished." (Chapter 3, Articles 3, 4.) Again: "As God hath appointed the elect unto glory, so hath he, by the eternal and most free purpose of his will, foreordained all the means thereto. Wherefore they who are elected, being fallen in Adam, are redeemed by Christ, are effectually called unto faith in Christ by his Spirit working in due season; are justified, adopted, sanctified, and kept by his power through faith unto salvation. Neither are any other redeemed by Christ, effectually called, justified, adopted, sanctified, and saved, but the elect only." (Chapter 3, Article 6.)

I would not accuse any one of believing what those confessions say unless he avows such belief. However, before a Presbyterian candidate for the ministry can be licensed, he must answer affirmatively four questions, one of which is "Do you sincerely receive and adopt the Confession of Faith and the Catechisms of this church, as containing the system of doctrine taught in the Holy Scriptures?" Then before he can be ordained as a pastor of any church, he must answer that question again. Hence if a Presbyterian preacher is truthful, he believes what his confession says about decrees. But how can he? God did "freely and unchangeably ordain whatsoever comes to pass; yet so as thereby neither is God the author of sin." That is, God ordained it, but is not the author of it! He ordained whatsoever comes to pass, but that does no violence to the will of the creatures! That is, God unchangeably ordained that a man should do a certain thing, but left him free to exercise his own will! His eternal and unchangeable decree does not take away the liberty or contingency of second causes! Can anyone believe these things?

The advocates of total depravity tell us that all infants, even the elect, are born dead, spiritually dead, subject to condemnation without defense or excuse. A part of the doctrine of the eternal decrees is the doctrine of eternal and unconditional election and reprobation, and this doctrine leaves all non-elect infants, who die in infancy with no provision for their salvation. But the London and Westminster Confessions make provision for elect infants: "Elect infants, dying in infancy, are regenerated and saved by Christ through the Spirit, who worketh when, and where, and how he pleaseth. So also are all other elect persons, who are incapable of being outwardly called by the ministry of the word." (Chapter 10, Article 3.) Again, "Neither are any other redeemed by Christ, or effectually called, justified, adopted, sanctified, and saved, but the elect only." So non-elect infants and idiots are doomed. But some have tried to soften this matter by saying that non-elect infants never die. On this point Mr. Rice in his debate with Mr. Campbell has this to say on page 680: "Are all infants, dying in infancy, elect? All Presbyterians, who express an opinion on the subject, so believe. So far as I know the sentiment on this subject of Presbyterians, they believe that all that die in infancy are of the elect—are chosen of God to eternal life, and are sanctified by the Holy Spirit, and saved according to his eternal purpose. Infants do not die by accident." And Mr. Rice did not mean the infant is elected because he died in infancy, for his confession says plainly that the number of both elect and non-elect is so exact that it cannot be either increased or diminished. He meant what he said, "That all that die in infancy are of the elect."

"Infants do not die by accident." Hence, no non-elect infants die in infancy—you could not kill one! Where did they find any authority for such a statement? No wreck, fire, storm, or atomic bomb could kill a non-elect infant! But this absurd interpretation of the Confession, which Presbyterians and other Calvinists give, is merely a weak effort to escape the clearly implied doctrine of infant damnation. But why the effort! If a child is a non-elect when he is born, he will never be anything else if he lives to be a hundred years old. And during all these hundred years of suffering and hardships, he can serve no one but the Devil, and be harassed with doubts about whether he is an elect or a non-elect. Always a non-elect is helpless and doomed, as helpless in maturity as in infancy. It is no more shocking to me to think that God would by arbitrary decree damn a helpless infant than that by an unchangeable decree he would damn the same infant after it becomes a man. To charge God with keeping the non-elect alive till they reach maturity to escape the charge of damning infants puts God in a bad light. According to the doctrine of decrees, the mature non-elect is as helpless as an infant, for he is not allowed any choice in the matter. How such arbitrary dealings with human beings can be for the glory of God is more than I can see. There is no mercy in it. It looks too much like a cat's playing with a helpless mouse before he decides to kill it and eat it! One of the glorious attributes of God is his mercy. If you will look carefully into the doctrine of election and reprobation, as set forth in the Westminster Confession of Faith, you will see that mercy for lost sinners was not what moved God to redeem even the elect. Where is mercy, when some are allowed to perish without remedy? Oh, I know the confession talks about grace and mercy; but where is there room for mercy in what is said about the decrees of God? "By the decree of God, for the manifestation of his glory, some men and angels are predestinated unto everlasting life, and others fore-ordained to everlasting death." Did mercy move God to make such a decree? No, he made it to manifest his glory. But does such a decree manifest any glory? Is any glory manifested in decreeing from all eternity that certain ones shall be saved regardless of their character, and certain ones damned without remedy? It seems to me that such decrees manifest neither the mercy nor the glory of God. The "decree" rather represents God as acting on a mere whimsey. And the makers of the confession thought there was also justice in such a decree. The larger Catechism tells us that God "in Christ hath chosen some men to eternal life, and the means thereof and also according to his sovereign power, and the unsearchable counsel of his own will (whereby he extendeth or withholdeth favor as he pleaseth) hath passed by, and fore-ordained the rest to dishonor and wrath, to be for their sins inflicted, to the praise of the glory of his justice." (Answer to question 13.) Now, is there any justice in decreeing that men shall follow a certain course, giving them no choice to do otherwise, and then inflicting punishment on them for so doing? It seems to me, that whatever they do would come under the head of what our courts of justice call "an act of God." It seems to me that the decree makes them no more responsible for what they do than is a bolt of lightning. And our courts do not regard it as just to punish anybody for "an act of God." But these decrees leave a man with no choice whom he will serve; that was settled by the eternal and unchangeable decree of God.

From my eighth year to my twentieth the nearest meeting house to our home was Old Center, a Primitive Baptist place of worship in Hickman County, Tennessee. I heard their preachers quite often, for they were rather numerous in our section and in some adjoining counties. At some time two schools of thought had appeared among them. One group held the old idea of the absolute predestination of all things —the eternal and unchangeable decree of God had marked out for every man his whole life to the minutest detail. If a man were born to be drowned, he would not be killed by a falling tree. But another group believed that the eternal decree applied only to election and reprobation, and a man had no choice as to whom he served; otherwise he was free to do as he pleased. These called the others absoluters. But the difference did not interfere with their fellowship. I never heard their differences publicly aired.

But does a man have any choice as to whom he will serve? "I call heaven and earth to witness against you this day, that I have set before thee life and death. The blessing and the curse; therefore choose life, that thou mayest live, thou and thy seed; to love Jehovah thy God, to obey his voice, and to cleave unto him." (Deut. 30:19,20.) Here God through Moses exhorts the people to choose life. It is folly therefore to say they had no ability to choose life. Joshua said to Israel, "And if it seem evil unto you to serve Jehovah, choose ye this day whom ye will serve; whether the gods which your fathers served beyond the River, or the gods of the Amorites in whose land ye dwell: but as for me and my house, we will serve Jehovah." (Josh. 24:15.)   Some one may say that these people were under the law of Moses.   True, but that part does not militate against the idea that people have the right of choice.   But why say more on this point; for every sane person is conscious that he can choose good or evil.

As the creeds have it, it is a dark picture.   In a discussion, Mr. Bogard stated that everything an unconverted sinner did was a sin.   When I reminded him that according to that statement, a sinner committed a sin when he prayed for salvation, Mr. Bogard avowed that the sinner sinned when he prayed for salvation.   But he spoke according to the creeds. And yet they contend that a sinner must pray for salvation.   If this also be so, then the sinner that wants to be saved sins in that act of heart and must add to all his other sins the sin of praying for salvation!   Without this added sin he cannot be saved!   Later I shall examine some Scripture relied upon to prove inherited depravity.

In the Bible, sin is never described as an inheritance.   In the very nature of the case, sin or guilt cannot be inherited.   As a matter of fact, it is impossible to inherit sin.   Sin is an act.   We cannot inherit an act.   We may sin in thought, word, or deed; but no one inherits a thought, a word, or a deed.   The creeds tell us that we are guilty of Adam's first sin.   If that is so, then we have inherited only

one sin. The creeds are very definite on this point;
they inform us that all this corruption results from
Adam's first sin. Why that first sin should so poison the stream of human life that the constant influx
of sin into that stream all down the ages did not make
it any worse is explained in their contention that the
first sin made the stream of life wholly defiled. It
just could not get any worse. But the inexplainable
part of the theory, even granting the possibility of
inheriting the guilt of sin, is, how do we inherit the
guilt of Adam's first sin and do not inherit the guilt
of his other sins, together with the guilt of all the
sins of all our ancestors from Adam on down to us?
Again, the theory is that Adam's guilt was transmitted to his children. Now, by what law of inheritance
would his children inherit his guilt and other people
not inherit their father's guilt? How comes it that
the law of inheritance operates only in the case of
Adam and his offspring? But if it could be proved
that we do inherit sin, would that inherited sin render
us unable to obey God? Suffering from the consequences of another's guilt is a very common experience, but there is a vast difference between the sin
and its consequences. A wife or a husband may suffer much from the sins of the other. Children may
suffer much on account of the wickedness of father
or mother. It is in this way that the sins of the
fathers are visited upon their children. The robber
may bruise your head and take your money. You
suffer the consequences of his guilt but certainly
you do not share in his guilt. And we suffer as a
result of Adam's sin without inheriting his guilt.

God made man in his own likeness and image. He

was not then partaker of any sin. God made man
upright, clean, and pure. And man then had all the
human nature that any one ever had. It is a mistake,
therefore, to think that sin is an essential part of human nature. Adam's sin is no more a part of human nature than are your sins. In a radio speech,
Mr. Ben M. Bogard (Baptist) accepted the scientific
dictum that acquired characteristics cannot be transmitted to the offspring. Then added that as righteousness is an acquired characteristic, the righteousness of parents cannot be transmitted to their children. He evidently did not see what that was doing
to his ardently advocated doctrine of inherited depravity. All the depravity or sin that Adam and
Eve ever had was acquired. This no one can deny.
Sin was not a part of their nature; it was acquired.
How then could they transmit it to their offspring?

It is not my purpose to notice all the false arguments and perversions of which religious people are
guilty—not even all I know. First, let us notice some
peculiar notions people have formed about the results
of the sin of Adam and Eve in the garden of Eden.
Read Genesis 3.

When I was in the Nashville Bible School, a visiting
preacher of great ability said in a sermon, "When
Adam sinned the seeds of mortality were sown in the
human body." I did not believe that theory then,
nor do I now. Recently some brother said that if
Adam had not sinned, we would have remained immortal. That is a wild guess. There is not the least
indication that man's physical nature was affected
by his eating the forbidden fruit. We are asked,
"If people are not born totally depraved, how comes

it that all people sin?" In reply we ask this question: "If Adam and Eve were not totally depraved, how came they to sin? So far as the record shows, they sinned the first time they were tempted; none of us now do any worse. Adam and Eve were as human before they sinned as after. Had they been permitted to have access to the tree of life they would have lived on in sin. You do not believe it? Then read this: "And Jehovah God said, Behold, the man is become as one of us, to know good and evil; and now, lest he put forth his hand, and take also of the tree of life, and eat, and live for ever—therefore Jehovah God sent him forth from the garden of Eden, to till the ground from whence he was taken. So he drove out the man; and he placed at the east of the garden of Eden the Cherubim, and the flame of a sword which turned every way, to keep the way of the tree of life." So it was the fruit of the tree of life that kept them alive; separated from it they died. And herein we suffer the consequences of Adam's sin. Death comes to us because we do not have access to the tree of life, and not because we are guilty of Adam's sin. To say that Adam and Eve by sinning changed their bodies from immortal bodies to mortal bodies is to say that by sinning they worked a great miracle on themselves! Then I have seen in print where brethren refer to "our fallen nature." I do not think they know what they mean by the expression. What do they think happened to our nature? Do they think our nature fell into a state of sin and depravity? What else can they mean, if they mean anything? It sounds very much like the Augustinian-Calvinistic doctrine of inherited depravity.

"And Jehovah saw that the wickedness of man was great in the earth, and that every imagination of the thoughts of his heart was only evil continually." (Gen. 6:5.) I think these people were totally depraved— there was no good in them. But there is not a hint that such wickedness was inherited from Adam. How came they so depraved? Verse 12: "And God saw the earth, and, behold it was corrupt; for all flesh had corrupted their way upon the earth." They corrupted their way. It should also be noted that Noah and his family were righteous. Did they inherit their righteousness? That could as easily be proved as that the others inherited their wickedness. And it will be noticed that God did not send a direct operation of his Spirit into their hearts to cure them of their corruption; but he did send a flood, and destroyed them. God does not regenerate totally depraved folks. Also when Sodom and Gomorrah reached the wholly corrupt condition, which the creeds wrongfully charge upon all men, the Lord destroyed them. So he did with Pharaoh and his hosts. And such endings come to people who were "utterly indisposed, disabled, and made opposite to all good, and wholly inclined to all evil."

"Behold, I was brought forth in iniquity; and in sin did my mother conceive me." (Ps. 51:5.) David did not charge his mother with sin; neither did he implicate Adam in his sin. David does not say that he was a sinner when conceived, nor that he was full of iniquity when brought forth. He was in a distressing emotional state of mind. This language is from the Psalm of penitence written by David after Nathan rebuked him for his immoral relations with Bath-Sheba, Uriah's wife, and his guilty connection with the husband's death. He bewails the fact that he was conceived and brought forth in a world of sin. On the great Pentecost, when the people heard the apostles speaking in so many languages, they were astonished, and said: "And how hear we every man in our own language wherein we were born?" (Acts 2:8.) This does not mean that they were born speaking a certain language, but that they were born where all spoke that language. Just so David: he was brought forth in a world of sin. He pleads that as an extenuating circumstance. It would save us from many blunders if we would give more attention to the language used. To say that he was brought forth in iniquity is quite different from saying he was brought forth with iniquity in him.

"Can the Ethiopian change his skin, or the leopard his spots? Then may ye also do good, that are accustomed to do evil." Jeremiah 13:23. This text does not say anything about inherited depravity. To help the depravity argument it would have to read, ". . . then may ye also do good, that were born totally depraved." Jeremiah did not use that expression to prove that these Jews needed a direct work of the Spirit. By it he meant that their case was hopeless; their reformation impossible. Neither are people accustomed to evil when they are born; to become accustomed to anything requires a period of practice. Because they could not change Jeremiah immediately adds: "Therefore will I scatter them as the stubble that passeth away, by the wind of the wilderness. This is thy lot, the portion measured unto thee from me, saith Jehovah; because thou hast forgotten me, and trusted in falsehood." (verses 24,25.) It is argued that a sinner cannot do anything toward changing his condition any more than an Ethiopian can change his skin or a leopard his spots—that this illustrated the condition of an unregenerate sinner. But some things are overlooked. It is not said that these Jews were born evil, but were accustomed to do evil; they were not alien sinners, but Israelites, God's chosen people. Also, Jehovah said evils would come upon them "because thou hast forgotten me." So they had known Jehovah, for people cannot forget what they have never known. Because they had become hopelessly corrupt, the Lord would "scatter them, as stubble that passeth away, by the wind of the wilderness." It is argued that nothing less than the mighty power of God can change a leopard's spots or an Ethiopian's skin. But did the Lord ever by direct power change people who have become wholly corrupt? Verse 27: "Woe unto thee, O Jerusalem! thou wilt not be made clean." Because Jerusalem had reached that condition the Lord abandoned them, and had them carried into captivity. And when the Jews again became so hopelessly corrupt that they crucified the Lord, and then, by bitter persecution and slaughter tried to destroy his church, the Romans utterly destroyed their nation, killing multiplied thousands of them carrying the remainder into captivity. That is the way the Lord deals with people when they become hopelessly corrupt.

Another argument is built upon an unwarranted use of the word *dead* in Eph. 2:1. It is believed that a dead man can do nothing—cannot even hear, and cannot believe, till God makes him alive by some direct influence of the Holy Spirit. But the Bible represents the sinner as being dead through his own trespasses. "Even when we were dead through our trespasses, . . ." Eph. 2:5. "And you being dead through your trespasses and the uncircumcision of your flesh, . . ." Col. 2:13. But even if we had inherited this dead state from Adam, we are no more dead to righteousness than Adam and Eve in their state of innocence were dead to sin. The Devil led them into sin by placing motives before them; he did not have to perform some direct inward change in their hearts to enable them to act. God places the highest imaginable motives before the sinner; but we are told God cannot undo by motives what the Devil accomplished by motives! The prodigal son was dead, but he returned to his father without any direct operation of the spirit of his father.

Eph. 2:3: "were by nature children of wrath." By nature a person does what he is in the habit of doing. When you began to drive a car, you were awkward; but by practice you reached the point where it became part of your nature to do things a certain way. You were not born talking; but you learned to talk, and then it was natural for you to talk. If you will read verses 1, 2, 3, of Eph. 2, you will see how these people became children of wrath by nature. They had indulged in sin till sinning was their nature. But even if by birth we inherited the wrath of God, that does not mean that it requires a direct impact of the Spirit on the sinner to remove God's wrath. God's wrath is not in the sinner. Does it not sound absurd to say that a direct operation of the Spirit in the sinner's heart would remove wrath from

God's mind? In Eph. 5:1-5 Paul mentions a number of sins, and then adds, "for because of these things cometh the wrath of God upon the sons of disobedience." It is not because of what we inherit, but because of what we do, or fail to do. (See also Col. 3:5,6.)

When I debated the Holy Spirit question with Ben M. Bogard, in his first speech he put in his time trying to prove that the sinner is so depraved, so dead, that he can do nothing till he is made alive by the regenerating power of the Holy Spirit in addition to the word. I knew he would accuse me of limiting the power of God; and so I decided to beat him to it and put him in a dilemma so that he would get hurt no matter which way he went. I began my reply by saying, "One objection I have to Mr. Bogard's theory is he limits the power of God. He has the sinner so depraved and so dead that God could not make a gospel that would reach him. I then waited for results—they came in his next speech. He came up waving his arms and talking louder than usual, saying, "It is not a question of what God can do. God can do anything he wants to. He could have made a gospel that would reach that dead sinner, if he had wanted to." I replied, "Oh, well, the sinner is not as dead as we have heard he is, for God could have made a gospel that would reach him, if-he-had-wanted-to. So the trouble is not the inability of the sinner at all: it is with the ineffectiveness of the gospel God made! But I maintain that God made the very gospel Bogard said he could have made, and I will proceed to prove it, for it is useless in the face of Bogard's admission to talk any more about depravity and the dead sinner." Then I proceeded to show by numerous passages that the gospel is God's power for salvation, and that sinners were able to hear, believe, and obey that gospel. Search the book of Acts, and not one time will you find that any sinner was told that he could not obey the gospel without a direct work of the Spirit. Will any one say that Luke an inspired historian failed to mention an absolutely essential thing; really the essential thing? He did, if the advocates of the direct operation theory are correct. Who can believe it?

Some confusion arises from putting undue stress on certain terms used in reference to the process of becoming children of God. Here are some of the terms used: born again, created, conversion, turn from darkness to light, turn from power of Satan unto God, translated into kingdom, obey from the heart, believe and be baptized, believe and turn to the Lord, baptized into Christ. All these terms refer to the same thing, that is, how people become children of God. To give a meaning to any of the terms that makes void the other terms, or any one of them, is, beyond question, wrong. And yet every advocate of the direct operation of the Spirit does that very thing. As an illustration, take "born again" and "created." When they talk of being created, they put a stress on it that puts "born again" out of the picture; and the reverse when they talk about being born again. A literal birth and a literal creation are two different things. The change in becoming a Christian is so great that it may figuratively be spoken of as being born again or as being created. Neither term, when applied to becoming a Christian, expresses a literal act. So far as the record shows, the apostles never told sinners that they must be born again, or that they must be created. To sinners they said, "Repent ye, and be baptized every one of you in the name of Jesus Christ unto the remission of your sins; and ye shall receive the gift of the Holy Spirit." (Acts 2:38.) "Repent ye, therefore, and turn again, that your sins may be blotted out, so that there may come seasons of refreshing from the presence of the Lord." (Acts 3:19.) Inspired Ananias said to Saul, "And now why tarriest thou? Arise, and be baptized, and wash away thy sins, calling on his name." (Acts 22:16.) They called their converts saints, new born babes, children of God, and new creatures, and told them that they had been baptized into Christ, and had been translated out of the kingdom of darkness into the kingdom of Christ.

There is one truth which is necessary to observe in studying the Bible, which denominational preachers seem never to learn, and that is, that commands are given in plain, unfigurative language, but conditions and relationships are frequently expressed in highly figurative language. No inspired man ever commanded an inquiring sinner to become a branch of the vine, or to become a sheep, or to become a child of God by being born again, or to become a member of the Lord's body, or to become an epistle of Christ, or to be a graft; but these terms are all applied to Christians. Figures of Speech abound in the Epistles; but if you want to read what inspired men in plain unfigurative language told sinners to do, read the book of Acts. Figures of speech abound in many speeches Jesus made, but there is no figurative language in the commands he gave the apostles in the great commission. Yet people will turn away from the plain commands and promises of Jesus and his apostles and hang their hopes of heaven on fanciful interpretations of figures of speech. These figures of speech enlarge the views of the Christian and comfort him in his struggles and trials, but no figure of speech tells a sinner what to do to be saved. Think on these things.

Anvil Sparks:

The noise of escaping gas does not interest me, whether it be from a leaky pipe or a man's mouth.

Innovations are usually adopted on the plea of expediency, and afterwards defended as Scriptural. Societies, sprinkling, and instrumental music, are all illustrations.

Some seem not to know the difference between prejudice and conscience.

In failing to be wise as serpents we sometimes also fail to be as harmless as doves.

Some folks have more of their think-sos than of the Lord's say-sos in their religion.

Some Brethren and Inherited Depravity

One of the peculiar things about human beings is that the doctrines they fight often seep into their thinking. Brethren sometimes speak of "our fallen nature," and yet I doubt they know what they mean. I would like for some brother who uses the term to tell us what it means. In an otherwise good article in the Gospel Advocate of Nov. 11, 1948, a brother is specific in giving what he considers the result of the sin of Adam and Eve. He says, "Deceived by the devil, who said 'ye shall not surely die' (Gen. 3:4) the woman was led to think that God would not keep his word. She and Adam ate the forbidden fruit. They thus challenged God to stand by his word. Results? The image of God in which they were created was blotted out, they lost their home in Eden, their oldest son killed his brother; the people of Noah's generation filled the earth with violence; and the story of wasted lives runs like a scarlet thread through the sorrowing centuries." Read again what the brother says. It is just a plain and forceful statement of the Augustinian-Calvanistic doctrine of hereditary total depravity. In his debate with Mr. Campbell (p. 630) Mr. Rice says the divine image has been "defaced." And "defaced" is not as strong a term as "blotted out."

A brother made a glowing report of the work being done in the Maude Carpenter Children's Home. I do not doubt that those who have that institution in their charge are doing a good work for the children; but I cannot go along with him in the following statement of the work being done in that home: "These children are being taken from ruined homes and reclaimed, transformed into the image of God." All advocates of inherited depravity will indorse all those expressions, excepting they would not agree with the brother as to how the image of God is restored. They would not agree for a moment that any children's home can transform people into the image of God. They claim that people are transformed into the image of God by the direct impact of the Holy Spirit, in regeneration. No, people are still made in the image of God.

Anvil Sparks:

Some preaching is food, some a tonic, and some an intoxicant. All Christians need food, some need a tonic, but none needs an intoxicant. And if your church shows no permanent improvement after a rousing meeting it is an indication that the rousing meeting was only a religious spree.

If a man is honest for policy's sake he is a rascal.

The devil is the best mixer the world has ever known.

The Direct Operation of the Spirit

Over against the doctrine of inherited sin let us place the words of the Lord: "The soul that sinneth, it shall die: the son shall not bear the iniquity of the father, neither shall the father bear the iniquity of the son; the righteousness of the righteous shall be upon him, and the wickedness of the wicked shall be upon him." (Ezek. 18:20.) I know of no other place where the Bible speaks so plainly on this doctrine of inherited sin. It is a death-blow to the doctrine of inherited sin. Read the entire chapter. Why people will argue against a plain statement of the Lord is hard to understand.

The present position of the Baptists on the doctrine of inherited sin is the very opposite of the doctrine of some through whom they seek to trace their line of succesion. The concluding clause of Article IV of the Mennonite "Confession" prepared by John de Rys and Lubbert Gertis in 1580 says: "So that none of his posterity, in respect of this restitution, is born guilty of sin or blame." Article V. of this "Confession" is lengthy. It affirms that as Adam and Eve, though righteous, had the power to admit or reject evil, "so after the fall, by hearing and admitting occurring good, he shows that he has the faculty of accepting it. But that faculty of accepting or rejecting the grace of God truly offered, remains, through grace, in all his posterity." A "Confession of Faith," supposed to have been prepared by John Smyth, whom Prof. W. J. McGlothlin calls "the founder of the English General Baptists," says "that original

(139)

sin is an idle term," and "that infants are born in innocency and without sin."

In these matters there has been quite a revolution among the Baptists. The present position of the Baptists, as set forth in their creeds and manuals, and affirmed by their debaters, is that a sinner must be regenerated before he can make any use of the Scriptures; whereas the "Confession" prepared by Smyth taught that the unregenerate man needed the Scriptures, but the child of God did not need them. "That such as have not attained the new creature have need of the Scriptures, creatures and ordinances of the church, to instruct them, to comfort them, to stir them up the better to perform the condition of repentance to the remission of sins. (2 Pet. 1:19; 1 Cor. 11:26; Eph. 4:12-23.)"

"That the new creature which is begotten of God needeth not the outward Scriptures, creatures, or ordinances of the church, to support or help him (2 Cor. 13:10,12; 1 John 2:27; 1 Cor. 1:15,16; Rev. 21:23), seeing he hath three witnesses in himself, the Father, the Word, and the Holy Ghost: which are better than all Scriptures, or creatures whatsoever."

So some of the people through whom the Baptists like to trace their so-called "line of succession" thought the unregenerate needed the Scriptures, but the new creature did not need them, for he had something better than all Scripture. The present-day Baptists think the Scriptures are a dead letter to the unregenerate, but useful to the new creature. But are they so useful, after all? They try to prove by profane history that they are the true church, claim that another power converts the sinner, and that the converted man cannot fall away, even if he never looks at a Bible! What essential place does the Bible fill in their program of things?

It is claimed in the creeds that the first sin of Adam caused all the corruption they attribute to our inherited nature. If that be so, then we cannot be worse by nature than Adam was after he committed the sin. After Adam sinned, God talked with him. If he could understand God in that condition, and we inherited the same condition, then we can also understand God. Also, it is distinctly stated that Adam and Eve in their fallen condition knew good and evil. They were not so dead that they could not hear God talk and understand him, and they were not too dead to know good and evil. The creeds, in making out such a desperate condition for us, and in attributing that condition to us on account of our inheriting the depravity brought upon Adam and Eve by their first sin, fail to take notice of the fact that Adam and Eve were not so dead as they say we are.

Adam and Eve could certainly hear and understand each other, just as we do today. It would be strange, indeed, if they could not hear and understand God. If a man states a proposition and backs it up with sufficient evidence, a sinner can believe him. It is almost blasphemy to say that God cannot so state matters that that same sinner can believe him. You can put motives before a sinner that will induce him to act; and will you say that God cannot do the same thing? It seems to me that the theory of total depravity reflects about as much on God as it does on the sinner. Besides, the theory limits the power of God. It implies that the sinner is so dead that God could not have made a gospel that would reach him. If God could make a gospel that would reach his heart, then the sinner is not so dead as the theory says he is. If God could have made a gospel that would reach the sinner's heart, but did not, as Mr. Bogard contended, then the deficiency is in the gospel and not in the sinner; and that is another reflection on God. If God did not make a gospel that would convert a sinner, and yet could have done so, will some one tell us why he did not? Does not the theory, at this point, reflect on his benevolence? If it be said that he could not have made a gospel that would reach the sinner's heart, then does not that idea reflect on the power of God? So it seems to me that, no matter from what angle you view this theory of the need of a direct operation of the Spirit, it slanders God about as much as it does man.

Sane people are moved by motive. Sometimes people who do not think much ask: "What Bible did Satan use to lead Adam and Eve into sin?" That question implies that the querist thinks he used some direct operation of his spirit on them. But he did not. He presented motives to move them—the most powerful motives that he could present. He showed them that the fruit was beautiful, that it was good for food, and that it would make them wise. These motives prompted their act. He induced them to do his will by putting motives before them. And yet the direct-operation theory would have us believe that God cannot accomplish as much by motive as the Devil did. And let it be remembered that Adam and Eve were as dead to sin as any sinner is to righteousness; they were as far removed from the devil as any sinner is from God. Yet it required no direct operation of the devil's spirit on their hearts to get them to do his will; he accomplished it all by motive. God presents to the sinner motives as high as heaven, and as deep and awful as hell, and as beautiful as perfect holiness and bliss.   These motives are presented to him in the Bible.   And consider this: every sensible act is prompted by a sensible motive.

In all their preaching, the prophets, apostles, and all inspired men proceeded with the understanding that their message was perfectly adapted to the people as they were. Jesus commanded the apostles to preach to every creature, without giving them one hint that the people could not obey the gospel. They "went everywhere preaching the word." If they prayed for power and boldness, it was to enable them to preach with more force. They did not pray for God to send his Spirit into the hearts of the people to enable them to hear. When people would not hear, they placed the blame on the people. They depended on the preaching of the gospel to produce action. They dealt in no sensational claptrap and announced no foolish themes for their discourses. They were fully persuaded that the gospel was "the power of God unto salvation." Believing that with all their souls, they preached it with no uncertain sound. When Paul and Barnabas went to Iconium, they "so spake that a great multitude both of Jews and of Greeks believed." (Acts 14:1.)

In Old Testament times the labors of the prophets were confined to the Jews. There is one notable exception—Jonah's mission to Nineveh. That was a corrupt, heathen city. If they were depraved by inheritance, they had added to that depravity by their own sins; yet Jonah's preaching brought the whole city to repentance. It is also said that "the people of Nineveh believed God." Nothing is said about any power other than preaching. Those who contend for a direct operation of the Spirit make that the essential thing in the conversion of sinners. Yet, in recording the conversion of this city, Jonah says not one word about such a power. Will any one contend that Jonah, in recording so great a happening, would fail to mention the main agency that caused it? This record of the conversion of that great city is "a Jonah" to the theory of direct operation of the Spirit in conversion!

Anvil Sparks:

It might lessen crime if an occasional jury would suspend the criminal instead of the sentence.

When a fellow brags about being a self-made man, he is giving proof that he did a poor job.

Direct Supernatural Influence

Pharaoh, king of Egypt, had two dreams; both had the same significance. (Gen. 41:1-36.) Joseph, having been called in to interpret the dreams, said to Pharaoh, "What God is about to do he hath showed unto Pharaoh." (V. 28.) "And for that the dream was doubled unto Pharaoh, it is because the thing is established by God, and God will shortly bring it to pass." (v. 32.) Hence, the dream was the result of supernatural influence, but nothing is said about any change in the King's character; neither was there any change in the character of the King's butler as a result of his inspired dream—he immediately ignored his obligation to Joseph. (Gen. 40:9-23; 41:9.)

When the children of Israel were settled in Canaan, the men went to a special place three times a year to attend the feasts required by law; and yet they were surrounded by enemy nations, who took advantage of any opportunity to invade their country. What an opportunity when all the men were gone from their homes! Three times a year their wives, children and property were without the protection of fighting men, and yet there was no enemy invasion while the men attended the feasts. Jehovah gave them assurance: "Neither shall any man desire thy land, when thou goest up to appear before Jehovah thy God three times in the year." (Ex. 34:24.) Jehovah exercised a direct influence on the desires of these enemies at stated times, but it made no change in their character. They did not even know that the God of Israel operated on their desires, and controlled their movements, at such times. May not Jehovah even now, when he so desires, exercise a like control over men and nations?

Balaam's case is another striking illustration of the truth that direct, supernatural influence does not renew the heart or change the character. (Read Numbers, Chapters 22-24.) When the children of Israel, in their journey to Canaan, reached the borders of Moab, Balak, the King, and all Moab were frightened. Balak sent for Balaam to come and curse them, promising Balaam great reward. Balaam wanted the reward, but he knew God would be in control of what he said. (22:20,35,38.) "The Spirit of God came upon him." (24:2.) He tried repeatedly to get Jehovah to curse Israel through him, so that he could receive the reward Balak had promised him—he "loved the hire of wrong-doing; but he was rebuked for his own transgression: a dumb ass spake with a man's voice and stayed the madness of the prophet." (2 Pet. 2:15,16.) As the Lord would not allow him to pronounce any curses upon Israel, he went amongst them and corrupted both their religion and their morals. (Num. 31:16; Rev. 2:14.) And so this direct spiritual influence did not regenerate him, nor prevent his becoming more and more degenerate, till he was finally slain by the people he tried to curse for pay. (Num. 31:8.) And by the direct power from heaven Balaam's ass spoke with the voice of a man, but no change in her character or habits.

A rather interesting bit of history is recorded in 1 Sam. 6:1-16. The Philistines had captured the Ark of God, and had carried it into their own country. The Philistines suffered many plagues, and decided that it was because of the ark. They asked their priests and diviners what to do. Their advice: Make a new cart, take two milch cows on which a yoke had never been placed and hitch them to the cart, and shut their calves up at home. No one to control the movements of the cows. If they went the right direction, the Philistines would know their troubles had been brought upon them by Jehovah. "And the kine took the straight way by the way of Bethshemesh; they went along the highway, lowing as they went, and turned not aside to the right hand or to the left." Evidently these heathen priests and diviners were influenced from above in giving their advice, and the cows were certainly controlled by Jehovah. If left to follow cow nature, these cows would never have left their calves. But this divine influence did not change the character of the heathen priests and diviners, nor the nature of the cows. Direct divine power was brought to bear on them, but changed them not.

Jehovah selected Saul to be the first King over Israel. He started out well, but soon became so involved in rebellion against Jehovah, that Jehovah disowned him. He became envious of David, and tried to kill him. David fled to Samuel at Ramah. Samuel and David then went to Naioth. Saul was told where David was. He then sent three groups of messengers, one after another, to bring David to him. There were prophets with Samuel and David. As each group of messengers came to the prophets, they also began to prophesy. These messengers went there to assist Saul in carrying out his murderous intentions; and yet "the Spirit of God came upon the messengers of Saul, and they prophesied." Then the degenerate Saul came to take David, and he also turned prophet. Some people today would pronounce such a scene as a great revival! But this direct operation of the Spirit on Saul and his messengers made no change in character or course of life. It was not intended to benefit them, but was done for David's sake. (See 1 Sam. 19:18-24.)

One incident in the life of Nebuchadnezzar gives us another illustration of direct spiritual influence on a sinner, heathen sinner. He had a dream, which bothered him greatly, for he could not interpret it. Daniel interpreted the dream. As the interpretation was from God, we know that the dream was from God also. In fact Daniel said to the King, "There is a God in heaven that revealeth secrets, and he hath made known to King Nebuchadnezzar what shall be in the latter days." But this direct operation of the Spirit upon the sleeping King made no change in him, for we next find him erecting a great image of gold and demanding that all worship it. Read Dan. 2:1-45; 3:1-23. A direct operation of the Spirit does not make saints of sinners.

Read John 11:45-53. Jesus had raised Lazarus from the dead; and, as a result many Jews believed on him. This made the leaders more determined to put him to death. A council was held to see what could be done. Caiaphas the high priest spoke, but God caused him to make a definite prophecy concerning Jesus. However that direct power upon him did not change him for the better in the least degree. He became more and more determined to have Jesus killed.

Before the coming of Christ God spoke to the people through prophets. (Heb. 1:1.) "Men spake from God, being moved by the Holy Spirit." (2 Pet. 1:21.) David said, "The Spirit of Jehovah spake by me, and his word was upon my tongue." (2 Sam. 23:2.) Through prophets God taught people and revealed things to come. Some of them had power also to work miracles; but they did not need the gift of tongues to speak to their own people. It may be that Jonah was an exception, when he was sent to preach to the Ninevites.

The part this direct Spirit power, or operation, had in revealing and confirming the gospel is interesting to any Bible student. A full discussion of the Holy Spirit would be set forth under the following divisions: 1. The Holy Spirit an intelligent being; 2. The miraculous endowments of the Holy Spirit, the baptism in the Holy Spirit, and Spiritual gifts; 3. The Holy Spirit in Conversion; 4. The indwelling of the Holy Spirit. No one can understand the work of the Holy Spirit, unless he gives attention to the divisions just mentioned. In giving attention to the subject with the foregoing phases in mind, it will be necessary at times to mention some matters already discussed.

"I indeed baptize you in water unto repentance: but he that cometh after me is mightier than I, whose shoes I am not worthy to bear; he shall baptize you in the Holy Spirit and in fire." (Matt. 3:11.) These are the words of John the Baptizer, and this is the first time baptism in the Holy Spirit is mentioned.

Though John had said that Jesus would baptize in the Holy Spirit, yet the language of Jesus himself shows that he did not baptize anyone in the Holy Spirit during his personal ministry. In fact, he taught very little about the Holy Spirit till the night of his betrayal. On that night he made the following statements: "These things have I spoken unto you, while yet abiding with you. But the Comforter, even the Holy Spirit, whom the Father will send in my name, he shall teach you all things, and bring to your remembrance all that I said unto you." (John 14:25,26.) The apostles would need this power to enable them to remember, as occasion demanded, what Jesus had said to them. In this same discourse Jesus told the apostles that he must go to the father, and sorrow filled their hearts. He then added:

"Nevertheless I tell you the truth: It is expedient for you that I go away; for if I go not away, the Comforter will not come unto you; but if I go, I will send him unto you. And he, when he is come, will convict the world in respect of sin, and of righteousness and of judgment: of sin, because they believe not on me; of righteousness, because I go to the father, and ye behold me no more; of judgment, because the prince of this world hath been judged. I have yet many things to say unto you, but ye cannot bear them now. Howbeit when he, the Spirit of truth, is come, he shall guide you into all the truth: for he shall not speak from himself; but what things soever he shall hear, these shall he speak: and he shall declare unto you the things that are to come. He shall glorify me: for he shall take of mine, and shall declare it unto you." (John 16:7-14.)

Read carefully again. If, as many contend, sinners can be convicted of sin only by a direct impact of the

Spirit on the heart, how would sending him to the apostles have anything to do with convicting the world? Jesus would send the Holy Spirit to the apostles; and when he came to them, he would convict the world of sin, of righteousness, and of judgment. The Spirit in them would convict the world, and do this by guiding them in presenting the truth to the people. The passage cannot be made to fit the direct operation theory. When the Spirit came to the apostles, he was to speak, not from himself; "but what things soever he shall hear, these shall he speak." The Holy Spirit would take possession of the vocal organs of chosen men, and by means of them speak to the people. On a former occasion Jesus told the apostles that they would be brought before authorities and gave them this assurance: "But when they deliver you up, be not anxious how or what ye shall speak: for it shall be given you in that hour what ye shall speak. For it is not ye that speak, but the Spirit of your Father that speaketh in you." (Matt. 10:17-20.) In this way the Holy Spirit would speak, and in this way convict the world. To say that the Spirit could not in this way convict sinners is to limit the power of the Holy Spirit. One who respects the Holy Spirit will not disrespect the Holy Spirit by saying he cannot convict sinners with his words.

After Jesus arose from the dead, he commanded the apostles to make disciples by preaching the gospel to the nations. (Matt. 28:19; Mark 16:15, 16.) By their own knowledge they would not know what to say. In their own wisdom and power, they would be helpless before an unbelieving world. So Jesus said to them: "Thus it is written, that the Christ should suffer, and rise again from the dead the third day; and that repentance and remission of sins should be preached in his name unto all the nations, beginning from Jerusalem. Ye are witnesses of these things. And behold, I send forth the promise of my father upon you: but tarry ye in the city, until ye be clothed with power from on high. (Luke 24:46-47.) "And being assembled together with them, he charged them not to depart from Jerusalem, but to wait for the promise of the Father, which, said he, ye heard from me: for John indeed baptized with water; but ye shall be baptized in the Holy Spirit not many days hence. They therefore, when they were come together, asked him, saying, Lord, dost thou at this time restore the kingdom to Israel? And he said unto them, It is not for you to know times or seasons, which the Father hath set within his own authority. But ye shall receive power, when the Holy Spirit is come upon you: and ye shall be my witnesses both in Jerusalem, and in all Judaea and Samaria, and unto the uttermost part of the earth." (Acts 1:4-8.) "And when the day of Pentecost was now come, they were all together in one place. And suddenly there came from heaven a sound as of the rushing of a mighty wind, and it filled all the house where they were sitting. And there appeared unto them tongues parting asunder like as of fire; and it sat upon each one of them. And they were all filled with the Holy Spirit, and began to speak with other tongues, as the Spirit gave them utterance." (Acts 2:1-4.) Jesus, according to promise, had sent the Holy Spirit to these waiting apostles to guide them into all truth; they were now clothed with power from on high; the Spirit was speaking through them in various languages, languages the apostles did not know; the Holy Spirit speaking through them would convict sinners; this was the baptism in the Holy Spirit. It was not a mere sprinkling of the Holy Spirit; they were completely overwhelmed by the power of the Holy Spirit.

"And when this sound was heard, the multitude came together, and were confounded, because that every man heard them speaking in his own language." (v. 6.) The multitude came together after the apostles were baptized in the Holy Spirit. Many Jews were there from various parts of the Roman Empire, and spake the language of the people where they were born and grew up. They were amazed to hear these Galileans speaking in all the languages represented there. But they did not see the significance of this speaking in tongues, neither do many today see its significance. It shows that the only way the Holy Spirit intended to reach the various nations was through the apostles—through his word. We have recorded what the Spirit said through Peter, and its effect on the people. "Now when they heard this they were pricked in their heart." Words brought conviction to their hearts, so intense that they wanted to know what to do. Peter was not like many deluded preachers of today; he did not say, "There is nothing you can do." Promptly the Holy Spirit said through him, "Repent ye, and be baptized every one of you in the name of Jesus Christ unto the remission of your sins; and ye shall receive the gift of the Holy Spirit." Yes, there was something they could do about it; "and with many other words he testified, and exhorted them, saying, save yourselves from this crooked generation. Then they that received his word were baptized." In the record of what occurred on this Pentecost day, we see exactly how the Holy Spirit convicted and converted sinners. And if a man were baptized in the Holy Spirit today, he would answer inquiring sinners exactly as the Holy Spirit did on that day.

Anvil Sparks:

Folks are so easily deceived that most of us deceive ourselves.

In cities you find one-way streets; in churches you find some one-way pockets.

A preacher who cannot preach better than he can practice is not worth listening to, and a preacher who will not try to practice what he preaches is not fit to listen to.

A man is a selfish fool who says it is nobody's business what he does.

If debating often makes a man a "professional debater," why does not preaching often make him a "professional preacher?"

Some friends are like your shadow. They are always near when the sun shines upon you; but when the clouds come and the darkness gathers about you, they have vanished.

You give a child candy to get him to do chores; you flatter grown-ups to get them to grind your ax.

Educate a wise man and he will be useful; educate a dunce and he will not be appreciated.

When a man can see danger in speaking where the Bible speaks and being silent where it is silent he is so intoxicated on fermented ego that he is liable to see anything.

Holy Spirit—Direct Spiritual Influence

The baptism of the apostles in the Holy Spirit on the day of Pentecost was not for their special good; but it enabled them to be of service to others. They were baptized in the Holy Spirit to enable them to fulfill their missions as apostles. Through them the Holy Spirit revealed the gospel, speaking, when occasion demanded it, in languages the apostles did not know. As God is not now calling and sending out apostles, no one is now baptized in the Holy Spirit. And yet it seems that some preachers talk more about "Holy Ghost baptism" than they do about Jesus the Christ. But the Holy Spirit, in his first sermon spoken through the apostles, preached Christ, and said nothing about "Holy Ghost baptism," or any other direct operation of the Spirit. Follow up the activities of the apostles and other inspired men, and you will see that these inspired men never told sinners that they could neither believe nor obey till regenerated by a direct work of the Holy Spirit, or they must first have an experience of grace. There is a striking difference between their preaching and much of the preaching of today. One wonders what would happen to the preacher and his hearers, if in the midst of the sermon the Holy Spirit should suddenly take possession of the vocal organs of the preacher and do the preaching!

After the incidents of Acts 2 the next recorded sermon is found in Acts 3. When a lame man had been healed, a crowd came together. Peter preached to them, and again reminded them that they had killed the Christ. The Holy Spirit was speaking through Peter. He did not tell them they must have "Holy Ghost baptism," or must be regenerated by a direct work of the Spirit, or must be born of the Spirit; neither did he tell them they could do nothing. But he did say, "Repent ye therefore, and turn again, that your sins may be blotted out, that so there may come seasons of refreshing from the presence of the Lord." If they did what the Holy Spirit commanded, they were led by the Holy Spirit.

Now read Stephen's speech in Acts 7. It is said of Stephen that he was "a man full of faith and of the Holy Spirit." "And Stephen, full of grace and power, wrought great wonders and signs among the people." "And they were not able to withstand the wisdom and the Spirit by which he spake." (Acts 6:5,8,10.) These verses show that Stephen had the power of the Holy Spirit upon him, and that the Holy Spirit spoke through him. His sermon was really a sermon spoken by the Holy Spirit. The Holy Spirit depended on words to convict the people. In the sermon nothing was said about regeneration by a direct work of the Holy Spirit. It was said, "Ye stiffnecked and uncircumcised in heart and ears, ye do always resist the Holy Spirit: as your fathers did, so do ye." And the next verse shows that their fathers resisted the Holy Spirit by persecuting and killing the prophets through whom the Spirit spoke; and the council was resisting the Holy Spirit in the same way. And they proceeded to demonstrate the truth of Stephen's statement, for they proceeded at once to kill him. People resist the Holy Spirit by resisting his words, nor could they resist him in any other way. No man could resist a direct impact of Almighty Power.

Read Acts 8:1-13. When the disciples were driven out of Jerusalem by a great persecution, Philip went down to the city of Samaria, and preached Christ to the people. Nothing is said about the Holy Spirit regenerating the people to enable them to believe; but Luke does say, "But when they believed Philip preaching good tidings concerning the kingdom of God and the name of Jesus Christ, they were baptized, both men and women." Philip preached, the people believed, and were baptized. So far as the record shows, the gospel was the only power brought to bear on them. The signs he performed attracted the attention of the people, and confirmed the preaching; but the preaching produced faith, and led to obedience. One thing is certain, and that is, these Samaritans had not been baptized in the Holy Spirit, or received any direct operation of the Holy Spirit before they were baptized; they did not receive any direct operation of powers, of the Holy Spirit till some days later when Peter and John came down from Jerusalem and laid hands on them.

In the conversion of the eunuch (Acts 8:26-40), an angel told Philip to "go toward the south unto the way that goeth down from Jerusalem unto Gaza." When he reached the designated point, there came into view a man of Ethiopia, the treasurer of the queen of Ethiopia. He was reading a portion of the prophet Isaiah. An angel had directed Philip to this point. Now the Spirit said to Philip, "Go near, and join thyself to this chariot." Philip said to the man, "Understandest thou what thou readest?" And he said, "How can I, except some one shall guide me?" Had Philip been imbued with the doctrine of total depravity he would have informed the eunuch that he could not understand what God says until he was regenerated, or made alive by a direct work of the Spirit, but fortunately Philip was under the influence of the Holy Spirit, not total depravity doctrine. So he guided the eunuch to an understanding by beginning from the scripture the eunuch was reading, and preaching to him Jesus, with such force and clearness that the eunuch said, "Behold, here is water, what doth hinder me to be baptized?" What hinders any to be baptized? Philip did not ask him, "Have you been regenerated by a direct work of the Spirit?" A lack of faith is the only thing that hinders anyone to be baptized. Philip had preached to him to produce faith; he believed and was baptized. Then he rejoiced.

Luke records the conversion of Saul in Acts 9:1-19. Saul, or Paul, gives an account of his conversion in Acts 22:1-16; 26:1-19. The student should read and compare these three accounts. Equipped with letters of authority from the chief priests, Saul was on his way to Damascus to bring bound to Jerusalem all the disciples in that city. As he neared Damascus about noon a great light shone about him, so intensely bright that it blinded him and he fell to the earth. A voice said to him, "Saul, Saul, why persecutest thou me? It is hard for thee to kick against the goads." And Paul said, "Who are thou, Lord?" He fell to the earth, because he knew he was in the presence of a heavenly being, though he did not know who it was. Back in the days when many of the denominations thought of conversion as a sort of convulsion, they said Saul was struck down. One preacher said, "Saul was knocked clean off his horse." Recently a preacher said Saul was born again on the highway, because Paul said, ". . . and last of all, as to the child untimely born, he appeared to me also." (1 Cor. 15:8.) Now is there, can there be, such a thing as an untimely spiritual birth? The thought is absurd. The meaning is, that the Lord's appearing to him was untimely; it had been a number of years since he had appeared in person to anyone. Saul was not saved when he saw the light. It was not Spiritual light shinning in his heart—shone round about him a light brighter than the sun. If he were saved —born again—at the moment, he was saved before he knew the Lord, or even believed in him; for he said, "Who art thou, Lord?" Neither had he received the Holy Spirit; for in Damascus Ananias said to him, "Brother Saul, the Lord, even Jesus, who appeared unto thee in the way which thou camest, hath sent me that thou mayest receive thy sight, and be filled with the Holy Spirit." But one preacher recently said, "Ananias called Saul brother; he was a brother in Christ when Ananias came to him." Such talk does not appear to be honest. Paul addressed as "brethren and fathers" the mob that had been trying to kill him. (Acts 22:1.) See also such passages as Acts 2:29,37; 3:17; 7:2; 13:15; 26:38; 23:1. Paul considered all Jews as his kinsmen and brethren. Neither the brilliant light nor Saul's blindness converted him, but that experience put him in a proper frame of mind to give heed to what he heard. He could not believe till the Lord said, "I am Jesus whom thou persecutest." He believed on that testimony—his faith came by hearing, and not by having it put into his heart by some mysterious operation. Then Saul said, "What shall I do, Lord?" The Lord said, "Arise, and enter into the city, and it shall be told thee what thou must do." Notice the emphatic "must do." In the city he was three days without sight, and so great was his distress of mind that he neither ate nor drank. Ananias came and said to him, "And now why tarriest thou? Arise, and be baptized, and wash away thy sins, calling on his name." "And he arose and was baptized; and he took food and was strengthened." Only then was his mind at ease, and his heart glad. If he had been saved on the highway, he would have gone into Damascus happy, even though he was blind; but he went into the city dejected and sad, blind both physically and spiritually, and remained so till Ananias led him into the light.

In the case of Cornelius (Acts 10; 11:1-18) he was divinely guided to send for Peter. The angel said to Cornelius, "Send to Joppa, and fetch Simon, whose surname is Peter; who shall speak unto thee words, whereby thou shalt be saved, thou and all thy house." While Peter spoke to Cornelius and those with him, the Holy Spirit fell on them with miraculous power; but that was not to save him, for they were to be saved by the words which Peter spoke to them. Peter told them what to do to be saved, and set motives before them to induce them to act. The gospel is God's power to save, and that was the power that was brought to bear on them.

At Iconium Paul and Barnabas "entered together

into the synagogue of the Jews, and so spake that a great multitude both of Jews and of Greeks believed." The miracles and signs performed through them confirmed the truthfulness of their preaching, but it was their preaching that caused many to believe. (See Acts 14:1-3.) No matter how many other things may happen to a person, he cannot believe in Jesus Christ if he has never heard of him. (Rom. 10:14-17.)

"And on the sabbath day we went forth without the gate by a river side, where we supposed there was a place of prayer; and we sat down, and spake unto the women that were come together. And a certain woman named Lydia, a seller of purple, of the city of Thyatira, one who worshipped God heard us: whose heart the Lord opened to give heed unto the things which were spoken by Paul. And when she was baptized, and her household, she besought us, saying, If ye have judged me to be faithful to the Lord, come into my house, and abide there. And she constrained us." (Acts 16:13-15.) To get the whole story of Lydia's conversion in mind, consider some things that led up to Paul's preaching in Philippi. After leaving Iconium the Spirit of the Lord kept Paul and his company on a direct course to Troas. Here "a vision appeared to Paul in the night: There was a man of Macedonia, standing, and beseeching him, saying, Come over into Macedonia and help us." They concluded that God had called them to preach the gospel to the people there. These are all significant words. Luke here joined Paul's company. The whole company decided that the help needed in Macedonia was just such help as they could supply by preaching the gospel. There is nothing strange about that. When Cornelius needed help, an angel told him to send for Peter; and when Saul of Tarsus needed help, the Lord sent Ananias to him. Now Paul and his company were to give to the people of Macedonia the help they needed. Is not that God's plan? He told his chosen to make disciples of the nations. These men were to do that by teaching—by preaching the gospel. Paul informs us that God had given to chosen men the ministry, or service, or work, of reconciling people to him; and he gave them the word, or gospel, as a means of accomplishing the work committed to them. These points are plainly stated in 2 Cor. 5:18-20. Christ's chosen ambassadors were acting on his behalf, persuading men to be reconciled to God. Said Jesus, "He that heareth you heareth me." (Luke 10:16.) And Jesus sent Paul to open the eyes of people, and to turn them from darkness to light. (Acts 26:16-18.) Paul told the Ephesians that they had formerly had the eyes of their heart enlightened. (Eph. 1:18.) Hence, to open the heart is to open the eyes of the heart. That was done by preaching, for that was the only way Paul could open the eyes of people. Lydia was a worshipper of God, but did not know Christ. Through Paul's preaching Lydia's heart was opened. Before it is said that the Lord opened her heart, it is said that she "heard us." Denominational preachers assume that the Lord opened Lydia's heart by a direct operation of the Spirit, and that sinners cannot listen to preaching till they are regenerated by a direct work of the Spirit, then why did not the Spirit operate on those who shamefully treated Paul and Silas? They certainly needed regenerating.

Notice Paul's work at Thessalonica. (Acts 17:1-9.) He preached three sabbath days in the synagogue of the Jews, proving to them that Jesus is the Christ. Notice verse 4: "And some of them were persuaded." His preaching persuaded them to obey the gospel. They were not so depraved that they could not be persuaded to accept Jesus the Christ. Christ gives life to those who come to him, and sinners are not so dead that they cannot come. On one occasion Jesus said to some dead sinners, "Ye will not come to me, that ye may have life." (John 5:40.) These people would not be persuaded to come to Christ, that they might have life; but many at Thessalonica were persuaded to come to Christ, that they might have life. They did not have life, they came, that they might have life.

Now read Acts 17:10-12. The Bereans "received the word with all readiness of mind, examining the scriptures daily, whether these things were so. Many of them therefore believed." Notice the force of therefore. They believed because they received the word with all readiness of mind. They did not believe because they had received a direct work of the Spirit, but because they received the word of God.

Of Paul's labors at Corinth it is said, "And he reasoned in the synagogue every sabbath, and persuaded Jews and Greeks. But when Silas and Timothy came down from Macedonia, Paul was constrained by the word, testifying to the Jews that Jesus was the Christ." The result is stated in verse 8: "And Crispus, the ruler of the synagogue, believed in the Lord with all his house; and many Corinthians hearing believed, and were baptized." To these Corinthians

Paul preached Jesus as the Christ: "For I determined not to know anything among you, save Jesus Christ, and him crucified . . . And my speech and my preaching were not in persuasive words of wisdom, but in demonstration of the Spirit and of power." (1 Cor. 2:2-4.) "Demonstration of the Spirit and of power" was not an invisible operation but a demonstration—a proof—that his preaching was from God. He conferred spiritual gifts and worked miracles. To this church he wrote, "Truly the signs of an apostle were wrought among you in all patience, by signs and wonders and mighty works." (2 Cor. 12:12.) These were demonstrations—proof—that Paul's preaching was from God, but only Paul's preaching gave life. "For though ye have ten thousand tutors in Christ, yet have ye not many fathers; for in Christ Jesus I begat you through the gospel." (1 Cor. 4:15.) That settles one thing—spiritual life was not generated in them by a direct operation of the Spirit.

Anvil Sparks:

"Conscience makes cowards of us all" is another old saying that is not always true. A good conscience gives courage, a guilty conscience sometimes makes a coward, but some consciences are too weak to make cowards of anyone.

Sometimes a man who is not a member of a congregation tries to run its affairs.

Improve your mind, learn to form correct judgments, and cultivate your conscience.

Holy Spirit An Intelligent Being

The Holy Spirit is an intelligent, speaking Being. The word person is not a very suitable word to apply to the Holy Spirit; for the Latin word from which it came was a stage, or theater word—"a mask (used by actors), a personage, part, or person." Later any human being was a person; and then the Father, Son, and Holy Spirit were said to be persons. For want of a better word we all use the word person in speaking either of the Father, Son, or Holy Spirit; but we need to realize that each one of these heavenly beings has a distinct work to do. A failure to recognize this has involved some people in much confusion. If you ever attended meetings in which they prayed long and loud for mourners, you likely heard them pray indiscriminately for God, Jesus, and the Holy Spirit to "come down and save these mourners."

There is an analogy between the first creation and the new, or spiritual creation. In Hebrews 1:1-2 we read, "God, having of old time spoken unto the Fathers in the prophets by divers portions and in divers manners, hath at the end of these days spoken unto us in his Son, whom he appointed heir of all things, through whom also he made the worlds." God planned, the Son executed the plans. (See also John 1:1-3, 10; Col. 1:16.) The Spirit was the finisher, the organizer, bringing order out of chaos. In the beginning it is said that "the Spirit of God moved upon the face of the waters." The marginal reading is more significant: for "moved upon," it has "was brooding upon." Job. 26:13: "By his Spirit the heavens are garnished." Psalms 104:30: "Thou sendest forth thy spirit, they are created; and thou renewest the face of the ground."

In bringing into existence and operation this great scheme of human redemption each member of the Godhead performed a work similar to that which each one performed in creating the world. It was done according to the Father's plan. "For God so loved the world, that he gave his only begotten Son, that whosoever believeth on him should not perish, but have eternal life. For God sent not the Son into the world to judge the world; but that the world should be saved through him." (John 3:16-17.) "For I am come down from heaven, not to do mine own will, but the will of him that sent me." (John 6:38.) In his prayer Jesus said, "I glorified thee on the earth, having accomplished the work which thou hast given me to do." (John 17:4.) "But God commendeth his own love toward us, in that, while we were yet sinners, Christ died for us." (Rom. 5:8.) But the death of Jesus left the disciples in despair, and even his resurrection left them in darkness as to the significance of all that went before. And after he ascended, they knew not what blessings to the world were made possible by his life, death, resurrection, and ascension. How was this spiritual darkness to be removed? If they remembered what Jesus had told them, they had grounds for hope that light would come.

But because I have spoken these things unto you, sorrow hath filled your heart. Nevertheless I tell you the truth: It is expedient for you that I go away; for if I go not away, the Comforter will not come unto you; but if I go, I will send him unto you. And he, when he is come, will convict the world in respect of sin, and of righteousness, and of judgment; of sin, because they believe not on me; of righteousness, because I go to the Father, and ye behold me no more; of judgment, because the prince of this world hath been judged. I have yet many things to say unto you, but ye cannot bear them now. Howbeit when he, the Spirit of truth, is come, he will guide you into all the truth: for he shall not speak from himself; but what things soever he shall hear, these shall he speak, and he shall declare unto you the things that are to come. (John 16.6-13).

Before Jesus ascended, he commissioned his apostles to preach to the whole world, but charged them to tarry in Jerusalem until they were clothed with power from on high. (Luke 24:45-49.) He also said to them, "Ye shall be baptized in the Holy Spirit not many days hence." (Acts 1:5.) Still in the dark, "They therefore, when they were come together, ask him saying, Lord dost thou at this time restore the kingdom to Israel? And he said unto them, it is not for you to know times or seasons, which the Father hath set within his own authority. But ye shall receive power, when the Holy Spirit is come upon you." (Acts 1:6-8.)

And when the day of Pentecost was now come, they were all together in one place. And suddenly there came from heaven a sound as of the rushing of a mighty wind, and it filled all the house where they were sitting. And there appeared unto them tongues parting asunder, like as of fire; and it sat upon each one of them. And they were all filled with the Holy Spirit, and began to speak with other tongues, as the Spirit gave them utterance. (Acts 2:1-4).

A great multitude came together. Then Peter, being filled with the Holy Spirit, preached to them, as the Spirit gave him utterance, proving to them that they, by the hand of lawless men, had crucified the Messiah, and closed with these words: "Let all the house of Israel therefore know assuredly, that God hath made him both Lord and Christ, this Jesus whom ye crucified." But they were still in the dark, for Peter had not told them what to do about it. So they, being pricked in their heart, said unto Peter and the rest of the apostles, "Brethren, what shall we do?" They realized that they must do something. Peter did not tell them, as many false guides do to-day, that there was nothing they could do; but he told them plainly what to do. "Repent ye, and be baptized every one of you in the name of Jesus Christ unto the remission of your sins; and ye shall receive the gift of the Holy Spirit." Now the plan of salvation had been completed, and these sinners had been told how to come into possession of its blessing. The next move was theirs and Peter exhorted them to make that move, saying, "Save yourselves from this crooked generation." The responsibility was now theirs; would they save themselves by obeying the Holy Spirit? "They then that received his word were baptized; and there were added unto them in that day about three thousand souls."

Read carefully Acts 2; here you learn how the Holy Spirit operates in the conversion of sinners. Of course we need not expect such an outpouring of the Holy Spirit on preachers today as came upon the apostles. That was God's way of revealing the gospel of Christ; without it they could not have preached the gospel, but the gospel has been fully revealed, and we have it recorded in the Bible. The multitude was not present when the apostles were baptized in the Holy Spirit. When the people came together the apostles preached the gospel to them, or rather the Holy Spirit took possession of the vocal organs of the apostles and used them to speak to the people. Hence the Holy Spirit was operating on them by means of his words. By means of his words he brought conviction to many, and they asked what to do. The Holy Spirit told them plainly what to do, and they did it. The Holy Spirit did not say, "You must be regenerated," or "You must be converted." The Holy Spirit told them what to do; and when they followed the leading of the Holy Spirit—when they obeyed the words of the Holy Spirit, they were regenerated, born again, became new creatures, were converted. The gospel preached on that day was, and is, God's power for saving people. As the gospel is God's power for saving people, then a direct operation of the Spirit is not his power for saving people. It is true that the Spirit quickens, that it gives life; but how? "This is my comfort in my afflictions; for thy word hath quickened me." (Psalms 119:50,93.) With those who respect what the Spirit says, statements like these end all controversy as to how the Spirit quickens; but strange it is, that those who talk loudest about the Spirit pay little attenion to what the Spirit says.

Now read carefully and thoughtfully the parable of the sower, recorded in Matt. 13:3-23; Mark 4:3-20; Luke 8:4-15. "The seed is the word of God," and the human heart is the soil. Life is in the seed; to germinate, the seed must be sown in the soil. That is why the gospel must be preached to all sinners; for there can be no spiritual life in them, till the seed is sown in their hearts. But it has been argued that the soil has to be prepared; and it is assumed that the soil is prepared by a direct operation of the Spirit, though such operation is not even hinted at in the parable or in the explanation Jesus himself gave of the parable. Stranger still, it is assumed that this preparation of the soil puts life in the soil. The fact is, you may put your soil in a perfect state of cultivation, but there is no life in it till the seed is planted. And even if there were such a thing as a direct operation of the Spirit on the sinner's heart, the seed, the word of God, must be sown in it to produce spiritual life—no seed, no life. Besides, the Lord holds every intelligent being responsible for the condition of his heart. "Keep thy heart with all diligence; for out of it are the issues of life." (Prov. 4:23.) In explaining to his disciples why he spoke in parables, Jesus said concerning the people to whom he had spoken, "For this people's heart is waxed gross, and their ears are dull of hearing, and their eyes they have closed; lest haply they should perceive with their eyes, and hear with their ears, and understand with their heart, and should turn again, and I should heal them." Their heart waxed gross, they closed their eyes; they were not born in such condition. If the sinner closes the eyes of his understanding and refuses to receive this spiritual seed, the word of God, then he alone is to blame. "Wherefore putting away all filthiness and overflowing of wickedness, receive with meekness the implanted word, which is able to save your souls." (James 1:21.) The Lord does not say "I will take all filthiness and wickedness out of your heart so that you can receive the implanted word"; the individual is to put these things away himself, and receive the word. When Paul and Silas preached at Berea, the Bereans "were more noble than those in Thessalonica, in that they received the word with all readiness of mind, examining the Scriptures daily, whether these things were so." (Acts 17:11.) They laid aside everything that might hinder their receiving the word. "Many of them therefore believed." (v. 12.) "Seeing ye have purified your souls in your obedience to the truth unto unfeigned love of the brethren, love one another from the heart fervently: having been begotten again, not of corruptible seed, but of incorruptible, through the word of God, which liveth and abideth. For, all flesh is as grass, and all the glory thereof as the flower of grass. The grass withereth, and the flower falleth; but the word of the Lord abideth forever. And this is the word of good tidings which was preached unto you." (I Peter 1:22-25.) The word which abides forever, the word by which these brethren had been begotten, was the word which had been preached to them, it is an incorruptible seed. It is the implanted word of James 1:21, the word sown in the heart. The only seed therefore that produces Christians is the word of God, which was announced through men that preached the gospel by the Holy Spirit sent forth from heaven. (See I Peter 1:12.) This word lives and abides; it has life in it—it lives, and therefore can impart life to the heart in which it is sown. If the word of God did not have life in it, it would not be seed. Those who claim that the sinner must have life imparted to him by a direct work of the Spirit before he can receive the word cannot regard the word as seed. We are told by some that the word is food for the Christian, but cannot put life into a sinner; but the truth is, it is both seed and food. The direct operation theory contradicts the statement that the word is seed.

Anvil Sparks:

Any religious body in the wrong is less harmful as an enemy than as an ally.

A person is never richly endowed with a virtue of which he boasts.

The Holy Spirit In Conversion

In the latter part of my previous article, I made some observations on the plain statement of the passages that speak of the word of God as seed. The purpose of seed is well known. If you want to produce plants in the spiritual kingdom, you must plant the seed, which is the word of God. Anyone who has sense enough to raise vegetables could understand that the word of God, the seed, is necessary to produce Christians, if he were not blinded by foggy theology. But here is one thing that should make people think: If the theory is true that life is generated in the sinner before he can understand or accept the word then the word of God is not seed! This thought has not had the attention its importance deserves. If "seed" is incapable of producing life, it is not seed.

Now read carefully Matt. 11:28-30: "Come unto me, all ye that labor and are heavy laden, and I will give thee rest. Take my yoke upon you and learn of me, for I am meek and lowly in heart: and ye shall find rest unto your souls. For my yoke is easy, and my burden is light." To whom is this invitation extended? Our hereditary depravity advocates tell us that a sinner cannot do anything till he is regenerated, or made alive, by a direct work of the Holy Spirit; and they tell us that when that occurs all burdens of heart are rolled away, and happiness reigns. If that is true, then Jesus is not inviting them—his invitation is to those who labor and are heavy laden, and who desire rest. Read the verses again. Jesus is not inviting those who have been made shouting happy

over being regenerated and thereby having their
burdens of sins rolled away. And certainly Jesus
would not be inviting people to come, who are so bound
by hereditary depravity that they cannot come. But
these advocates are wrong, as wrong as wrong can
be. Jesus is inviting those who labor against the ad-
verse forces of the world and who are burdened with
sin and doubt; and he places motives before them
to induce them to come—rest, sweet rest, and association with Jesus. If the promises of the gospel and
the dread of punishment do not move sinners, nothing
will.

To show the helplessness of the sinner John 6:44
is quoted and wrongly applied: "No man can come
to me, except the Father that sent me draw him: and
I will raise him up at the last day." It is assumed
without any sort of proof that God draws the sinner
by direct operation of the Spirit. It is hard to believe that such argument is made ignorantly, for in
the next verse Jesus says: "It is written in the prophets, and they shall all be taught of God. Everyone
that hath heard from the Father, and hath learned,
cometh unto me." There is therefore a drawing and
a coming. What is learned through being taught
draws people, and they come. "I drew them with
cords of a man, with bands of love. (Hos. 11:4.)
"Yea, I have loved thee with an everlasting love;
therefore with loving kindness have I drawn thee."
(Jer. 31:3.) God does not draw people to him by
physical power. He draws with the power of the
gospel, and that is done through teaching. But no
one will be drawn by this teaching, unless he believes;
"for he that cometh to God must believe that he is,

and that he is a rewarder of them that seek after him." (Heb. 11:6.) The sinner must be taught, must believe and then come; in this way God draws.

> "The word is nigh thee, in thy mouth and in thy heart: that is, the word of faith, which we preach: because if thou shalt confess with thy mouth Jesus as Lord, and shalt believe in thy heart that God raised him from the dead, thou shalt be saved: for with the heart man believeth unto righteousness; and with the mouth confession is made unto salvation. For the Scripture saith, Whosoever believeth on him shall not be put to shame. For there is no distinction between Jew and Greek: for the same Lord is Lord of all, and is rich unto all that call upon him; for, Whosoever shall call upon the name of the Lord shall be saved. How then shall they call upon him in whom they have not believed? and how shall they believe in him whom they have not heard? and how shall they hear without a preacher? and how shall they preach, except they be sent? even as it is written, How beautiful are the feet of them that bring glad tidings of good things! (Rom. 10:8-15).

To understand this Scripture we need first to notice some of the terms used by Paul. "The word" and "the word of faith, which we preach" of verse 8 are the "Glad tidings of good things" of verse 15. In the New Testament a preacher was "God's ambassador, and the herald or proclaimer of the divine word." —Thayer. Paul says he was made a preacher and an apostle. (I Tim. 2:7; II Tim. 1:11.) God qualified and sent certain men, called apostles, to proclaim the gospel—to reveal it. No one could reveal the gospel unless God sent him. And if these men had never proclaimed the gospel, no one could have heard it, and therefore no one could have believed. But as it was written for us, we can read and believe. "Many other signs therefore did Jesus in the presence of his disciples, which are not written in this book: but these are written, that ye may believe that Jesus is the Christ, the Son of God; and that believing ye may have life in his name." (John 20:30-21.) Life or salvation, depends on hearing, and hearing depends on the original proclamation of the gospel. No hint is here given that some direct power is necessary to enable anyone to believe; but it is plainly taught that the original proclamation of the gospel is the only thing that is necessary to enable anyone to believe. "For seeing that in the wisdom of God the world through its wisdom knew not God, it was God's good pleasure through the foolishness of preaching to save them that believe." (I Cor. 1:21.) Or, through the foolishness of the thing preached. To the Greek philosophers the gospel was foolishness, but it was God's means of saving all who would believe it. Not a hint is here given that any other power was necessary, or that any other means would be used.

When I was teen-age I frequently witnessed rousing mourner-bench exercises in revivals of a church which then thought that such exercises were the supreme method of converting sinners. When they succeeded in getting several mourners to come to the mourner-bench, they sang to them, and talked to them, prayed for them, and shouted over them. One man of years and of more than average intelligence, seemed to be the main one to pray. One of his petitions was, "O God, try some untried means on these hard-hearted sinners." He wanted God to experiment on them to see if he could find something that would work. That sort of prayer was made when a group of mourners could not be excited into raising a shout. He reminds me of the rich man's prayer in Hades to father Abraham when he thought of his hard-hearted brethren back home: Send Lazarus to testify to my five brethren, lest they also come into this place of torment. He wanted Abraham to try something on his brethren that had never been tried before; but Abraham said, "They have Moses and the prophets; let them hear them." But the rich man knew they would not pay any attention to Moses and the prophets; "but if one go to them from the dead, they will repent." But Abraham knew it was useless to try some untried means on them; so he said, "If they hear not Moses and the prophets, neither will they be persuaded, if one rise from the dead." (Luke 16:19-31.) In view of what we hear today, is it not singular that neither the rich man nor Lazarus thought of the direct operation of the Spirit—no untried means was used on these five brethren, though the rich man asked to have it done.

The Jewish Sanhedrin, or council, opposed the gospel and antagonized and persecuted God's preachers. For this reason Stephen said to the council, "Ye stiffnecked and uncircumcised in heart and ears, ye do always resist the Holy Spirit: as your fathers did, so do ye." Surely no one thinks these men were able to resist a direct impact of the almighty power of God! But they could, and did, resist, or oppose, the preaching the Holy Spirit did through chosen men. The connection and circumstances show clearly that this was the way of explaining how they resisted the Holy Spirit. Stephen, by way of explaining how they resisted the Holy Spirit said, "Which of the prophets did not your fathers persecute? and they killed them that showed before of the coming of the righteous one: of whom ye have now become betrayers and murderers; ye who received the law as it was ordained by angels, and kept it not." (Acts 7:51-53.)   To illustrate further, read Nehemiah 9:20, 30: "Thou gavest also thy good Spirit to instruct them." This instructing had been done through Moses and the prophets. "Yet many years didst Thou bear with them, and testifiedst against them through thy prophets; yet would they not give ear." In this way they resisted the Holy Spirit. To attempt to do so would be an uneven wrestling match. But to resist any person does not necessarily mean a personal impact, or wrestling match. Paul resisted Peter; that is, he opposed what Peter was doing. (Gal. 2:11-14.)   James said, "Resist the devil." (Jas. 4:7.)   Jesus resisted the devil with words; and the Jewish council had been resisting the Holy Spirit with words up to the time Stephen said, "Ye do always resist the Holy Spirit." Because they could not answer Stephen's arguments, they had decided to kill him. The Spirit had been striving with them, but they had resisted him.

The people before the flood became very wicked— "all flesh had corrupted their way upon the earth." Noah preached to them, but apparently made no impression. It was by his preaching that God's Spirit was striving with them; and so God said, "My Spirit shall not strive with man forever." Yet God gave them one-hundred and twenty more years of probation. But they grew worse; "and Jehovah saw that the wickedness of man was great in the earth, and that every imagination of the thoughts of his heart was only evil continually." They had reached the limit of wickedness, even though God's Spirit was striving with them through Noah's preaching. Surely no one is simple enough to think God's Spirit made a direct assault on them, but they were too powerful to be subdued.

Anvil Sparks:

We sometimes learn our lesson too late to profit by it. On the scaffold, just before adjusting the black cap, the sheriff asked the darkey: "Sambo, have you anything to say to these people?" "Yes, suh; jist one wu-ud, boss: Dis sho' goin' to be a lesson to me."

I have heard many big fish yarns, but the evolutionists ask us to believe the biggest one yet. Somewhere in the remote past, they say, a fish flapped out on dry-land and his fins turned into legs. After that, the story of Jonah and the whale seems easy.

Who Received Holy Spirit Baptism

In recent years there seems to be more talk about the baptism in the Holy Spirit among some groups than ever before, but they usually speak of it as "Holy Ghost baptism." I think they prefer to say "Holy Ghost baptism," rather than Holy Spirit baptism, because the word "Ghost" fits in better with their mystic ideas. It sounds more ghostly and weird. But there is a lack of agreement among the advocates of "Holy Ghost baptism." I think it is safe to say that the majority of such advocates contend that sinners are regenerated and saved by this "Holy Ghost baptism," and that every such regeneration is a miracle. One such advocate argued that it was a mistake to say that Jesus saves sinners, that he only made it possible for sinners to be saved, but that the Holy Spirit really brings salvation to the sinner in this Holy Spirit baptism. I judge he was stating what most of them believe. One group of Holiness folks, according to one of their representatives with whom I had a small debate, advanced this theory: A sinner is justified by faith only, then by faithful living grows into sanctification, and then may receive Holy Ghost baptism in answer to prayer. He claimed that such baptism neither justifies nor sanctifies, but that it gives power to speak in tongues, and heal the sick, etc. All these groups quote passages that applied only to the apostles.

"And even now the axe lieth at the root of the trees: every tree therefore that bringeth not forth good fruit is hewn down, and cast into the fire. I indeed baptize you in water unto repentance: but he that cometh after me is mightier than I, whose shoes I am not worthy to bear: he shall baptize you in the Holy Spirit and in fire: whose fan is in his hand, and he will thoroughly cleanse his threshing-floor; and he will gather his wheat into the garner, but the chaff he will burn up with unquenchable fire." (Matt. 3:10-12.)

Two classes of people are here included, the wicked and the righteous. Jesus had not then begun his personal ministry, and therefore had at that time no apostles and disciples. The baptism in fire is for the wicked, as may be seen by noticing the use of fire in verses 10 and 12; the fulfillment is recorded in Revelation 20:11-15. If the wicked, the chaff, are to be baptized in fire when cast into the lake of fire, why not conclude that all the righteous, the wheat, be baptized in the Holy Spirit when they are gathered into the garner, that is, into heaven.

Jesus had a special work for a special group whom he selected and called apostles. They therefore needed special preparation. It should be plain to any one who has any ability to understand the simplest matters, that other disciples would not need the same qualifications that apostles had to have to enable them to do their special work. If you do not claim to be an apostle, why should you claim to have that which enabled them to be apostles?

Of course he gave his apostles a period of teaching, but other disciples were also with him. (Acts 1:21,-22.) But on the night of his betrayal only the apostles were with him. (Matt 26:20; Mark 14:17; Luke 22:14.) On that night Jesus told the apostles what the Holy Spirit, when he came, would do for them, though he did not use the term "baptism in the Holy Spirit," but we shall see that what he promised was the baptism in the Holy Spirit. Be honest with what Jesus said, and see if you think it can possibly apply to you: "Nevertheless I tell you the truth: It is expedient for you that I go away; for if I go not away, the Comforter will not come unto you; but if I go, I will send him unto you. And he, when he is come, will convict the world in respect of sin, and of righteousness, and of judgment: of sin, because they believe not on me; of righteousness, because I go to the father, and ye behold me no more; of judgment, because the prince of this world hath been judged. I have yet many things to say unto you, but ye cannot bear them now. Howbeit when he, the Spirit of truth, is come, he shall guide you into all the truth: for he shall not speak from himself; but what things soever he shall hear, these shall he speak: and he shall declare unto you the things that are to come. He shall glorify me: for he shall take of mine, and shall declare it unto you." (John 16:7-14.)

After his resurrection he said to them: "Thus it is written, that the Christ should suffer, and rise again from the dead the third day; and that repentance and remission of sins should be preached in his name unto all nations, beginning from Jerusalem. Ye are witnesses of these things. And behold, I send forth the promise of my father upon you: but tarry ye in the city, until ye be clothed with power from on high." (Luke 24:46-49.)

At that time they had not received what he promised them on the night of his betrayal. He here refers to it as being "clothed with power from on high." They could not reveal the gospel without this power from on high. Luke gives some additional information in his report of what occurred just before Jesus ascended: "The former treatise I made, O Theophilus, concerning all that Jesus began both to do and to teach, until the day in which he was received up, after that he had given commandment through the Holy Spirit unto the apostles whom he had chosen: to whom he also showed himself alive after his passion by many proofs, appearing unto them by the space of forty days, and speaking the things concerning the kingdom of God: and, being assembled together with them, he charged them not to depart from Jerusalem, but wait for the promise of the Father, which said he, ye heard from me: for John indeed baptized with water; but ye shall be baptized with the Holy Spirit not many days hence. They therefore when they were come together, asked him, saying, Lord, dost thou at this time restore the kingdom to Israel? And he said unto them, It is not for you to know times or seasons, which the Father hath set within his own authority. But ye shall receive power, when the Holy Spirit is come upon you: and ye shall be my witnesses both in Jerusalem, and in all Judaea and Samaria, and unto the uttermost part of the earth." (Acts 1:1-8.)

Here again we have the apostles whom Jesus had chosen. The commandment given them was the great commission, which, as recorded by Matthew, Mark, and Luke, was a condensation of "the things concerning the Kingdom of God." After their return from Galilee they were commanded "not to depart from Jerusalem," but to wait for the promise of the

Father, which he had repeated to them, as told in John 16:7-14. In fulfillment of this promise they would "be baptized in the Holy Spirit not many days hence." They would thus receive power—"be clothed with power from on high"—and thereby be fully qualified to be his witnesses. At no other time, so far as the record shows, did Jesus use the term baptize in referring to the miraculous giving of the Holy Spirit; and as in the promise previously made, so here, he was speaking to his apostles. "Not many days hence," "when the day of Pentecost was now come, they were all together in one place. And suddenly there came from heaven a sound as of the rushing of a mighty wind, and it filled all the house where they were sitting. And there appeared unto them tongues parting asunder, like as of fire; and it sat upon each one of them. And they were all filled with the Holy Spirit, and began to speak with other tongues, as the Spirit gave them utterance." (Acts 2:1-4.) Jesus had said, "Howbeit when he the Spirit of truth is come, he shall guide you into all the truth: for he shall not speak from himself; but what things soever he shall hear, these shall he speak: and he shall declare unto you the things that are to come." ". . . as the Spirit gave them utterance." The Holy Spirit spoke by the mouth of these Apostles, and he was declaring things to them as well as to the people who heard them; and the people who heard them knew what they were saying as well as did the apostles. By speaking through these Holy Spirit filled men, he would bring to pass these words of Jesus: "And he, when he is come will convict the world in respect of sin, and of righteousness, and of judgment." And this Holy Spirit baptism, this being clothed with power from on high, enabled them to work all sorts of miracles. Now, can you carefully look into all the things this baptism of the Holy Spirit enabled the apostles to do, and then honestly claim that you have been baptized in the Holy Spirit?

According to the plain words of Jesus, he had promised this power to none but the apostles. And as further proof, notice these words: "But Peter, standing up with the eleven," and "For these are not drunken." (Acts 2:14,15.) And yet as plain as the record is, I heard a man quote the record as saying, "But Peter, standing up with the hundred and twenty," etc. My credulity will not stretch sufficiently to allow me to believe the man was honest. Again, when the words of the Holy Spirit convicted the multitude, they said unto Peter and the rest of the apostles, "Brethren, what shall we do?"

So many people utterly misunderstand the purpose of the baptism in the Holy Spirit. Their ideas lead some into all sorts of hurtful and fanatical notions. Witness, the snake handlers. They deliberately and foolishly tempt, or make trial of God. Others, less fanatical, put their feelings above what God plainly says. Otherwise intelligent people have been heard to say that they would not give their feelings for a stack of Bibles as high as a house. Hence, they would not give their feelings for all that God says. They thus give God the lie. It is a fearful state of mind to get into. I heard one prominent preacher say, "If Jesus Christ was to come down the aisle, and tell me that I was wrong, I would tell him he did know what he was taking about." And when a man can say, as one said to me, that he had an unction from on high and did not need any body to teach him, and that he could get along without the Bible as well as with it, it is time we were doing all we can to recover people from such blasphemous foolishness. What did the baptism in the Holy Spirit accomplish? And what did it not accomplish? It is well to sum up some things.

1. No man was baptized in the Holy Spirit for his own individual benefit. In olden times prophets were not inspired for their own individual benefit. Being "clothed with power from on high," the apostles were enabled to reveal the gospel, and to confirm it —to prove that it was from God—by miracles and signs. "Concerning which salvation the prophets sought and searched diligently, who prophesied of the grace that should come unto you: searching what time or manner of time the Spirit of Christ which was in them did point unto, when it testified beforehand the sufferings of Christ, and the glories that should follow them. To whom it was revealed, that not unto themselves, but unto you, did they minister these things, which now have been announced unto you through them that preached the gospel unto you by the Holy Spirit sent forth from heaven; which things angels desire to look into." (1 Pet. 1:10-12.) "For no prophecy ever came by the will of man: but men spake from God, being moved by the Holy Spirit." (2 Pet. 1:21.) Hence Peter was to tell Cornelius and his company words whereby he and his house should be saved. And Paul tells us that the gospel is God's power unto salvation—"the word of this salvation."

2. Faith is not produced in an individual by his being baptized in the Holy Spirit. Faith comes by hearing the word of God. (Rom. 10:17.) At Iconium Paul and Barnabas, "so spake that a great multitude both of Jews and Greeks believed." (Acts 14:1.) Much other evidence could be given; but it is not necessary, for it stands to reason no one can believe in a person of whom he has never heard. Said Paul, "How shall they believe in him whom they have not heard." (Rom. 10:14.)

3. People are not converted, begotten or born again, or regenerated, by a baptism in the Holy Spirit. These terms—some of them figurative—mean about the same thing, and what they express is effected by the word of God. The only thing that hinders the word from bringing about this change is a condition of heart. "For this people's heart is waxed gross, and their ears are dull of hearing, and their eyes they have closed; lest haply they should perceive with their eyes, and hear with their ears, and understand with their heart, and should turn again, and I should heal them. (Matt. 13:15.) This is conversion —*hearing, understanding, turning*. "For though ye have ten thousand tutors in Christ, yet have ye not many fathers; for in Christ Jesus I begat you through the gospel." (1 Cor. 4:15.) "Having been begotten again, not of corruptible seed, but of incorruptible, through the word of God, which liveth and abideth." (1 Pet. 1:23.) "Of his own will he brought us forth by the word of truth, that we should be a kind of firstfruits of his creatures." (Jas. 1:18.)

4. Hearts are not cleansed, or purified, by Holy Spirit baptism. In speaking of his preaching at the

house of Cornelius, Peter said, "And God, who knoweth the heart, bare them witness, giving them the Holy Spirit, even as he did unto us; and he made no distinction between us and them, cleansing their hearts by faith." (Acts 15:8,9.)   So Peter here shows clearly that it was not the outpouring of the Spirit on Cornelius and his company that cleansed their hearts, but it was done by faith.   According to the Greek text Peter said their hearts were cleansed by the Faith.   The Faith is the gospel.   (Compare Acts 6:7, Gal. 1:23.)   "A great company of the priests were obedient to the faith"—obedient to the gospel. Paul preached "the faith"—he preached the gospel. Hence, the Gentiles' hearts were cleansed by obedience to the gospel.   "Seeing ye have purified your souls in your obedience to the truth . . . " (1 Pet. 1:22.) If you still contend that hearts are cleansed by the baptism of the Holy Spirit, then you do not believe what the Holy Spirit says in these scriptures just quoted.   Remember this: not one time does the Bible say that the heart, or soul, is cleansed, or purified, by Holy Spirit baptism.

5. Holy Spirit baptism was never intended to subdue the rebellious hearts of those who received it so as to bring them into subjection to God's will.   No direct operation of the Spirit ever changed the moral or spiritual nature of its recipient.   "The law of Jehovah is perfect, restoring the soul." (Ps. 19:7.) It restores the soul to right relations with God and man.   The gospel is called "the word of reconciliation." (2 Cor. 5:19.)   It requires thinking.   "I thought on my ways, and turned my feet unto thy testimonies." (Ps. 119:59.)   There is only one thing that

will subdue a hard heart. "Is not my word like fire? saith Jehovah; and like a hammer that breaketh the rock in pieces?" (Jer. 23:29.) No one's character can be improved while his eyes are closed and he walks in darkness of sin and ignorance. Bent on persecuting disciples at Damascus, Saul was on his way thither, when the Lord appeared to him and said, "I am Jesus whom thou persecutest. But arise, and stand upon thy feet: for to this end have I appeared unto thee, to appoint thee a minister and a witness both of the things wherein thou hast seen me, and of the things wherein I will appear unto thee; delivering thee from the people, and from the Gentiles, unto whom I send thee, to open their eyes, that they may turn from darkness to light and from the power of Satan unto God, that they may receive remission of sins and an inheritance among them that are sanctified by faith in me." (Acts 26:15-18.) This would all be done by preaching Christ to them. While on this matter as to what changes people and develops character, let us go a little farther.

There is great power in an idea, or thought when spurred to action by motive. Thoughts are powerful only when carried into action. The old colored man, too old to work much, when asked what he did, said, "Sometimes I sets and thinks, and sometimes I just sets." He did not have sufficient motive to move him. But there is great power in a thought. Thoughts control actions. If you can get people to think the way you want them to think, they will act the way you want them to act. Every educator, reformer, or propagandist knows this. The politician makes speeches and writes articles to get his thoughts into the minds of the people. To that extent he fills them with thoughts, to that extent he works in them to will and do his pleasure. And how much more wonderful are God's thoughts! "For as the heavens are higher than the earth, so are my ways higher than your ways, and my thoughts than your thoughts." (Isa. 55:9.) As we learn the word of God and cherish it we are imbibing the thoughts of God. In this way he works in us; "for it is God who worketh in you both to will and to work, for his good pleasure." (Phil. 2:13.) Transformation of character is not effected by a baptism in the Holy Spirit. "And be not fashioned according to this world; but be ye transformed by the renewing of your mind." (Rom. 12:2.) This puts the responsibility on the individual. Renew the mind—fill it with God's thoughts, and the transformation results. "Think on these things."

Anvil Sparks:

Humility on display is hypocrisy.

You cannot fight the devil with your hands tied.

The optimist of yesterday is the grouch of today.

Spiritual Gifts

"Now there are diversities of gifts, but the same Spirit. And there are diversities of ministrations, and the same Lord. And there are diversities of workings, but the same God, who worketh all things in all. But to each one is given the manifestation of the Spirit to profit withal. For to one is given through the Spirit the word of wisdom; and to another the word of knowledge, according to the same Spirit: to another faith, in the same Spirit; and to another gifts of healings, in the one Spirit; and to another working of miracles; and to another prophecy; and to another discernings of spirits: to another divers kinds of tongues; and to another the interpretation of tongues: but all these worketh the one and the same Spirit, dividing to each one severally even as he will." (1 Cor. 12:4-11.)

In the first verse Paul said, "Now concerning spiritual gifts, brethren, I would not have you ignorant." Though this church was richly endowed with spiritual gifts, many, at least, were ignorant of their purpose and the proper use of them. And even today there is, among religious people, a lamentable amount of ignorance concerning spiritual gifts. It seems that the baptism of the Holy Spirit conferred all the gifts on its recipients. We conclude therefore that each apostle had all the spiritual gifts mentioned, and that any operation of the Holy Spirit that did not confer all these gifts is not the baptism of the Holy Spirit.

The Holy Spirit distributed these gifts according

(191)

to his own will—"but all these worketh the one and the same spirit, dividing to each one severally even as he will." But even so, those who had spiritual gifts were responsible for the way they used them, as may be seen by reading 1 Cor. chapter 14.

These miraculous manifestations of the Holy Spirit —Spirit baptism and gifts of the Holy Spirit—were not conferred upon chosen ones for the sole benefit of the recipients. "But to each one is given the manifestation of the Spirit to profit withal." The words, "to profit withal," has no clear meaning to the average reader. MacKnight gives this translation: "And to each is given the manifestation of the Spirit for the advantage of all." Conybeare and Howson gives this: "The gift whereby the Spirit becomes manifest is given to each for the profit of all." No extraordinary power of the Holy Spirit was ever conferred upon any one for his own personal benefit. When churches began to dot the country in those days, the Apostles could not be present in every church, the New Testament had not been written. As they could not hand a New Testament to a person, translated into his own language, it was necessary that some one be empowered to preach to him in his own language. Hence the gift of tongues. Those who now claim to have this gift of tongues are utterly at sea on that question. In every congregation some inspired person was needed to reveal the will of God on matters as they came up. The gift of prophecy enabled the recipient to reveal unerringly the will of God. Christianity was a new thing then, and the early preachers needed some way to convince the people that their preaching was from God. In fact, the people had a right to demand that the preacher prove to them that God had sent him with his teaching. God enabled them to work miracles of healing, as proof that God was with them. But evidently not all members received spiritual gifts; they were distributed according as the Holy Spirit willed. The conferring of these spiritual gifts had two objects in view—namely, the conversion of sinners and the building up of the saints. But it cannot be proved that a spiritual gift conferred upon a person worked any moral change in him. Inspiration enabled him to preach the gospel, and miracles gave him a favorable hearing. But these miraculous powers did not convert people—they were not God's power for saving people. The gospel which these miracle-working men preached was their sole reliance for converting men. "And they went forth, and preached everywhere, the Lord working with them, and confirming the word by the signs that followed." (Mark 16:20.)

The Holy Spirit bestowed these gifts according to his own will, but how? Seeking an answer to that question may seem to some to be impractical. Perhaps so, but it is an interesting study. Evidently they were bestowed by the laying on of hands. Some argue that none but apostles could confer these gifts, but the proof offered does not seem to me to be conclusive.

An argument is built on the fact, that, after Philip's great success in Samaria, the apostles sent down Peter and John. "Then laid they their hands on them, and they received the Holy Spirit." (Acts 8:17.) It seems certain that Philip did not have power to bestow the Holy Spirit by the laying on of his hands, though he was inspired and could perform miracles; but does that prove conclusively that none but the apostles had power to impart spiritual gifts? Might we not prove as conclusively, that of the apostles only Peter and John had such powers, for they were the ones sent? But in either case we would be drawing a universal conclusion from a particular incident. Besides, when Simon asked for power to impart the Holy Spirit to others by laying his hands on them, had Peter said, "Thou hast neither part nor lot in this matter, for thou art not an apostle," that would have shown that none but apostles had such power; but the answer Peter gave shows that he might have been granted the power he asked, if his heart had been right. Think as you read Peter's answer: "Thou hast neither part nor lot in this matter; for thy heart is not right before God." (Acts 8:21.) Does not this language imply as plainly as language can, that the only thing that hindered the granting of his request was the condition of his heart? But when a person gets an idea firmly fixed in his mind, contradictory language does not seem to him to mean what it says.

I Timonthy 4:14, "Neglect not the gift that is in thee, which was given thee by prophecy, with the laying on of the hands of the presbytery." The presbytery was the eldership of a church; and no hands are here mentioned, except the hands of the elders. But we are referred to 2 Tim. 1:6: "For which cause I put thee in remembrance that thou stir up the gift of God, which is in thee through the laying on of my hands." Here the presbytery is not mentioned; in the other verse Paul does not mention himself. This difference indicates that Paul had two different instances in mind. That should not be cause for wonder or doubt, if we remember that some men—examples, Stephen, and Philip—had more than one gift bestowed on them.

Let us get back to the quotation at the beginning of this article and consider the phrase, "to another workings of miracles." For "miracles" the marginal reading says the Greek word means *powers*. That is mentioned as distinct from the other miracle working powers, such as prophecy, healing, speaking in tongues, etc., and could not therefore be a general term including all the miraculous powers mentioned. The phrase itself forbids such an idea. Notice the phrase—"to another workings of powers." It was therefore a distinct gift. But what does it mean? MacKnight gives this rendering and comment: *"To another the inworkings of powers,* that is, an ability to work in others the spiritual gifts and miraculous powers."

I am not dogmatic on this point, but it seems to me that the evidence shows that the Holy Spirit conferred on some who were not apostles the power to impart some spiritual gifts by the laying on of hands. But no matter which view you take, it is a thing that none of us can now practice.

The Indwelling of the Holy Spirit

We can believe revealed truths and facts, though we may be unable to understand all about them. I cannot understand how the Holy Spirit can be in different people at the same time; but to say such is impossible is to contradict plain statements of Holy Writ. On Pentecost twelve apostles "were all filled with the Holy Spirit." (Acts 2:4.) See also Acts 4:31. I do not understand it, but I believe it. Let us not try to measure the operations and possibilities of Deity by our own limitations. On this, as on other points of Christianity, the Bible is our only source of information; and what it says should be the end of controversy.

I have heard this argument on the setting up of the church before Pentecost, though it never did seem to me very conclusive: "The church is a body; and if it was set up before the Spirit was given on Pentecost, it was a body without a spirit; and a body without a spirit is dead." And the one who made the argument was likely to deny that the Spirit now dwells in the church! Is the church now a dead body? Think on these things.

"And we are witnesses of these things; and so is the Holy Spirit, whom God hath given to them that obey him." (Acts 5:32.) Have you obeyed God? One good brother said, "I know I haven't the Holy Spirit in me; if I had I could feel it." A denominationalist rises up in meeting and says, "I know I have the Holy Spirit, for I can feel it." So there you are —both depend on their feelings as evidence. In such talk God's word is ruled out of court. Is not that so? "Or know ye not that your body is a temple of the Holy Spirit which is in you, which ye have from God?" (1 Cor. 6:19.) "Know ye not that ye are a temple of God, and that the Spirit of God dwelleth in you?" (1 Cor. 3:16.) Not by feelings, but only by revelation, may we know this. I do not even feel my own spirit, neither do I know much about how it dwells in my body. I think I know my spirit is not in the food I eat, and I know, that, if I do not eat food, my spirit will leave my body. The word of God is the Christian's food. You can follow up the analogy, and yet the analogy may not be conclusive proof to you. "But if the Spirit of him that raised up Jesus from the dead dwelleth in you, he that raised up Christ Jesus from the dead shall give life also to your mortal bodies through his Spirit that dwelleth in you." (Rom. 8:11.)

But I have been met with this statement: "The Holy Spirit dwells in us, just as Christ does — by faith" — "that Christ may dwell in your hearts through faith." (Eph. 3:17.) And it is also said that we are justified by faith. In both cases is not faith the condition? On that condition the facts stated are based—faith is the condition, not a substitute for the thing affirmed. Jesus said, "I will not leave you desolate (Margin *orphans*): I come unto you." (John 14:18.) He would come to them in the person of the Holy Spirit. Again he says, verse 23: "If a man love me he will keep my word: and my Father will love him, and we will come unto him, and make our abode with him." Does this mean anything to you? Jesus and the Father are so closely united

that he could say, "I and the Father are one." (John
10:30.)   And after the Holy Spirit came, the Father
and the Son act through the agency of the Spirit.
Hence Paul could say of Christ the Lord and God,
" . . . in whom each several building, fitly framed
together, groweth into a holy temple in the Lord; in
whom ye also are builded together for a habitation
of God in the Spirit." (Eph. 2:21,22.)

What does the indwelling Spirit do? What if I
am unable to answer that question? And what if
no one else can give a definite answer, would our
inability to answer the question nullify what God
has said? If we cannot explain a thing, shall we say
there is no such thing? Let us not jump to unwarranted conclusions. This we do when we say, that,
if the Holy Spirit really dwelt in us, we could speak
by inspiration and work miracles. John was filled
with the Holy Spirit from his mother's womb. (Luke
1:15.)   I hardly think any one will say that John
worked miracles and spoke by inspiration as soon as
he was born. And he never did work any miracles,
even though he was a prophet. (John 10:41.) If an
apostle were living today, I feel sure he could not
speak by inspiration or work a miracle. The whole
plan of salvation has been fully revealed, confirmed,
and recorded; no additional revelations are needed.
But let us think of one idea that has been with me for
years. Did you brother preacher, ever pray for the
Lord to lead you into the places where you can do
the most good? No? Well, you should; the Lord
knows you and he knows the fields, and he therefore
knows where you can do the most good. You do not
know. For a long time I have prayed for the Lord

to lead me into places where I could do the most good. Why not?

If preachers would seek places where they can do the most good, instead of seeking places where they can get the most material good—what a blessing to the cause and to them that would be! If a preacher really wants to go where he can do the most good, he can then sincerely pray for the Lord to lead him to such places. If all preachers were of that mind, there would be no job-hunting preachers. There would be no scheming for good paying places. I think I am old enough and near enough to the grave to say without the appearance of boasting that I was never knowingly a candidate against any other for any place.

Anvil Sparks:

Ingorance is usually dogmatic.

And remember brother, that playing a tune with your mouth is not singing.

A man may slander me or he may preach to me; but he shall not do both, if I know it.

The Holy Spirit Baptism Controversy

It seems that some have concluded that a figure of speech is fiction. Once a brother asked me if I thought the baptism of the Holy Spirit (Acts 2) was figurative, and I replied, "Yes, I think so." He replied, "I don't; I think it was real." Now, cannot a real incident or a real person or thing be spoken of in figurative language? What is figurative language? What is a figure of speech? When we deviate from the plain ordinary mode of expression, we use figurative language. We use the word dull in its plain ordinary use when we say that the edge of a cutting tool is dull; but we use it figuratively when we speak of a dull sermon, or a dull preacher, or a dull student. When Paul called the church at Corinth an "epistle," he used a figure of speech, though the church was real, not a fictitious thing. When James spoke of bridling the tongue, he used a figure of speech. Now take the word baptize: in its plain ordinary use it refers to dipping or immersing in water. When Jesus spoke of his coming trials and crucifixion as baptism, he used figurative language, even though his sufferings would be awfully real. He was turning the word baptism from its ordinary use. And what the apostles experienced on Pentecost was real, but to speak of it as baptism is to turn the word baptism from its ordinary use. And notice, too, that Jesus spoke of that occurrence as being "clothed with power from on high." That, too, is figurative language; for in the plain ordinary use of the word clothe it means, to put on garments. Now could it have been that "clothed" and "baptized" were both figurative speech?

But in the estimation of many in the denominations the plain ordinary use of the word baptism refers to the "baptism of the Holy Ghost." With them that is the one baptism, and water baptism is merely symbolic, a picture of the real baptism. But they have the whole thing turned around.

But what about John's language in Matt. 3:11? As to the baptism in fire, verse 10 and 12 show plainly what that is, and Rev. 20:11-15 shows when that will occur. In so far as the apostles were concerned, their baptism in the Holy Spirit occurred on Pentecost when they were "clothed with power from on high." But when John uttered that language, there were no apostles, nor were there any disciples of Christ at that time. John had two classes of people before him, the good and the bad, but certainly John did not mean that only the wicked before him would be baptized with fire. It seems therefore that he was contrasting what was in store for the two classes that were before him, and for all others falling in either class. And yet, just before his ascension, when addressing his chosen witnesses, his apostles, Jesus said to them, " . . . ye shall be baptized in the Holy Spirit not many days hence." (Acts 1:1-5.) Not a word here about baptism in fire; neither did he so much as hint that those the apostles would baptize on that day would also be baptized in the Holy Spirit. And Peter's question from Joel did not mean that on that day God would pour out his Spirit on all his servants and hand maidens any more than it meant that on that day he would "show wonders in the heaven above, and signs on the earth beneath: blood and fire, and vapor of smoke: the sun shall be turned into darkness, and the moon into blood."

After Pentecost there was the imparting of the Holy Spirit, or spiritual gifts, by the laying on of hands, and this impartation was subject to the will of the Spirit, or of God (1 Cor. 2: 4-11). But this impartation of the Spirit by the laying on of hands is never called baptism in the Holy Spirit. If all Christians had been baptized in the Holy Spirit, there would have been no need to lay hands on any one to impart to him the Holy Spirit. So far as the record shows no disciple of the Lord received the baptism in the Holy Spirit after the apostles received it on Pentecost, unless Paul is an exception. It has been my idea that Saul of Tarsus was baptized in the Holy Spirit when he became Paul the apostle, though there is no statement to that effect in Acts. In all records after Pentecost of Acts 2: 1-4 we do not find either in Acts or in the Epistles any statement or hint that Christians were baptized in the Holy Spirit. There would not have been that silence, if all Christians had been so baptized. There is something wrong with a man, if these facts have no weight with him.

The idea that the baptism of a man in the Holy Spirit subdued the soul of man, or directly influenced his moral nature, finds no support in the word of God. An inspired man was infallible in his teaching, but not in his daily conduct. So far as the record shows the apostles received no more benefit from their baptism in the Holy Spirit than did those to whom they revealed and confirmed the word, or than we receive today from their baptism in the Holy Spirit. With all the powers of the Holy Spirit that rested upon Paul, he had to buffet his body and keep it under, lest he be a castaway. The Holy Spirit spoke through the apostles, and they had the revelation thus made to go by, even as we.

When I was in the Nashville Bible School, I heard Brother Harding advance the idea that the righteous would be baptized in the Holy Spirit at the time the wicked would be baptized with fire. That sounded reasonable to me, for it fits in with John's language. Besides, we will need some power to enable us to talk with people from all nations. "Fantastic," do you say? Perhaps so; but try to combat the idea, and see what headway you make. If you want to deny the idea, all right; I shall not defend it. But in that way both classes, the righteous and the wicked, will be baptized, as John prophesied.

Anvil Sparks:

It is said that every dog has its day. The pity of it is that every day has its dog.

Knowledge is power, and so is dynamite. Both are dangerous unless handled wisely.

Unity

If a man urges unity, he should preach and practice those things that promote real Christian unity. He cannot, of course, sacrifice a command of God or faith in the Lord Jesus Christ; but his own opinions and speculations must be sacrificed for the sake of unity.

Not so many years ago we often heard sermons and read articles on unity and union. Why has there been a falling off in such sermons and articles? Perhaps, in view of so much strife and division in the churches of Jesus Christ, preachers hesitate to preach on unity. But do not conditions demand that we study the subjects more carefully and prayerfully and preach on it more earnestly? Why hesitate in the midst of such need? Have we a condition for which we have no remedy? If so, we show a lack of faith in the gospel of Jesus Christ.

Someone propagates a theory or a speculation and thereby divides a church of Jesus Christ. Is there no remedy?

Two brethren fall out about some business transaction, the brethren take sides, and the church is divided. Is there no remedy?

A preacher stays with a church till the church divides over him. Is there no remedy?

If I should cause division in any of these ways, am I better than any other sectarian? What right would I have to claim to be a gospel preacher? What right have I to claim the support of any church, if my presence is a menace to their peace and well-being?

A division in a church hurts every member of that church. Even those who are in the right will be provoked into thinking and doing things injurious to their Christian character. Few people, if any, can maintain a proper balance in the midst of misrepresentations and abuse. And a church fuss injures the influence of that church. The world reads your religion in what you do. They figure that if your religion will not save you from the devil now, it will not in the world to come. And your actions thus hinder the prayer of Jesus. He prayed that his followers might be one, that the world might believe. Here we have a fearful responsibility. God hates one who sows discord among brethren. The sower of discord among the brethren is one of the devil's best servants, no matter what his pretentions may be. Am I helping the world believe, or am I serving the devil by sowing discord among the brethren? Make that question a personal matter.

Because of its bearing on the matter of this article and because of its historic value, I here append an excerpt from Rupp's "History of Denominations in this Country":

"As a striking instance of the necessity and importance of the proposed reformation, we present the following extract from the Boston Anthology, which, with too many of the same kind that might be adduced, furnishes a mournful comment upon the text— we mean upon the sorrowful subject of our woeful divisions and corruptions. The following reply to the Rev. Mr. Cram, missionary from Massachusetts to the Senecas, was made by the principal chiefs and warriors of the Six Nations, in council assembled at

Buffalo Creek, State of New York, in the presence of the agent of the United States for Indian Affairs, in the summer of 1805: "I am come, brethren," said the missionary, "to enlighten your minds, and to instruct you how to worship the Great Spirit agreeably to his will, and to preach to you the gospel of his Son, Jesus Christ. There is but one way to serve God, and if you do not embrace the right way, you cannot be happy hereafter." To which they replied: "Brother, we understand your religion is written in a Book. You say there is but one way to worship and serve the Great Spirit. If there is but one religion, why do you white people differ so much about it? Why not all agree, as you can all read the book. Brother, we do not understand these things. We are told your religion was given to your forefathers. We also have a religion which was given to our forefathers. It teaches us to be *thankful* for all the favors we receive, to love one another, and to be united. We never quarrel about religion. We are told you have been preaching to the white people in this place. Those people are our neighbors; we are acquainted with them. We will wait a little, to see what effect your preaching has upon *them*. If we find it does them good, makes them honest and less disposed to cheat Indians, we will then consider again what you have said." (Copied from the Millennial Harbinger, April issue, 1854.)

Do you love the church as Jesus loved it? What would you give for its glory and honor? How do you regard divisions in the church which Jesus purchased with his blood? Will you trample that blood under your feet in a mad scramble to have your own way? "Oh, no," you say. Good! But what is your attitude toward the man who does such things? Do you follow Paul's demands? "Now I beseech you, brethren, mark them that are causing the divisions and occasions of stumbling, contrary to the doctrine which ye learned: and turn away from them. For they that are such serve not our Lord Christ, but their own belly; and by their smooth and fair speech they beguile the hearts of the innocent." (Rom. 16:-17,18.) Many churches have suffered, and been permanently injured, because they paid not heed to this solemn injunction. Will we wake up? Will we cultivate a conscience on this matter that will rise above personal considerations? Have we forgotten that Rom. 16:17,18 is in the Bible? Does it mean anything to you? But you want a man of smooth and fair speech? Page Absalom!

Anvil Sparks:

Where you are on the road is not as important as which way are you headed.

Some writers sharpen their pencils before they write; others sharpen their wits.

In some places the young folks sit back and chew gum while the old folks sit up front and chew the rag.

If you will listen to some incessant talkers you will decide that practice does not make perfect.

Straight living cannot come out of crooked thinking.

It is easy to abuse other folks for the troubles one's own sins have brought upon him.

If no one ever abused you because he could not use you, I fear you let him use you.

The person who shows spite and hatred will reap his share of it.

Logic—The Argumentum Ad Hominem

Without taking part in the discussion between writers on logic as to whether it is a science or an art, or a combination of both, we shall, for the present, consider it in its application to discourse as the art of correct reasoning. Every one uses logic, even though many have never looked into a textbook in logic. Perhaps no one has so mastered logic as to always reason correctly. But the more a person knows of the laws of correct reasoning, the easier it is for him to avoid fallacies in his own reasoning and to detect them in the reasoning of others. Not enough attention is given to the study of logic. In this matter our educators do greatly err. There is no excuse for compelling a student to wait until he reaches the university to acquaint himself with the laws of reasoning. No preacher should be satisfied to go through life without studying logic. It might be a good idea for religious journals occasionally to give a series of logic lessons, because reasoning is so intimately connected with studying and teaching the Bible. One should be able to reason correctly both in learning and in teaching. And a knowledge of the laws of correct reasoning will save a speaker or writer from being put to shame by a shrewd critic. To make a fallacious argument, even in support of the truth, gives an opponent an opening for attack. The pity is that in showing the fallacy of your argument he is likely to make many think he has disproved your position. Also, a fallacy in your sermon may be detected by some silent listener. If so, your sermon loses force with him.

But some arguments are classed as fallacies that are not always fallacies. Hill's Jevons puts the *argumentum ad hominem* down as a fallacy, but it is not always a fallacy. It may be as valid as any other argument. The *ad hominem* argument is an argument to the man; it is an appeal to his interests, his pride, his sense of justice and right, or his passions, etc. It depends upon the circumstances and the motive as to whether it is a fallacy. If in trying to save a man from disgraceful conduct I appeal to his family pride and to his self-interest, I am using the *argumentum ad hominem,* but there is no fallacy. If your opponent is practicing some things that in principle are exactly like the thing he opposes, you may charge the inconsistency upon him with the hope of getting him to see the point and abandon his position. That is the *argumentum ad hominem,* but where is there any fallacy? If a man is opposing one wrong thing and practicing a similar wrong, you may show him his inconsistency, and thereby induce him to abandon the wrong that he is practicing. Some one opposes the use of printed helps in teaching the Bible. You charge him with inconsistency, in that he uses song-books and the marginal references in the Bible, which in principle are like the helps he opposes, hoping to get him to see the point and abandon his opposition. You are not appealing to his prejudice, nor his passions, nor any other unholy feeling. There is no fallacy in that sort of argument, yet it is the *argumentum ad hominem.* But the *argumentum ad hominem* is fallacious when it is an unfair appeal to personal opinions, or to one's vanity or prejudice or passions. Much of the flattery from the pulpit comes under this head. It is also a fallacy when an appeal is made to a person's hatred of sectarianism to induce him to do or not to do a certain thing.

Noah K. Davis does not class the *argumentum ad hominem* as a fallacy, but puts it under the heading, *"Modified Forms."* Concerning it he says: "The *argumentum ad hominem* is arguing from the premises of an opponent merely to defeat him. We accept his principles on which to base a counter argument, even if believing them false, our argument being directed against him personally, *ad hominem*. It aims to convict him of ignorance, bad faith, inconsistency, or illogical reasoning, and so to put him ex curia (out of court). Usually it attempts no more. . . . Criticism is mostly in the form *ad hominem,* and should be distinguished from proof of the opposite or controversy."

Henry Coppee, page 147, says: "The *argumentum ad hominem* is not a fallacy when the design is to teach pure truth, and when no *unholy passion* or emotion of man is appealed to. In this application it was used by our Saviour himself to the Jews on many occasions with great force and beauty. His touching and yet searching appeal to them for the woman taken in adultery sent them out *one by one* before his power. Each one felt the argument and admitted the conclusion." But some one may say: "To charge her accusers with the same crime did not prove her to be innocent." Certainly not; neither did the Savior intend that it should. But he intended to stop the unholy mouths of her hypocritical accusers. He knew these men cared nothing about the woman's guilt. He knew they were after him, and not her, and were using her in an effort to get him to commit himself in such a way that they could make out a case against him. The woman's guilt was a mere pretext. And the fact stands out clearly that Jesus stopped their mouths by charging that they were as guilty as she.

Again Jesus used the *argumentum ad hominem*. He healed a sorely afflicted woman on the sabbath. The ruler of the synagogue became very indignant. Jesus replied: "Ye hypocrites, doth not each of you on the sabbath loose his ox or his ass from the stall, and lead him away to watering? And ought not this woman, being a daughter of Abraham, whom Satan had bound, lo, these eighteen years, to have been loosed from this bond on the day of the sabbath?" Jesus virtually said: "If I am guilty, you are even more so, for you do a less needful thing. If you are justified in what you do, I am even more so."

Other instances could be given, but these are sufficient to show that the Savior frequently used a form of argument that is now condemned by some Christians. And yet some who condemn it use it in its fallacy form. To create the impression that all *ad hominem* arguments are fallacious, and then seek to create prejudice against an opponent by calling his argument an *ad hominem*, is an *argumentum ad hominem* fallacy.

Reason for Hope—God Is

"But sanctify in your hearts Christ as Lord: being ready always to give answer to every man that asketh you a reason concerning the hope that is in you, yet with meekness and fear." (1 Pet. 3:15.)

At the time these lines were written Christians were surrounded by either Jews or idolaters, or by both. Men who believed in no religion at all were not so plentiful. They did not have the present-day demonstrations to contend with, but as their religion was such a new thing and was so challenging in its nature, they would be assailed by both Jews and Gentiles. The Jew would ask them why they believed in Jesus as the Christ, and the Gentile idolaters would ask them why they believed in the one God, as well as why they believed in the Lord Jesus Christ. As all Christians were expected to give a reason for their hope, it is certain that they were not expected to give such reasons as only profound scholars could give. The unlearned, as well as the learned, were admonished to be ready always to give a reason for their hope. Each one would give an answer according to his ability; and they would try to give such reasons as their critics could understand, for their primary object would be to convert them.

Of course a Christian should always be able to meet the members of the various denominations in their attacks upon religion. He should be able to state clearly the reason for any distinctive feature of his religion, whether it be immersion, believer's baptism, the Lord's Supper, the manner of conversion, his antagonism to denominationalism, or what not. But that is not enough in this age of unbelief. The world is fast drifting back to the point where Christians will be confronted with the problems the early Christians had to meet. We must be able to give answer to the atheist and all sorts of skeptics.

Usually the books and essays on Christian evidences are too scholarly and technical to be of much help to the ordinary person. Such books and essays are useful enough in their field, and yet they are a little discouraging to the ordinary Christian, for they are likely to make him feel that Christian evidences are matters with which he is unable to deal. Have not the common man's needs in this field been too much overlooked? Are there not facts and truths which any thoughtful person can offer as sufficient grounds for his faith? There certainly are; otherwise Peter would not have admonished all Christians to be ready to give a reason for their hope. I present a few, but to me conclusive, arguments, hoping that others may add to them.

Twice did David say: "The fool hath said in his heart, There is no God." A fool may have much knowledge or he may be ignorant, but he lacks wisdom; he lacks what is known as common sense. If a man thinks and acts contrary to what experience and observations teach, he is a fool. Experience and observation both teach us that fire burns. The man who disregards that teaching, and, contending that fire will not burn, thrusts his hand into the fire, is a fool. Both experience and observation teach us that every design has a designer and that every made thing has a maker. Wisdom, or common sense, recognizes this basic principle and acts accordingly. The machine on which I am now writing shows design and workmanship. Only a fool would say that it just happened to be, or was created by resident forces. And yet it is a simple affair compared to many other machines, and they are simple affairs compared to the universe. As small a thing as the tiniest wrist watch does not happen to be, and yet compared to the earth the wrist watch is only a speck, and still the earth is only a speck in the solar system. And yet there is perfect time in the movements of the various planets. If a man is a fool who says no one made the watch, how much greater fool is he who says no one made the universe, or even the solar system? The simplest and yet sublime statement of Moses is the only sensible explanation of the origin of the material universe: "In the beginning God created the heavens and the earth."

And there is life—whence came it? Observation and experiments show that all life is the product of life. Scientists have tried to produce life; they have also tried to prove that life may come into existence by spontaneous generation. In both they have failed. So far as they know, all life comes from previously existing life. Their talk about evolution does not ex-- plain the origin of life. They begin with a small and low form of life, and tell us that all living things come from that; but where did that life come from? Here they are lost, and must take refuge in a supposition that the original spark of life just happened to be. But that supposition is contrary to all that they know of life; it is contrary to all observation and human experiments, and is, therefore, the foolish guess of fools. Not all scientists belong to this class of guessers; many of the greatest of them realize that back of all made things is a Maker, who is also the source of all life. But the atheist is forced to say that life just happened to be.

And to the scientist, as well as to the rest of us, life is an undiscovered mystery. We know that in the grain of corn there is the germ of life. The chemist can analyze that grain and tell us its chemical composition, but he cannot find life in it. If he should say that chemical analysis reveals no life in the grain, and therefore, there was no life in it, he would be classed as a fool, for observation and experiments have taught us that there is a germ of life in the grain. No matter how wise the chemist is, he cannot put that grain of corn back together in such a way as to make it sprout. Does it not show that a wiser Intelligence than the chemist made the grain of corn?

It is astounding how irrational and foolish the atheist is. On every hand he sees things that have been created, but denies there is or was a Creator; he sees design in all the workings of nature, but denies there was or is any Designer; he sees results, but will not recognize any adequate Cause for them. He disdains superstition, but is himself as superstitious as the most ignorant negro. A superstitious person attributes results to things that cannot in any sense be even a contributory cause. And does not the atheist do the same? His "concourse of atoms" can have no more to do with producing life than the black cat that crossed before you had to do in causing trouble to you after you had passed on down the road. Yes, atheists are overly superstitious.

But why argue the existence of God? Disbelief in God is not due to a lack of evidence, but to a desire, for one reason or another, to eliminate God. A belief in God brings with it a feeling of responsibility, and a feeling of responsibility stirs the conscience. If a man wants to live as he pleases, he prefers not to be bothered with the idea of God. Some want to escape a feeling of responsibility; they prefer to believe that all things are driven along by forces over which they have no control. They do not like to retain God in their knowledge; they refuse to believe.

Anvil Sparks:

If you have fallen into a hole, remember the only way out is up.

In a factional fight the more hatred the leader can stir up in his followers for the other side the more loyally they will stand by him.

Reason for Hope

A man may know that a watch did not just happen to be, but he cannot tell by the closest inspection whether it was made by one man or a hundred men. If he ever knows, he will have to gain his information from some source other than the watch itself. Neither can any one determine by studying nature whether the world had one Maker or many makers. "The world through its wisdom knew not God." The cultured Athenians illustrated this truth when they dedicated an altar to *an unknown God*. Only by revelation may we learn of the oneness of God and of his majesty and glory. Hence, Paul said to the Athenians: "What therefore ye worship in ignorance, this I set forth unto you." And only by revelation can we know that "God so loved the world, that he gave his only begotten Son, that whosoever believeth on him should not perish, but have eternal life." Neither is there an inner light to guide us in the way of life. "O Jehovah, I know that the way of man is not in himself; it is not in man that walketh to direct his steps." And we never could by our unaided powers have found out the glories prepared for the redeemed; only by revelation can we know them. "Things which eye saw not, and ear heard not, and which entered not into the heart of man, whatsoever things God prepared for them that love him. But unto us God revealed them through the Spirit: . . . that we might know the things that were freely given to us of God. Which things also we speak." (1 Cor. 2:9-13.) Many have so perverted this passage as to lose its meaning entirely. It teaches us plainly that God has revealed to us the things that man could not find out by his own unaided powers. To one who believes that God is, it is perfectly reasonable that God should reveal to man the things that man needs to know.

Christians everywhere and in all ages have believed with good and sufficient reason that Christianity is of divine origin, and that the Bible is also of divine origin. And these Christians who have been reformed by its transforming power and who have been sustained and comforted by it in the trials of life and the horrors of death, many suffering death by torture, are in better position to judge of its truth than is one who has never experienced its power. By experience he has demonstrated the power of Christianity; he has given it a practical test. By others the Christian was led to believe there was transforming power in Christianity; he tried it out by an experiment, so to speak, in the laboratory of life, and found it to be as represented. Will not even a scientist accept a formula, or theory, that has been often tested by experience? The good wife may find a new recipe and believe that it will work out as represented, but when she gives it a practical test she knows. Her test demonstrates its value. But we cannot find out in this life the full results of Christianity, because its promises reach into the future; but experience will demonstrate that it transforms, sustains, and comforts us even in this life. And any man knows that if Christianity were not true it would be the biggest lie ever palmed off on people; but any man also knows that the biggest lie cannot transform, purify, and ennoble human character as Christianity does. If the infidel insists that Christianity is worth nothing to a person in this life, what does he know about it? He has never tried it. He, therefore, cannot speak from experience, and he will not accept the testimony of those who are competent to testify. Having no experience in the matter, he cannot be a competent witness; and rejecting all reliable testimony, he cannot be depended on to give any judgment in the matter. On his own showing he is ruled out of court.

But am I right in saying that the one who is devoted to Christianity can know it is of divine origin? Hear what Jesus says: "If any man willeth to do his will, he shall know of the teaching, whether it is of God, or whether I speak from myself." (John 7:17.) The leaders of the Jews thought Jesus was only a man; and knowing that he had never attended their schools, they wondered how he acquired such learning as his speeches indicated he had. Jesus replied: "My teaching is not mine, but his that sent me." Of course they should have known as much because of the miracles he did. But now he tells them that if any one wills—is determined—to do God's will, he shall know that his teaching is from God and not from men. "Shall know"—what? That his teaching is from God. That is a fair test. You have been led to believe that a certain food is delicious and wholesome; you then eat it and find it has been correctly represented. By experience you know it is good food. Certainly the man who eats a certain food knows more of its taste and wholesomeness than does the person who has such an unreasonable prejudice against it that he will neither believe what others say nor taste it himself. That is the infidel's attitude toward Christianity. But those who love the Lord and are faithfully following him know that his teaching is not of men. With Job and Paul the devout Christian can say: "I know . . ."

If I were to tell a chemist that his theory concerning a certain point in chemistry was wrong and that no informed person thought as he did, he would likely tell me that I did not know what I was talking about, and that the theory had been demonstrated by experiments times without number. But my knowledge of chemistry is very limited, and I would not think of denying what had been demonstrated by all the best chemists. Why, then, are some scientists in all branches so ready to dispute the claims of Christianity? Usually the noisy scientist knows less about Christianity than the ordinary Christian knows about science; it is, therefore, amazing how dogmatic he frequently becomes in discussing Christianity. If he should be so dogmatic in a branch of science which he had not studied, other scientists would consider him a fool. Suppose a chemist should say to a biologist, "There is no life in a grain of corn, for I have made complete analysis of many grains, and have found in them no such thing as life," what would the biologist say to him? He would likely think more than he would say.

The truth is that scientists, though they have made many wonderful and useful discoveries, are unable to explain some of the most common things in nature. Why, then, are some of them so dogmatic about things the Bible teaches? They should confine their speech to subjects they can discuss without talking foolishness. But a foolish talker never knows how foolish he sounds. The true student of any branch of science does not study and experiment in order to prove some theory, but to find out the truth. Let him study the Bible in the same spirit of devotion to truth, and he will not go astray. But he must not come to the Bible in a know-it-all spirit; God does not reveal himself to that sort. "Let no man deceive himself. If any man thinketh that he is wise among you in this world, let him become a fool, that he may become wise." (1 Cor. 3:18.) He must come to the Bible as one who does not know, but craves to learn the truth. "Blessed are they that hunger and thirst after righteousness: for they shall be filled." (Matt. 5:6.)

Anvil Sparks:

Narrow-minded? Well, a person's mind should be narrow enough to shut out everything but truth, and broad enough to accept all truth.

The pessimist has no motor; the optimist has no brakes.

Superstition is ignorant reverence; rationalism is irreverent reasoning.

Moreover, with some the principal involved has a greater urge than the principle.

Walking By Faith

"For we walk by faith, not by sight." (2 Cor. 5:7.) Not many verses in the Bible have been more generally misused than this verse. It is too often assumed that faith ends where sight begins, and this verse is appealed to as proof. "When faith is lost in sight" has been a favorite clause, and yet before our eyes is the statement of Jesus to Thomas: "Because thou hast seen me, thou hast believed; blessed are they that have not seen, and yet believed." (John 20:29.) In this case faith began with sight—or, rather, faith was revived by sight. It certainly was not lost in sight. There is no reason for singling out Thomas and calling him "doubting Thomas," for the faith of the others had suffered an eclipse till they saw Jesus after he arose. If their faith was not produced by sight, it certainly was not lost in sight; it was revived by sight. The same Paul who wrote 2 Cor. 5:7 also wrote in the first letter (9:1): "Have I not seen Jesus our Lord?" He also said: "I know him whom I have believed." Paul saw the Lord, and yet who had greater faith than he? The truth is that faith in a person may exist where there is the most intimate association and the clearest knowledge, for faith in a person means much more than a belief that he exists. It is to have confidence in his power, wisdom, honesty, and goodness—to trust him unreservedly. And the more you see of some people the more faith you have in them. No, faith is not, and will not, be lost in sight. I cannot think my faith in the Lord will ever end—not even when I stand in glory and am permitted to see the face of my Redeemer. Perhaps we shall not be able to know to what heights and depths faith may attain till we see our Lord face to face.

But someone may say: "Does not the Bible say that faith will end when we are saved in heaven?" I recall no such statement, though 1 Pet. 1:9 is sometimes used as if it said that very thing. It says: "Receiving the end of your faith, even the salvation of your souls." It does not say that we shall receive salvation at the end of our faith, nor that faith ends when we receive salvation. "Receiving" is present participle. They were rejoicing in that they were receiving the end of their faith, the salvation of their souls. The word *end* does not mean *the termination, the limit at which a thing ceases*. It frequently means *the purpose, the result, or the issue*. "Jehovah hath made everything for its own end." (Prov. 16:4.) He created everything to serve his own purpose, not that it might cease to be. "But the end of the charge is love out of a pure heart and a good conscience and faith unfeigned." (1 Tim. 1:5). "Love out of a pure heart and a good conscience and faith unfeigned" is the purpose or aim of the charge, not its termination, not the limit of its existence. "Ye have heard of the patience of Job, and have seen the end of the Lord, how that the Lord is full of pity, and merciful." (James 5:11.) Certainly no one has seen the end of the Lord's existence, the time when he ceased to be! But they had seen the purpose and the results of his dealings with Job. "The end of the Lord" — "the end of your faith." Salvation is the purpose and the result of faith. Without faith there would be no such result. Without faith there would be no such result as the salvation of our souls. The passage shows that there is no such thing as unconditional salvation.

But what does all this have to do with 2 Cor. 5:7? It shows that faith does not end with possession, or with sight. Notice the marginal reading in the American Standard Version. For some purpose the American Standard translators followed the King James Version, though they tell us in the margin that the Greek word means "appearance." The Greek word which is here translated *sight* is defined by Thayer as follows. *"The external appearance, form, figure, shape."* He then gives this note on 2 Cor. 5:7: "Commonly explained, by sight—that is, *by beholding;* but no example has been adduced from any Greek writing in which *eidos* is used actively, like Latin *species,* of vision." Paul does not, therefore, say that we walk by faith, not by seeing. "We walk by faith, not by appearance." We walk by faith, not by the way things seem to us, or by the way things appear to be. People are controlled too much by appearance. "Man looketh on the outward appearance." The devil baits his trap with *appearance,* and he catches every man that walks by appearance rather than by faith. The devil could never sidetrack so many Christians into various schemes if it did not appear that good could be accomplished by such schemes. Often you hear religious people defend a certain course by saying, "It appears to me," or "It seems to me." The end of the way that seems right unto man is death. Jesus said: "Judge not according to appearance." (John 7:24.) Certain brethren at Corinth gloried in appearance. (2 Cor. 5:12.) Anyone should know that things are not always what they seem. Any well-informed Christian knows that one ceases to walk by faith when he begins to be guided by appearance.

The passage gains in force and beauty when it is properly understood. We walk by faith, not by the appearance of things. Even men may appear to be righteous, but inwardly be "full of hypocrisy and iniquity." (Matt. 23:28.) When life, or happiness, or health is at stake, we cannot afford to depend on appearance. I stood by a bold spring of cold water, clear as crystal, gushing forth at the foot of a mountain. It appeared to be just the kind of water that would be food for a thirsty man, but I did not drink. Laboratory tests had proved it to be laden with typhoid germs. Faith in that report, not the appearance of the water, guided my actions. Human organizations and humanly-devised forms of worship may appear to be attractive and effective, but they contain the deadly germs of human wisdom. We pass them by; for we walk by faith, not by appearance. But if faith leads you in a certain way, follow it, even if that way appears to be ruinous. "We walk by faith, not by appearance."

Anvil Sparks:

If an exception proves the rule, then two exceptions would be double proof.

Some preachers act and talk as if the devil had sent them out as a burlesque on preaching.

How Faith Comes

God does not give us faith by any direct operation of the Spirit. If he did, he would not command us to believe, nor would he condemn us for not believing; neither would he give us evidence to be believed. If man did not have the ability to believe, God would not condemn him for not believing. Even the devil knows that man can believe, and he also knows what produces faith. "And those by the way side are they that have heard; then cometh the devil, and taketh away the word from their heart, that they may not believe and be saved." It takes clear evidence to produce assured faith. Even opinion must have some basis. What some people call faith is not even an opinion, but a wild guess generated in their own imaginations. A matured person said: "I do not read the Bible much; I know what I believe before I ever read it." That person did not really believe anything. It takes evidence, solid evidence, to produce faith. A person can make a wild guess without evidence; he can form an opinion on meager evidence.

FAITH: Genuine faith is more than an intellectual assent to a truth. "And without faith it is impossible to be well-pleasing unto him; for he that cometh to God must believe that he is, and that he is a rewarder of them that seek after him." (Heb. 11:6.) It is not enough simply to believe that God is; the demons believe that. One must also believe that he is a rewarder of them that seek after him. God has promised to render eternal life to them that seek for glory and honor and incorruption. (Rom. 2:6,7.) We

(226)

must believe that he will fulfill every promise; we must believe that he is not slack concerning his promises—that is, we must have confidence in him, we must trust him. In carrying out his mission as preacher, apostle, and teacher, Paul suffered much; and at the time he wrote his second letter to Timothy he was about to suffer death, but he gave Timothy this assurance: "Yet I am not ashamed; for I know him whom I have believed, and I am persuaded that he is able to guard that which I have committed unto him against that day." (2 Tim. 1:12.) In this expression, and in many other expressions, Paul states his full confidence in God.

Without confidence faith is defective; it is little. The incident related in Matt. 8:23-27 and Mark 4:35-41 shows this to be true. While Jesus and his disciples were crossing the Sea of Galilee, Jesus fell asleep; "and there ariseth a great storm of wind, and the waves beat into the boat, insomuch that the boat was now filling." In their distress the disciples "awake him, and say unto him, Teacher, carest thou not that we perish?" "Save, Lord; we perish." Jesus said to them: "Why are ye fearful, O ye of little faith?" In what respect was their faith little? Their plea to him shows that they believed that he had power to save them from the fury of the storm. In this respect their faith was not defective. Their language also plainly shows that they had begun to doubt that he had sufficient interest in them to save them from perishing in that storm. "Carest thou not that we perish?" To doubt his love for them and his care for them was a serious defect in their faith—they were lacking in confidence. Every Christian should examine himself to see if there is a similar defect in his faith. Here is both a preventive and a cure for this sort of defective faith: "Humble yourselves therefore under the mighty hand of God, that he may exalt you in due time; casting all your anxiety upon him, because he careth for you." (1 Pet. 5:6,7.)

Abraham is set before us as a man of great faith and the father of the faithful; yet on one occasion he doubted the word of Jehovah. "And he said unto him, I am Jehovah that brought thee out of Ur of the Chaldees, to give thee this land to inherit it. And he said, O Lord Jehovah, whereby shall I know that I shall inherit it?" (Gen. 15:7,8.) For the moment he doubted. He wanted some assurance in addition to the plain promise of Jehovah. Jehovah showed his displeasure by bringing him through a harrowing experience in connection with offerings which Jehovah required him to make, and by revealing to him the future bondage of his offspring.

Another good man fell into a like error. Zacharias and his wife Elizabeth "were both righteous before God, walking in all the commandments and ordinances of the Lord blameless." Zacharias had prayed for a son, but Elizabeth was barren. They were too old now, according to nature, to become parents. Zacharias was a priest. While he was burning incense in the temple of the Lord, and the multitude of the people were praying without, "there appeared unto him an angel of the Lord standing on the right side of the altar of incense. And Zacharias was troubled when he saw him, and fear fell upon him. But the angel said unto him, Fear not Zacharias: because thy supplication is heard, and thy wife Elizabeth shall

bear thee a son, and thou shalt call his name John.
. . . And Zacharias said unto the angel, Whereby shall
I know this? for I am an old man, and my wife well
stricken in years." And because Zacharias doubted
the word of the angel and called for additional proof,
he became dumb, not being able to speak till the word
of the angel was fulfilled. This was proof that the
angel's word would be fulfilled, and also punishment
for his doubt. We should not be much surprised at
the doubts of Zacharias. The course of nature was
well against such an event as the angel promised.
Even today what we call the laws of nature have more
weight with some Christians than do the promises
of God.

Sometimes a man's confidence is in himself and
his own way rather than in Jehovah and his way.
That was the trouble with Cain. He believed in the
existence of Jehovah, but he undertook to worship him
in his own way. He thought to make improvement
in his worship, or else he thought his way was as
good as God's way. His confidence was in self, not
in God. Abel believed that God's way was the only
way—he had confidence in God, not in self. God accepted his offering, but rejected Cain's. Abel did
what God said because he had faith in God. Any man
now will seek to follow God's way if he has faith in
God. Faith never seeks to improve on God's way, nor
offers any substitute for what God requires. There
are too many Cains in the religious world.

Sometimes men want to put themselves forward
and leave God in the background. Especially is this
true when they have a crowd before whom they want
to make a show. They arrogate to themselves powers

that belong only to God. Moses and Aaron once fell into that grievous sin. When the people of Israel complained because of a lack of water, "Jehovah spake unto Moses, saying, Take the rod, and assemble the congregation, thou and Aaron thy brother, and speak ye unto the rock before their eyes, that it give forth its water. . . . And Moses and Aaron gathered the assembly together before the rock, and he said unto them, Hear now, ye rebels; shall we bring you forth water out of this rock? And Moses lifted up his hand, and smote the rock with his rod twice: and water came forth abundantly, and the congregation drank, and their cattle. And Jehovah said unto Moses and Aaron, Because ye believed not in me, to sanctify me in the eyes of the children of Israel, therefore ye shall not bring this assembly into the land which I have given them." (Nu. 20:7-13.) Moses and Aaron both believed in the existence of God, but they turned aside from the thing God commanded them, arrogating to themselves all the honor. They did not follow God's way—they did not believe in him. And so it is with any man who does not honor God in what he does.

You have faith in a certain physician, and call him to administer to your ailments. Will you follow his directions? That is the real test of your faith in him. If you vary the treatment according to your own notions, you thereby dismiss him as your doctor and become your own doctor. You come to realize that your sin-sick soul needs to be cleansed and healed. You call on the Great Physician. He has the necessary remedies already prepared, and the course of treatment mapped out. You have nothing to do with preparing the remedies, nor with arranging the course of treatment. Your part is to follow directions. If your faith—your confidence—is what it should be, you will diligently do as directed. If you begin to invent remedies of your own, or change the course of treatment the Great Physician prescribes, you dismiss him as your physician and become your own physician, your own savior. If you follow your own notions, you trust yourself not him.

No wrong teaching is so popular in religious circles as the doctrine of justification by faith only, unless it be the doctrine of direct operation of the Holy Spirit in conversion. It is strange how two false doctrines became so popular.

The advocates of the doctrine of justification by faith only take a too limited view of faith; they do not give proper weight to the fact that there are degrees of faith, and they fail to tell us what degree of faith justifies. Is it little faith? weak faith? dead faith? or perfect faith? On this point James is better authority than denominational preachers. Read his second chapter from verse 14 to the close of the chapter.

Verse 14: "What doth it profit, my brethren, if a man say he hath faith, but have not works? can that faith save him?" This is really an affirmation that faith without works cannot save a man. You will notice that James does not say, "if a brother have not works;" but, "if a man"—any man, saint or sinner. To show the worthlessness of faith without works, James gives a pointed illustration.

Verses 15, 16: "If a brother or sister be naked and in lack of daily food, and one of you say unto them,

Go in peace, be ye warmed and filled; and yet ye give
them not the things needful to the body; what doth
it profit?" James was not here teaching a lesson on
feeding the hungry and clothing the naked, but was
showing by this illustration that faith without works
was as worthless as it would be to say to a naked and
hungry person, "Be ye warmed and filled," and then
do nothing about it. There is no profit in such talk;
it is barren of results. Such talk is dead talk; it is
inactive. "Even so faith, if it have not works, is dead
in itself." And the only way a man can show his
faith is by his works. It is well to believe that God
is, but the demons do that. Their faith is faith only;
they do not do any willing service. "But wilt thou
know, O vain man, that faith apart from works is
barren?" "Barren"—it produces nothing, is devoid
of blessings or benefits; and the man who thinks otherwise is vain, so says James. It is a vain man, therefore, who claims that a man is justified by faith only
—faith without works. There is a vast difference
between being justified by works of the law and being
justified by works of faith, and the man who fails to
recognize this difference will never understand justification by faith.

Verses 21-23: "Was not Abraham our father justified by works, in that he offered up Isaac his son
upon the altar? Thou seest that faith wrought with
his works, and by works was faith made perfect; and
the scripture was fulfilled which saith, And Abraham
believed God, and it was reckoned unto him for
righteousness; and he was called the friend of God."
Abraham was not justified by works of law, but by
deeds of faith. The command to offer up Isaac tested

his faith to an extreme degree, and in obeying that command his faith reached its peak, and his justification became full and complete. Previous to this he had been declared justified. It is here declared that that statement was fulfilled when he offered up Isaac. This statement shows that his previous justification had been tentative, or provisional, conditioned on this severe test of his faith. When his faith was shown to be equal to any test, his justification became absolute, and he was thenceforth called the friend of God. It is true that Abraham was not an alien sinner when he offered up Isaac. The faith-alone advocate grabs this fact, as a drowning man grabs a straw, and argues that, as an alien sinner, Abraham was justified by faith only, but as a servant of God he had to work to be justified. But, strange to say, these same faith-only advocates argue that an alien sinner must be justified by faith only in order that justification may be by grace; that grace rules out all works. But that involves an absurdity; for if works rule out grace, and a Christian must work to be justified by works, then there is no grace for the Christian! Yes, we are told that works and grace cannot go together, but that a Christian must work to be justified! A bare statement of that doctrine condemns it.

It is also argued that Abraham was justified in the sight of God by faith only, but was justified in the sight of men by works. But James is here speaking of Abraham's offering up Isaac; and not a man, not even his servants, saw that deed. If any man had chanced to see him in that act, he would have condemned, rather than justified, Abraham. The argument is a dodge. No one thinks God commanded

Abraham to offer up Isaac to satisfy the demands of men, or to gain favor with men.

The Scripture quoted by James is Gen. 15:6. It is assumed that Abraham was then justified as an alien sinner. Why this assumption is generally allowed to go unchallenged is a mystery. Look at the record. Before that statement was made to Abraham he was a man of faith and obedience. God had called him out of Ur of the Chaldees and delivered to him the promises recorded in Gen. 12:1-3. Surely no one will argue that God made such promises to an alien sinner. He was then a man of faith. "By faith Abraham, when he was called, obeyed to go out unto a place which he was to receive for an inheritance; and he went out, not knowing whither he went." (Heb. 11:8.) God appeared to Abraham at Schechem, and Abraham built an altar. (Gen. 12:7.) At Bethel also he built an altar, and there called upon the name of Jehovah. Again he worshipped Jehovah at Bethel. (Gen. 13:3,4.) Again Jehovah appeared to him and renewed the land promise and the promise concerning a numerous seed; again Abraham built an altar. (Verses 14-18.) And Melchizedek, "priest of God Most High," said to Abraham, "Blessed be Abram of God Most High." And finally: "After these things the word of Jehovah came unto Abram in a vision, saying, Fear not, Abram: I am thy shield, and thy exceeding great reward." (Gen. 15:1.) That would be strange language for Jehovah to utter to an alien sinner. Gen. 15:6 does not, therefore, refer to the justification of an alien sinner. But from the principle involved in the facts presented James draws a conclusion that applies to "a man"—any man, saint or sinner. Faith without works is as worthless to a sinner as to a saint. "Ye see that by works a man is justified, and not only by faith." That he does include the sinner as well as the saint is shown by the next example he adduces: "And in like manner was not also Rahab the harlot justified by works, in that she received the messengers, and sent them out another way?" (James 2:25.) To see what Rahab did, read Josh. 2. "In like manner"—As Abraham was justified by a faith that worked, so also—"in like manner"—was the harlot justified by works. The writer of Hebrews says this: "By faith Rahab the harlot perished not with them that were disobedient, having received the spies with peace." (Heb 11:31.) So it is seen that this harlot was justified by faith and by works—justified by a faith that worked. It does not seem to be by mere chance that James uses two examples—one a servant of God, the other an alien—to show that both saint and sinner are justified by a faith that works. "Even so faith, if it have not works, is dead in itself." "For as the body apart from the spirit is dead even so faith apart from works is dead." Evidently some early Christians, having learned that justification was not by works of the law, but by faith in Christ, had concluded that faith without works would justify. James corrects that idea. It is a pity that so many people of today will not see the truth James sets forth.

The religion of our Lord is intended to make people better here and now. It is not a sort of grabhooks arrangement by means of which the Lord yanks sinners out of the kingdom of the devil and lands them into the certainty of eternal life, and that without any effort on their part. No Bible teaching leads to such an idea. One must seek that he may find, and one must strive to enter. That develops character. But the doctrine of unconditional salvation, or the doctrine of faith only, does not make folks better. A conditional promise invites people to come up higher so as to obtain the promise. To lead a man to believe that he is saved eternally as soon as he believes is to administer to him a spiritual opiate. There is nothing about such a doctrine to cause one to strive to live on a higher plane.

Recently a man said over the radio that all a man had to do was to trust in Christ, and he was then saved for all eternity. Fortunately for the world, some people are better than the doctrine they preach; they are really not fully committed to their doctrine.

We have seen that the faith that saves is a faith made perfect by works. A faith that does nothing receives nothing; it has always been so. Even the cases of healing during the personal ministry of Christ are no exception. For the most part, those that were healed showed their faith by voluntary actions; but Jesus specified certain conditions, those conditions had to be fulfilled. An example or two will suffice to prove this point. On one occasion ten lepers said to Jesus as he was passing by: "Master, have mercy on us." Jesus said to them: "Go and show yourselves unto the priests. And it came to pass, as they went, they were cleansed." They obeyed promptly and were healed as they obeyed. Can anyone believe they would have been healed had they refused to do what Jesus commanded them to do, even though they had kept up their cry for mercy?

And there was a condition stipulated when Jesus gave sight to the man who was born blind. (John 9.) Jesus anointed his eyes with clay, "and said unto him, Go, wash in the pool of Siloam. . . . He went away therefore, and washed, and came seeing." If he had not rendered prompt obedience, he would never have seen. In both these cases faith gave prompt obedience, and the blessings came promptly. Contrast these cases with the rulers who believed, but did nothing about it. "Nevertheless even of the rulers many believed on him; but because of the Pharisees they did not confess it, lest they should be put out of the synagogue: for they loved the glory that is of men more than the glory that is of God." (John 12:42,43.) They would rather please men than God. Their faith was dead—barren of any profit to themselves. But if men are saved by faith only, these men were saved; but who believes they were saved? "But they did not put their trust in Christ." Certainly not, for trust and obedience go together. Witness the prompt obedience of all who accepted the preaching of the apostles and other inspired men.

On Pentecost those who accepted Peter's preaching were commanded to repent and be baptized in the name of Jesus, the Christ, unto remission of their sins, and about three thousand rendered prompt obedience. And so in other cases. In the reports of the cases of conversion under the preaching of these inspired men there is not a hint that sinners were saved the moment they believed. "And the hand of the Lord was with them: and a great number that believed turned unto the Lord." (Acts 11:21.) If they were saved the moment they believed, they were saved before they turned unto the Lord; but healing, or salvation, follows the turning to the Lord. (Isa. 55:7; Matt. 13:15; Acts 28:27.)

No arguments of the faith-only advocates can do away with the plain statements of our Lord and his inspired preachers on the necessity of obedience. The fact is that in their arguments they array Scripture against Scripture. Our Lord makes this plain statement: "Not every one that saith unto me, Lord, Lord, shall enter into the kingdom of heaven; but he that doeth the will of my Father who is in heaven." (Matt. 7:21.) To say, "Lord, Lord," shows some degree of faith; but it is dead faith, for there is no obedience to God's will. Such faith profits nothing— puts no one into the kingdom of heaven. The writer of Hebrews says of Jesus, the Christ: "Though he was a Son, yet learned obedience by the things which he suffered; and having been made perfect, he became unto all them that obey him the author of eternal salvation." (Heb. 5:8,9.) No one can misunderstand that plain statement, nor twist its meaning into something that it does not say. Some are so set on evading its force that they seek to array some other passage against it, and that is not fair dealing with the word of God. If a man does not obey the Lord Jesus Christ, he is not the author of salvation to such a man. "And to you that are afflicted rest with us, at the revelation of the Lord Jesus from heaven with the angels of his power in flaming fire, rendering vengeance to them that know not God, and to them that obey not the gospel of our Lord Jesus: who shall suffer punishment, even eternal destruction from the face of the Lord and from the glory of his might, when he shall come to be glorified in his saints, and to be marvelled at in all them that believe (because our testimony unto you was believed) in that day." (2 Thes. 1:7-10.) Two things will occur when Jesus comes again: He will take vengeance on them that obey not the gospel—such shall suffer eternal punishment; also in that day Jesus will be glorified in his saints. Now, a person either obeys the gospel or he does not obey it. It is easy to see what is to be the fate of those who do not obey it. But this obedience does not make void faith—in fact, such obedience is what Paul calls the obedience of faith. (Rom. 1: 5.) That faith only does not fill the measure of the required obedience is clear from the following: "But thanks be to God, that, whereas ye were servants of sin, ye became servants of righteousness." (Rom. 6:17,18.) In believing one does not obey from the heart, for believing takes place in the heart; but the obedience to which this faith leads is obedience from the heart. When faith is as strong as it should be, it produces obedience. When one obeys from the heart, not in the heart, he is made free from sin and becomes a servant of righteousness.

It has been often argued that justification must be by faith only that it may be by grace. They array grace against obedience. With them there is no obedience in salvation by grace, and no grace in salvation by obedience to the gospel. The greatest manifestation of God's grace was giving of his Son to die for man; the next greatest manifestation of his grace is seen in the commands he gave in the gospel. Did you ever think what a favor to the traveler the highway signs are? Well, the commands, cautions, and prohibitions given in the gospel of Christ are God's highway signs. What a favor they are to the one who seeks to travel the highway to heaven! By carefully observing these highway signs you do not have to guess as to whether you are on the right road. You cannot, therefore, separate the grace of God from his commands—his highway signs.

When denominational preachers and writers discuss their doctrine of justification by faith only, they try hard to make it appear that justification must be by faith only in order that it be by grace. Making no distinction between the works of the law and the obedience of faith, they seem to think they build an impregnable argument on Paul's language in Rom. 3:27; 4:1-5, 16. As their arguments on these Scriptures are so misleading, and therefore hurtful, the cause of truth demands, and the salvation of souls requires, that their arguments should be met and the real teaching of the passage be shown.

Rom. 3:27: "Where then is the glorying? It is excluded. By what manner of law? of works? Nay: but by a law of faith." By the works of the law of Moses no flesh was justified, for the simple reason that no one kept the law perfectly. If a man were to live a perfect life, he would have grounds for boasting that he had always done the right thing, that no taint of sin ever soiled his spotless character, and that he stood justified on his own record; and all this without favor, or grace, of anyone. But none so live, for all sin. In recognizing one's self as a condemned sinner, there is cause for humility, but no grounds for boasting; and there is additional ground for humility in submitting one's self into the hands of another to be buried in baptism to obtain pardon. This is the law of faith that excludes boasting.

Rom. 4:4: "Now to him that worketh, the reward is not reckoned as of grace, but of debt." The reward is reckoned to the person that works, for that is his due; he has worked so as to merit reward. Paul is not here condemning salvation by works; he is merely stating that the works he has in mind bring salvation as a matter of debt, and not of grace. And we can rest assured that if a man should perform the works that make salvation as of debt, God would pay that debt—the man's salvation would be secure. In view of the plain language of the verse, it is strange that denominational preachers use the verse in an effort to condemn baptism as a condition of salvation. If baptism is the works Paul here mentions, then the baptized person has salvation as of debt; his salvation is certain, for God will pay a debt. But their argument, instead of condemning baptism, exalts it out of all reason. The truth is that Paul was speaking of works of law, such works as would make salvation as a debt. To do this, a man's obedience to the law would have to be perfect; he would have to be entirely without any taint of sin. But if a man sins once, salvation can never come to him as a debt; neither can such a man ever be justified by works of the law. He needs forgiveness, and the law does not forgive; it condemns. No perfection of works will blot out, or forgive, a sin already committed, nor make void grace in the forgiveness of that one sin. This verse has been terribly perverted and made to do service in an effort to prove that a sinner could do nothing in order to be saved. Paul had no such point in view. He was showing that works of law could not save, for all under law had sinned; but that salvation comes through faith in Christ, or, as he puts it in chapter 1, verse 5, through the obedience of faith; or, as stated in chapter 6, verses 17, 18, freedom from sin arises from obedience from the heart to the form of doctrine to which they had been delivered. Paul was not arraying faith against obedience to the gospel but faith in Christ against the works of the law.

"But to him that worketh not, but believeth on him that justifieth the ungodly, his faith is reckoned for righteousness." (Verse 5.) The reader will notice that Paul says nothing about "the one who depends on works," nor about "the one who depends not on works." He speaks of the one who *works* and the one who does *not work*. *Works* must have the same significance in both verses (verses 4,5), for Paul had not changed the subject. Only perfect works as measured by law—works without any guilt of sin—can bring salvation as of debt. The one who "worketh" is, therefore, the one whose works are so perfect as to make his salvation as of debt. Hence, to the sinner, the one whose works are not perfect, but who believes in Jesus Christ, God reckons, or counts, his faith for (eis, in order to) righteousness—that is, in order that, on the basis of his faith, he may forgive his sins and thus constitute him a righteous person. The one who thinks Paul was speaking of the obedience of faith instead of works of law will never understand the doctrine of salvation by grace through faith. The man who switches Paul's line of reasoning so as to make it apply to acts of obedience required in the gospel perverts his language. Certainly Paul did not mean to say that God makes the person righteous who will not obey him, the person who simply does nothing. If so, he puts a premium on the very thing from which the gospel is intended to save us, and contradicts other things said by him.

Eph. 2:8,9 is another text wrongly used. "For by grace have ye been saved through faith; and that not of yourselves, it is the gift of God; not of works, that no man should glory." "That" refers to the whole matter of being saved by grace through faith. The phrase "not of works" does not refer to the obedience to the gospel; there is nothing in obedience to the gospel to cause anyone to boast. To believe in him who died for us, to repent in humility of sins committed, and to surrender one's self into the hands of another to be buried in baptism—how can anyone see any grounds for boasting in that sort of humiliation? Here, as in Rom. 4:4,5 Paul was writing about works that gave grounds for boasting. To believe in Christ is to accept him at his word and do what he says. In these references Paul was showing that works without faith would not save, and James showed that faith without works will not save. God has joined the two together, and woe to him that separates them.

The faith-only advocates realize that they must prove, if possible, that baptism is not a condition of salvation. In addition to the passages already considered, they hopefully appeal to Tit. 3:4,5: "But when the kindness of God our Savior, and his love toward man, appeared, not by works done in righteousness, which we did ourselves, but according to his mercy he saved us, through the washing of regeneration and renewing of the Holy Spirit." If we were saved by the perfection of our works, there would be no grace or mercy about it; but if Paul is here speaking of the conditions, or commands, of the gospel, his language would come nearer militating against believing and repenting than against baptism. The works of which he speaks are things "which we did ourselves." In believing and repenting, the sinner is active; these are things which he does himself; but in baptism he is passive—it is something done to him. He is commanded to believe and to repent. He is not commanded to baptize, but to "be baptized." But who does it? In John 4:1-3 we learn that Jesus made and baptized disciples through the agency of his disciples. A man is said to do what he does through his agents. Everyone who is now baptized by the authority of the Lord Jesus Christ is as truly baptized by the Lord as were those mentioned in John 4:1-3. Hence, baptism, even should it be called a work of righteousness, is not a work of righteousness "which we did ourselves," but which the Lord did to us through his agents. By baptism, "the washing of regeneration," the Lord saves us, according to his mercy and grace.

The advocates of the doctrine of the justification of sinners by faith only think they believe their doctrine; but in reality they do not believe it, for they readily admit, and even contend, that other things are necessary. They believe that sinners must love God, must be moved by godly sorrow to repent, and must pray. Certainly love, godly sorrow, fear, repentance, and prayer are not faith only. If so, baptism might be included and still have faith only! All recognize love, godly sorrow, fear, repentance, and prayer as conditions of salvation, though they are not all mentioned in any one verse. We must, therefore, recognize that there may be more conditions of salvation than are mentioned in any one verse, and that there can never be fewer conditions than the sum of all conditions mentioned in various passages. One item of command, mentioned alone, may stand for all the other conditions—this by a common figure of speech. It is easy to see from examples which we shall later examine that faith, mentioned alone, stands for all the requirements to which it leads. The word *repentance* sometimes stands for the whole process of becoming a Christian. In Paul's statement that God commands all men everywhere to repent (Acts 17:30,31), the term *repent* includes the whole process of becoming a Christian, for nothing else is there mentioned as necessary. Certainly he did not mean that now God commands only the simple act of repentance. Now read and ponder Acts 11:18, "And when they heard these things, they held their peace, and glorified God, saying, Then to the Gentiles also hath God granted repentance unto life." This passage has been so persistently and wrongly used to prove that repentance is only unto life—that is, in the direction of life—that the significance of the word *repentance* in this verse is lost. It is true that repentance, as distinct from other conditions of salvation, does merely lead in the direction of life; but these Jerusalem brethren did not mean that Cornelius and his company were as far as repentance on their way to life! For they had obeyed the gospel some days before this language was used—they meant that God had granted to the Gentiles the right to obey the gospel. Repentance here covers the whole process of becoming Christians. When salvation is attributed to faith, or repentance, or confession, or calling on the name of the Lord, or baptism, a common figure of speech is used, a figure in which a part is put for the whole. In such a figure a part really includes the whole. The word *only* cannot be applied to either condition mentioned without doing violence to the word of God. It would be doing no more violence to the word of God to say that baptism only doth now save us than to say that we are justified by faith only.

Rom. 5:1: "'Being therefore justified by faith, we have peace with God through our Lord Jesus Christ." In their use of this verse the faith-only advocates fail to realize that a faith that God approves, a faith that justifies, is a living faith, a faith made perfect by works. It is not difficult to determine from Bible usage what the phrase *by faith* means. An examination of a few of the many examples of its use will show what it includes, as well as what it excludes. Read Heb. 11.

"By faith Abel offered unto God a more excellent sacrifice than Cain, through which he had witness borne to him that he was righteous, God bearing witness in respect of his gifts: and through it he being dead yet speaketh." Certainly the phrase *by faith* here does not mean faith only; why should we conclude that it does in Rom. 5:1? The phrase includes all that was done in making that offering. "By faith Enoch was translated that he should not see death."

Moses gives us this bit of information about Enoch:
"And Enoch walked with God: and he was not; for
God took him." His faith was, therefore, a faith
that walked—walked with God. This was also true
of Abraham's faith, and he is the father of those
who walk in the steps of his faith. "And the father
of circumcision to them who not only are of the circumcision, but who also walk in the steps of that
faith of our father Abraham which he had in uncircumcision." (Rom. 4:12.) Faith only does not walk
—it does not take steps. And Paul says that we walk
by faith. Justified by faith—walk by faith.

"By faith Noah, being warned of God concerning
things not seen as yet, moved with godly fear, prepared an ark to the saving of his house." The phrase
by faith here includes all that Noah did in building
that ark. Noah did not just sit down and *trust* God,
and the ark was built by that sort of trust or faith;
yet it was built by faith. Justified by faith—ark
built by faith. As the phrase *by faith* cannot mean
faith only in the one, by what law of language or of
exegesis can it mean faith only in the other? Let the
Bible interpret its own words and phrases.

"By faith Abraham, being tried, offered up Isaac."
Read of this in Gen. 22. The long distance which
Abraham traveled to reach the appointed place of
sacrifice, the building of the altar, and all the other
incidents connected with the offering, are included
in the phrase *by faith*. That transaction was not done
by faith only; and yet it was done by faith, just as
we are justified by faith.

"By faith Moses, when he was born, was hid three
months by his parents." There was a three months'

period of anxious care and vigilance covered by the phrase *by faith*. These parents, Amram and Joche-bed, had faith; but it was not faith only, not the faith that sits and trusts God to do it all. Theirs was a living, active faith, a faith perfected by works. By faith Moses was hid three months—by faith we are justified. And by faith Moses forsook Egypt, but it certainly was not done by faith only.

"By faith the walls of Jericho fell down, after they had been compassed about for seven days." Read the account in Josh. 6. Here the phrase *by faith* covers thirteen trips around the city. As the phrase cannot mean faith only here, by what process of reasoning can anyone persuade himself that it means faith only in Rom. 5:1?

"By faith they passed through the Red Sea as by dry land." Read the account of this in Ex. 14:10-30. Here the phrase *by faith* spans the Red Sea from shore to shore, and includes all that was done in passing. But Paul says: "For I would not brethren have you ignorant, that our fathers were all under the cloud, and all passed through the sea; and were all baptized unto Moses in the cloud and in the sea." (1 Cor. 10:1,2.) As the phrase *by faith* covers, or includes, all that was done in passing through the sea, it includes baptism. And in that baptism they were saved from the wrath of the Egyptians. "Thus Jehovah saved Israel that day out of the hand of the Egyptians." (Ex. 14:30.) And that salvation is usually considered a type of our deliverance from sin. As their deliverance was by a faith that included baptism, we would naturally expect the anti-type to include baptism; and so it does. "For ye are all sons of God, through faith, in Christ." On what grounds did Paul make that affirmation? He immediately tells them: "For as many of you as were baptized into Christ did put on Christ." (Gal. 3:26,27.) They were children of God through faith, because they had been baptized into Christ.

Anvil Sparks:

We worry about our children, and forget that our parents used to worry about us.

No, no, beloved; elders are not infallible. Neither are majorities. Besides, a majority in a church manipulated absolutely by one man is in reality a minority, for it expresses the thinking of only one man. Think on this.

Some Points Discussed

The Prayers of Aliens and Patriarchy

Many things that will not stand the test of reason and revelation have been said about the prayers of aliens. I use the term aliens, instead of alien sinners, advisedly; for sometimes there is a difference between an alien and an alien sinner. But of that, more later.

In the ninth chapter of John we have an account of the controversy between the Pharisees and a man whose eyes Jesus had opened. The Pharisees contended that Jesus was a sinner. These Pharisees knew that Jesus was not an alien, but a member of the covenant, as also did the man whose eyes Jesus had opened—all knew he was a Jew and therefore in the covenant. So the man born blind had no reference to an alien sinner when he said, "'We know that God heareth not sinners: but if any man be a worshipper of God, and do his will, him he heareth." (John 9:31.) He was not speaking by inspiration, but was drawing his conclusion from the Old Testament scriptures; and for any one to make his statement refer to an alien sinner is such a perversion of his words as almost to put the perverter in the class whom the man said God would not hear. One grows weary of hearing brethren quote the blind man's words as if they were the words of an inspired apostle, and then wrongly make them apply to an alien, and then condemn sectarians for perverting the word of God.

But what is the difference between an alien and an alien sinner? In most cases, no difference; but when an alien "from the life of God" believes in the

Lord Jesus Christ and repents of his sins, he is not then a sinner—he has put sin out of his heart and quit sinning, though he has not yet had the penalty of his sins removed. The truth is, one must cease to be a sinner before he can be forgiven. Saul of Tarsus is an example. When the Lord made himself known to Saul on the highway, Saul ceased from his sinful course and became a deeply penitent man—not a penitent sinner, for in reality there is no such thing as a penitent sinner. He was not forgiven till he did what Ananias told him to do. It will not do to say that he was in covenant relations with God, when God said to Ananias, "Behold, he prayeth;" for the covenant with Israel had been abrogated—all Jews at that time were aliens, as much so as were Gentiles. Hence Saul was an alien, not an alien sinner, when God approved his praying. Yes, God was pleased with the prayer of an alien.

It appears therefore that it is anti-scriptural to say that God will not in any case hear the prayers of aliens. Such an idea is also unreasonable. I heard one preacher illustrate his idea in this way: "If a man is not a citizen of this government his name on a petition to the authorities would not be considered; it would count for nothing." Of course such a man has no citizen rights; but the preacher forgot to say that the first right an alien has, if he wants to become a citizen of this government, is the right of petition. If he has not sense enough to know this, he remains out. If some ill-informed person should tell him that he had no such right, I imagine the alien would know better. But even so, his petition would not be considered, if by law this government had debarred any one of his race or nation from obtaining citizenship. But God has never debarred any one of any race or nation from seeking and obtaining citizenship in his kingdom. Every one therefore has the right of petition, if he wants to become a citizen of God's kingdom. The fact therefore that God heard the prayers of Cornelius when he was praying to know what to do to be saved, is far from being proof that he was in covenant relations with God.

Yes, we should always observe closely the context; and we should also give due attention to the conditions and circumstances connected with any passage, event, or incident. If we will study the context, and the circumstances and conditions surrounding the controversy between the Pharisees and the man born blind, we will know better than to apply his language to an alien; and so with Saul of Tarsus. We would know that he was not an alien. Nor can I see how any one can prove conclusively that Cornelius was in covenant relations with God.

With the ideas some have, I do not see how they have any grounds for urging aliens to repent. We have been told that aliens are not in covenant with God—are not under his law, and therefore the Lord takes no notice of what they do. If this be true, they violate no law, and are therefore not sinners. Where then is there grounds for urging them to repent? Repent of what? It was put this way in a sermon I heard: "When a man becomes a Christian he obligates himself to do right." And that is saying that a man is under no obligation to do right till he becomes a Christian. If an alien is under no obligation to do right, then he commits no sin in failing to do right—he commits no sin no matter what evil he does. He would be under no obligation even to believe in God or the Lord Jesus Christ, and would have no sins to repent of. Can you think of a more vicious doctrine? It sounds like some of the phases of Russellism. Here is the way Scofield's Bible states the doctrine: "Acts is in two chief parts: In the first section, 1:1-9:43, Peter is the prominent personage, Jerusalem is the center, and the ministry to the Jews. Already in covenant relations with Jehovah, they had sinned in rejecting Jesus as *the Christ*. The preaching, therefore, was directed to that point, and repentance (i. e. a change of mind) was demanded. . . In the second division (10:1-28:31) Paul is prominent, a new center is established at Antioch, and the ministry is chiefly to the Gentiles who, as 'strangers from the covenants of promise' (Eph. 2:12), had but to 'believe on the Lord Jesus Christ' to be saved." These are strange statements, but consistent with the notion that aliens are not responsible to God for what they do. It is plainly implied that, if the Jews had not been in covenant relations with God, they would not have needed to repent of crucifying Jesus! And the Gentiles had no sins to repent of; so they had only to believe to be saved! But saved from what? If they had no sins to repent of, then they had none from which to be saved. Besides, no Jew today was ever in covenant relations with God, as had been the Jews to whom Peter preached; for that covenant had been nailed to the cross. If Scofield were correct, neither Jew nor Gentile would now need to repent. But Scofield's Bible and God's Bible do not agree. Jesus said that repentance should be preached among all nations. And when Peter explained his preaching to Gentiles, the brethren at Jerusalem "held their peace, and glorified God, saying, Then to the Gentiles also hath God granted repentance unto life." And Paul told the Athenians that God now "commandeth men that they should all everywhere repent." It is a pity that a man who professes to be a teacher of God's word will ignore plain statements of the Scriptures because he cannot fit them into a fanciful theory. Of course, repentance in the passages mentioned includes more than a mere change of mind.

As to the condition of the Gentiles there is little difference between Scofield and Pastor Russell. In a debate with a Russellite several years ago, one of the propositions I affirmed and he denied was, that baptism was for the remission of sins to Jew and Gentile alike. He readily granted that baptism to Jews was for the remission of sins, but denied that any Gentile was ever baptized for the remission of sins. Even so, it is easy to see that both Scofield and the Russellite were more consistent on that point than brethren who contend that baptism is for the remission of alien sins, and yet contend that the alien, not being under any law to God, violated no law of God. But brethren who so contend are as wrong on this point as Scofield and Russell. Paul speaks of "sinners of the Gentiles." (Gal. 2:15.) If the theory were correct, we might well repeat Paul's question, "Then how shall God judge the world?" The Jews had been intrusted with the oracles of God, but had made such poor use of their great blessings, that Paul makes this observation concerning them and

Gentiles: "What then? are we better than they? No, in no wise: for we before laid to the charge of both Jews and Gentiles, that they are all under sin." (Rom. 3:1-9.) And to see the degrading sins into which Gentiles had fallen read Rom. 1:18-32. And the Jews were no better—"all under sin." Jesus came to save sinners, not to make sinners; the gospel is God's power to save sinners, not to make sinners of those who hear it.

How came Cornelius to need salvation? One writer said "that Cornelius was doubtlessly serving the God of his fathers under patriarchy." But patriarchy was not a religion, nor a form of worship, but a form of government. Webster defines Patriarchy to be "a state of social development characterized by the supremacy of the father in the clan or family." The father was the ruler. He was also the priest and prophet for the family or clan, whether they worshipped God or idols. Again the writer said: "The patriarchal dispensation did not end at Sinai except to the descendants of Abraham. . . . While the offspring of Abraham was amenable to God under the law of Moses, Gentiles, to whom Moses' law was never given, could serve him under the law that had been in effect since Eden was lost to Adam and Eve." But many of Abraham's descendants were not included in the covenant made at Sinai. The word "dispensation" occurs a few times in the New Testament, but never in the sense we attach to it when we speak of the three dispensations.

So far as we know Abel was the first one to offer a God-appointed sacrifice, and it does not appear that he was the head of a family or clan. He was there-

fore not a patriarch, and it is certain that he did
not pass on to Cain or any other what God had revealed to him. I do not think any one will contend
that the commands to Cain and Abel were recorded
for the guidance of following generations. It seems
that the head of a family or clan, if he worshipped
God, received revelation direct from God, just as
did Abel. Joshua said to Israel, "Your fathers dwelt
of old time beyond the River, even Terah, the father
of Abraham, and the father of Nahor: and they
served other gods." (Joshua 24:2; see also verses
14, 15.) So Abraham came from idol-worshipping
patriarchs. "Fathers" would include at least his
father and grand-father, and perhaps farther back:
and so he did not learn true worship from them. God
spoke to him as he did to others before his time. You
will search in vain for any line of true worshippers
from creation to Abraham, and on down to Cornelius.
And I have seen no indication that any directions for
patriarchal government or worship was ever written
for their guidance.

I have never been dogmatic as to the patriarchal
dispensation among the Gentiles during the reign of
the law of Moses. From Paul's language in Romans
1:18-32 it seems that the whole Gentile world had
ceased to recognize God at all, and that God therefore
had completely given them over to their own folly.
Paul says also at that time they were "strangers from
the covenants of the promise, having no hope and
without God in the world." (Eph. 2:12.) Notice Romans 2:14. When Paul spoke of the law of Moses
he used "the" before "law"—"the law." When other
laws were spoken of, he did not usually use "the"

before law, especially when a contrast was made, as in
Rom. 2:14. Our translators did not follow Paul's
use and non-use of "the." Following the American
Version, but observing Paul's use and non-use of "the"
we have: "For when the Gentiles that have not law
do by nature the things of the law, these not having
law are law unto themselves." It seems to me that
this means that they had no revealed law, and therefore had to depend on such laws as they themselves
made for their own guidance. Possibly here and
there some families held to the idea of one true God.
It seems that Balaam was at one time a true prophet,
But where does any one read about a patriarchal
covenant? And where does one read that Cornelius
was a member of any covenant? There is no proof
that any revelation made to the early patriarchs re-
duced to writing for the benefit of succeeding generations of the Gentiles. That Cornelius was ruler,
prophet, and priest for his family or clan is a mere
guess, with no hint on which to base a guess.

Many Gentiles by contact with the Jews learned
of the one true God. Most likely Cornelius learned
of God in that way. At least he observed the Jewish
hour of prayer and gave much alms to the Jewish
people. But the fact that God heard his prayers is
no proof that he was in any covenant that God ever
made.

Here is a strange statement from our writer: "We
firmly believe that Cornelius was not a sinner until
the appearance of the angel with instructions that
brought him and the entire Gentile world in covenant
relations with Christ. Inspiration records, without
correction, the statement of the man that had been

healed of his blindness by the Lord (John 9:31),
'Now we know that God heareth not sinners.' God,
then, will not hear a sinner, but he did hear and answer the prayers of the Roman centurion. Therefore
the man was not a sinner at the time his prayers were
ascending unto the throne of God." Strange notion
—did the angel cause Cornelius to be lost so that Peter could tell him how to be saved? What next?
Perhaps some one will tell us that the Jews became
lost when the Holy Spirit came upon the apostles
at Pentecost! That would round out the picture. The
Jewish authorities said Jesus was a sinner, but they
knew he was not an alien—they knew he was in the
covenant. The man born blind knew Jesus was not
an alien; and to make his language apply to an alien
is inexcusable. Saul of Tarsus prayed before he became a Christian—prayed while he was still an alien,
and the Lord was pleased that he did pray. Nor was
Cornelius sinning when he was praying for more
light. If you will notice the answer he got you will
know what he was praying for. The angel told Cornelius that his prayer was heard; "Send therefore
to Joppa, and call unto thee Simon, who is surnamed
Peter, who shall speak unto thee words, whereby thou
shalt be saved, thou and all thy house."

I do not think I ever read a more startling notion
by any brother than that the visit of the angel to Cornelius made Cornelius a sinner and brought the entire Gentile world in covenant relations with Christ.
He was righteous till the angel spoke to him and that
turned him into a sinner! How come? Did not Cornelius immediately set about doing what the angel told
him to do? What sin did he commit? The visit of

an angel turned a righteous man into a sinner, and also the entire Gentile world became sinners! Another strange thing—a righteous man prayed and was heard, but the prayer was answered after he became a sinner. Cornelius the righteous man prayed, but Cornelius the sinner received the answer. And just how did the angel's visit to Cornelius bring the "entire Gentile world in covenant relations with Christ?" What is the nature of that covenant that the entire Gentile world is in. I cannot see wherein the state of the Gentiles is different now from what it was before the angel appeared to Cornelius, nor in what sense it could be different.

At the risk of being criticized, I make one personal reference, that may help some young preachers. I have said both publicly and privately, "I have been given credit for knowing more about the Bible than I really know, and I think the reason for that is, I do not know so many things that are not so." Think on this. If you do a lot of guessing, and make a lot of assertions for which you have no sure basis, people will rightfully conclude that you are not a careful Bible student.

The Apostles In Jerusalem

We do not know how long the apostles remained in Jerusalem after Pentecost. There was a period of about ten or twelve years between Pentecost and the conversion of Cornelius. What were the apostles doing during this time? Why did they not go on preaching tours among the Gentiles immediately after Pentecost? If a man would give a casual consideration to the conditions and needs, he would not say they failed to do so on account of Jewish bigotry and stubborn prejudice. It is my conviction that their labors in and around Jerusalem were necessary, and that they never in later years did a more fruitful work in the same length of time. They were working according to God's purpose, and did a great work.

The church began in Jerusalem with about three thousand members, and soon the number was increased to five thousand; and then "believers were the more added to the Lord, multitudes both of men and women." (Acts 5:14.) Again, "And the word of God increased; and the number of the disciples multiplied in Jerusalem exceedingly; and a great company of the priests were obedient to the faith." (Acts 6:7.) The apostles likely made many more believers in Jerusalem and surrounding territory than they would have made in the same time had they immediately gone among the Gentiles.

There is another important work that required their presence in Jerusalem for a time. These many thousands of believers needed teaching. And God saw to it that the apostles remained in Jerusalem to teach and train these new converts so that they would know how to live the Christian life, and be able to carry the gospel to other countries. "And they continued steadfastly in the apostles' teaching"—that is, they continued to be taught by the apostles. Read carefully Acts 2:42. Four distinct things which they did are mentioned. To moke the first phrase, or clause, mean that they continued to do what the apostles taught would make Luke say they continued to do what the apostles taught and three additional things. This church was a great school, and the apostles were the teachers; and these early disciples were eager and faithful pupils. They continued under the instruction of the apostles, and put into practice what they learned—continued steadfastly in "fellowship, in the breaking of bread and the prayers."

Some, perhaps many, of these new converts were from other countries; some of them remained in Jerusalem to be taught, otherwise they would have known nothing about what to do when they returned to their homes. God held in check the fury of the Jews till the disciples were prepared to preach the word. When God allowed the wrath of the Jews to break loose, the disciples had been so thoroughly taught and trained that they were able to "go about preaching the word." What a tragedy it would have been, if some of the critics had been managing the apostles. So the preaching of the gospel to the Gentiles had not been postponed on account of the supposed Jewish bigotry and stubborn prejudice of the apostles. (One postponement theory is one too many; let us not have another.) Yes, it took a series of divine visitations to convince Peter that he should go to the house of Cornelius; but who will say that God could not have done that immediately after Pentecost? And is it not strange that God worked so marvelously with the apostles, if they were remaining in Jerusalem in rebellion against his command? It sounds too much like blasphemy against God to say these apostles remained in Jerusalem for a time on account of Jewish bigotry and stubborn prejudice.

And finally: The face of the Lord is against those who are doing evil, but not against those who have repented of their evil doings.

The Word of Truth

"Jesus answered, My kingdom is not of this world: if my kingdom were of this world, then would my servants fight, that I should not be delivered to the Jews: but now is my kingdom not from hence. Pilate therefore said unto him, Art thou a king then? Jesus answered, Thou sayest that I am a king. To this end have I been born, and to this end am I come into the world, that I should bear witness unto the truth. Every one that is of the truth heareth my voice. Pilate said unto him, what is truth?" (John 18:36-38.) John does not tell us what Jesus said in answer to that question, but he did so enlighten Pilate concerning the nature of his kingdom that Pilate said, "I find no crime in him." John says, "For the law was given through Moses; grace and truth came through Jesus Christ." (John 1:17.) Jesus is the embodiment of truth. Said he, "I am the way, and the truth, and the life." "Howbeit, when he, the Spirit of truth is come, he shall guide you into all the truth." (John 16:13.) The whole revelation, therefore, made by the Holy Spirit through the apostles is truth. The truth spoken of in the New Testament is the scheme of redemption through Christ. In Galatians 2:5,14, Paul calls it "the truth of the gospel." This truth must be obeyed (Gal. 5:7.) It is called the word of truth. (Eph. 1:3; Col. 1:5; 2 Tim. 2:15; Jas. 1:18.) This word of truth is the gospel of our salvation, as is stated plainly in Eph. 1:13. And we are begotten, or brought forth, by the word of truth. (Jas. 1:18.) The New Testament writers never refer to the Old Testament, or law of Moses, as "the truth of the gospel," or "the word of truth." Hence to show distinction between the Old Testament and the New is not dividing the word of truth either rightly or wrongly. Yes, I used to call it "rightly dividing the word of truth," and preached sermons along the usual lines, but have not done so for many years—I learned better. Since then I have preached on the two covenants and showed the Old Testament ended at the cross of Christ, and that we are now under the New, which is the word of truth, the gospel of our salvation. Let us handle aright the word of truth. This we fail to do when we show we are not under the old covenant, and then call our effort "rightly dividing the word of truth." If our assumption were true, we would show that some of the word of truth does not apply to us.

"Therefore seeing we have this ministry, even as we obtained mercy, we faint not: but we have renounced the hidden things of shame, not walking in craftiness, nor handling the word of God deceitfully; but by the manifestation of the truth commending ourselves to every man's conscience in the sight of God. And even if our Gospel is veiled, it is veiled in them that perish." (2 Cor. 4:1-3.) "This ministry" is the ministry of the new covenant discussed in chapter 3. But read on through verse 7, and see how many terms are used in referring to this new covenant— "the word of God," "the truth," "our gospel," "the gospel of the glory of Christ," "the knowledge of the glory of God," "this treasure." And in ministering this new covenant they were preaching Jesus as Lord. In these verses there is material for a great expository

sermon.   God had made the apostles sufficient as
ministers of the new covenant—made them so by
their training and their baptism in the Holy Spirit.

"We faint not;" the apostles did not give up under
the severest trials and difficulties.   No other man
ever suffered more for an ideal than did Paul.   "Re-
nounce the hidden things of shame;" Paul indulged
in no secret sins—did nothing under cover.   "Not
walking in craftiness."   Paul was not a sly, cunning
schemer; he resorted to no underhand tricks to gain
personal advantage.   "Nor handling the word of God
deceitfully"—or, not adulterating the word of God.
A man may adulterate the word in ignorance or in
a deliberate effort to deceive others.   A man who
tries to deceive others as to what the Bible teaches,
lies about its teaching, and steals the word of God
from the people.   "Therefore, behold, I am against
the prophets, saith Jehovah, that steal my words
every one from his neighbor." (Jer. 23:20.)   And
the sad part is, that so many people like to have
straight Bible teaching stolen from them.   "A wonderful and horrible thing is come to pass in the land:
the prophets prophesy falsely, and the priests bear
rule by their means; and my people love to have it
so." (Jer. 5:30,31.)   People will find preachers who
will preach what they want to hear.   "Having itching
ears, they will heap to themselves teachers after their
own lusts."   "By the manifestation of"—by making
clear—"the word of truth commending ourselves to
every man's conscience in the sight of God."   Do not
darken counsel—make clear your teaching of the
word.   This will require more than just reading the
Bible; it will require study—not of somebody's ser-

mon outlines, but study of the Bible. Diligent study is required. "Give diligence to present thyself approved unto God, a workman that needeth not to be ashamed, handling aright the word of truth." (2 Tim. 2:15.) "Handling aright the word of truth," and not "handling the word of God deceitfully" amount to the same thing. Any sincere preacher or teacher is eager to be a worker that God will approve. To be such a worker he must give diligence to handle aright the word of truth, such a worker will not inject into his teaching his own notions, nor the doctrines of men. And he knows that he is not serving Christ, if he tries to please people. (Gal. 1:10.) He will not pervert, will not adulterate a passage of scripture to support a proposition, even if the proposition is true; but sometimes brethren do that very thing, though they berate sectarians for doing so.

Many years ago, while in a meeting in a small town in another state, I made my home with a successful business man, an old schoolmate of mine. He told me about a debate they had in that town. The brethren had secured the services of an experienced debater, who has since passed to his reward. In one speech the opponent gave a twist to a verse to make it sustain his position. The brother gave it another twist to show it did not support his opponent's position. At home the local brother said to the debater, "That verse does not mean what you said it does, does it?" The debater replied, "No, of course not." Said the brother, "Why did you say so?" "Well," said the debater, "he could not do anything with what I said; and when I am in a debate, I do not intend to let the truth suffer." In other words he would twist the truth all out of shape before he would let it suffer! But he was not handling aright the word of truth.

Another brother, in a radio sermon, in seeking to establish a true proposition, namely, that any one who really seeks to know the truth can find it, misquoted John 7:17 as follows: "If any man will do his will, he shall know the doctrine." But that is not what Jesus said. The King James version has, "If any man will do his will, he shall know of the doctrine, whether it be of God or whether I speak of myself." The American Standard version is a little plainer: "If any man willeth to do his will, he shall know of the teaching, whether it is of God, or whether I speak from myself." The Jews thought that Jesus was a mere man, and an imposter, and that he was preaching a doctrine of his own making. He had just said, "My teaching is not mine, but his that sent me." Then he asks them to put his teaching to the test, virtually saying, "If any man sets his heart on doing the will of God, he will come to know that what I teach is from God, and that I am not preaching my own opinions." Yes, the man who sincerely practices the teaching of Christ comes to know that it is from God, and not from man. "But he that doeth the truth cometh to the light, that his works may be made manifest, that they have been wrought in God." (John 3:21.) "And let us know, let us follow on to know Jehovah." (Hosea 6:3.)

In conclusion ponder the following statements. If the gospel of Christ is not true, then it is the biggest falsehood ever propagated. And yet it has done more to lift people out of sin and corruption, and done more to refine and civilize people, and has made its sincere converts more helpful and considerate toward others, than all other systems of philosophy and religion. The biggest falsehood cannot do the most good. A fair consideration of these things will lead any one to know that the gospel of Christ is from God and not from man.

Anvil Sparks:

Knowledge without wisdom is as dangerous as a car with neither steering gear nor brakes.

"Nothing in a name." Well, there is nothing in some names I know.

Also, it is just as evident that elephants were once boll weevils, for both have snouts.

Man of God

A prepositional phrase attached to a noun greatly limits the application of the noun; and sometimes such an expression, by usage, is restricted to a more limited meaning than the phrase itself would seem to indicate. Such is true of the phrase, "man of God." We are likely to assume that any man who served God would have been called "man of God," but not so. This term appears twice in the New Testament, both times in Paul's letters to Timothy—1 Tim. 6:11; 2 Tim. 3:17. The term occurs not less than seventy-five times in the Old Testament, and always refers to a prophet or public teacher of God's law. It was never applied to a man just because he was a servant of God. This fact gives some additional light on what is said in 2 Timothy 3:16,17: "Every scripture inspired of God is also profitable for teaching, for reproof, for correction, for instruction which is in righteousness: that the man of God may be complete, furnished completely unto every good work."

The Primitive Baptists, thinking that the term "man of God" meant any regenerated, or saved, man used to make an argument on these verses. If you quoted it to one, he would reply, "Of course, the scriptures thoroughly furnish the man of God unto every good work, but do not furnish the unregenerated man anything—he is not a man of God, and cannot even understand the scriptures." If you still think the term "man of God" refers to any Christian, how would you answer him? But they were mistaken in their use of the term. A man of God was a prophet, a teacher of God's word—a man to direct people right. Is a preacher thoroughly equipped for the work he should do? What is his work? If he is really engaged in the work of the Lord, he seeks to convert sinners and to edify saints. For that work the scriptures furnish him with everything he needs for his God-appointed work. To become Christians people must be taught. The scriptures are profitable for teaching—in teaching sinners, the preacher needs nothing else. In teaching sinners the preacher should have a definite purpose, and should therefore teach the sinner the things he needs to know. He needs to be made to realize that he is a sinner and needs salvation. It is the business of the man of God to do that essential thing, but what shall he use to accomplish that work? The scriptures are profitable for teaching. The scriptures are profitable for reproof. The Greeks had two words for reproof, but there was a difference. One simply meant to reprove, or rebuke, with no implications as to results. The other meant to so reprove a person as to make him realize his guilt—that is the word used here. Hence, the scriptures are profitable for conviction. Hence, the scriptures so teach a sinner as to bring him to a knowledge of his sinfulness. Jesus said of the Holy Spirit, "And he, when he is come, will convict the world in respect of sin . . ." (John 16:8-11.)

In this scripture we have in the Greek the verb form of the word translated "reproof" in 2 Tim. 3:16. Hence, the Holy Spirit and the scriptures, the written words of the Holy Spirit, convict sinners, but that does not mean that there are two methods of conviction. The scriptures are the words of the Holy

Spirit—these words convict sinners. But to convict a man that he is a lost sinner, and offer him no way of escape, only adds to his misery; but the scriptures, the written words of the Holy Spirit, do not stop there. The inspired scriptures are profitable for correction. The word correction is specific—the word conversion simply means a change. To convert a person is merely to change him from one thing to another, whether for the better or for the worse; but to correct a person is to get him out of the wrong way into the right way. A person may be converted from one wrong doctrine, or way, to another wrong doctrine, or way; but that is not correction. To correct him is to set him right—to put him in the right way. David expresses the same idea in other words: "The law of Jehovah is perfect, restoring the soul" (Psa. 19:7, American Standard Version.) To restore anything is to get it back where it belongs—back to its proper place. But to correct a man, or, what is the same, to restore him to his right place, and then leave him without any further guidance, is of little benefit, for it is not in man to direct his own steps. The person therefore who has been corrected and restored to the right way needs to know how to live right. The scriptures fill that need—they are profitable for instruction in righteousness. "Thy word is a lamp unto my feet, and light unto my path." (Psa. 119:105.) So the scriptures thoroughly furnish the preacher or teacher with everything he needs in teaching people, convicting them, correcting them, and instruction them in the right way. Thus equipped, he is complete, furnished completely unto every good work. He is lacking in faith, if he injects some

of his own wisdom and inventions. Any addition to
that which is complete makes it incomplete. You may
know many things, but you will never know as much
as God knows. So do not deify yourself by following
your own ways.

Anvil Sparks:

Much falsehood lies wrapped up in the old sayings.
for instance: "Honesty is the best policy." But honesty
is not a "policy"; it is a principle. There is no such thing
as honesty for policy's sake.

A hint to speakers and writers: There are only two
adjectives in the twenty-third Psalm.

Who Are the Sound?

"The time will come when they will not endure sound doctrine." (2 Tim. 4:3.) To be sound is to be healthy. In the Greek New Testament there are two words, an adjective and a verb, translated "sound," that refer primarily to bodily health or a sound body. The Greeks also applied the idea to the mind—a sound mind. Metaphorically, it refers to the condition of man's moral or religious character, or to his teaching. The verb means, *to be healthy, or sound,* or *to become healthy,* or *sound.* An understanding of its literal use will help us to see more clearly its figurative use. In its primary, or literal sense, the verb is found in these passages. "They that are in health have no use of a physician, but they that are sick." Luke 5:31. "And they that were sent, returning to the house, found the servant whole." Luke 7:10. The servant had been restored to health. "Beloved, I pray that in all things thou mayest prosper and be in health, even as thy soul prospereth." (3 John 2.) The adjective is used in its primary, or literal, sense in Matt. 12:13; 15:31; Mark 3:5; John 5:6,9,11,14,15; 7:23; Acts 4:10.

When is a person's body sound? It does not take a doctor to give a general answer to that question. It is sound when every part is acting, or is able to act, in harmony with the laws of its being; there must be no abnormal growths. Some people think they are sound physically when they are not. To say you are sound does not make it so. The laws governing our physical being are God-given laws and must be respected, else we shall not long have a sound body.

It should be easy for us to see the significance of the word *sound* when applied to our moral and spiritual nature. In this realm the Bible is the law we must respect; our whole being must be brought into harmony with God's will, if we would be sound morally and spiritually. There will then be symmetry of development, and there will be no abnormal growths, which are always an indication of unsoundness somewhere. If one of my arms were to develop in strength so that I could at one blow crush the skull of an elephant, the other arm perishing all the while, there would be a lack of soundness somewhere. Some brethren gain the name of being very sound because they have developed great strength along certain lines, while much of their character remains undeveloped. It is not soundness; it is an abnormal growth.

Some develop courage and boldness, but neglect meekness and kindness. Another is very earnest in contending for the faith, but is very deficient in forbearance. He becomes dogmatic and troublesome in the congregation. We forget that these opposing characteristics must be developed in the Christian. He must be brave and firm, yet meek and forbearing; uncompromising with reference to the truth, but yielding all his opinions or preferences for the sake of peace; otherwise, he is not sound.

More than fifty years ago a persistent effort was begun to lead churches away from the New Testament way of work and worship, and much harm was done. Those who fell in love with the move—instrumental music in the worship, the various societies, etc.,—called themselves Progressives. Many brethren opposed them on the ground that they had departed from sound doctrine; and so we began to hear such expressions as "sound brethren," "sound preachers," "sound churches." Too many took it for granted that opposition to innovations constituted soundness. To be sound you must oppose many things, but you may oppose all innovations and still be unsound. You do not have to run a high fever to be unsound physically —you may have a chill. While those who called themselves Progressives ran such a high fever that they, as a negro said of a drunkard, talked like a man with "delirium tremendous," a lot of the rest of us had a chill. Most of us recovered from the chills, but with our Progressives the "delirium tremendous" has become permanent, so much so that there is no hope of a cure. It is a sad sight to see a man with "delirium tremendous."

I would like to impress upon all that the requirement to be sound in faith and doctrine is not fulfilled by simply opposing. A man may oppose every departure from the truth and still be unsound, simply because he fails to come up to the standard of his duty. The requirement covers the whole of life. "But we may know that the law is good, if a man use it lawfully, as knowing this, that law is not made for a righteous man, but for the lawless and unruly, for the ungodly and profane, for murderers of fathers and murderers of mothers, for man slayers, for fornicators, for abusers of themselves with men, for men stealers, for liars, for false swearers, and if there be any other thing contrary to the sound doctrine." (1 Tim. 1:8-10.) Notice the long list of criminals for whom the law was made, and the significant expression, "and if there be any other thing contrary to sound doctrine." This shows that every form of sin is contrary to sound teaching. Do you practice sin? Is there any irregularity in your life? Then you are unsound. Verse 11 is directly connected with what had been said, and shows that the gospel is the final standard by which a thing is to be tested as to whether or not it is sound. Sound doctrine—teaching —is gospel teaching. Is it important that we hold on faithfully to this sound teaching? "If any man teacheth a different doctrine, and consenteth not to sound words, even the words of our Lord Jesus Christ, and to the doctrine which is according to godliness; he is puffed up, knowing nothing but doting about questionings and disputes of words, whereof cometh envy, strife, railings, evil surmisings, wranglings of men corrupted in mind and bereft of the truth, supposing that godliness is a way of gain." (1 Tim. 6:3-5.) Notice especially what Paul here says of the man who teaches a different doctrine and consents not to sound words. And this charge to the preacher: "Hold the pattern of sound words, which thou hast heard from me, in faith and love which is in Christ Jesus." (2 Tim. 1:13.) The words delivered to us by inspired men is our pattern, and we must hold to it in faith and love. "But speak thou the things which befit the sound doctrine: that aged men be temperate, grave, sober-minded, sound in faith, in love, in patience: that aged women likewise be reverent in demeanor, not slanderers nor enslaved to much wine, teachers of that which is good; that they may train the young women to love their husbands, to love their children, to be sober-minded, chaste, workers at home, kind, being in subjection to their own husbands, that the word of God be not blasphemed: the younger men likewise exhort to be sober-minded: in all things showing thyself an ensample of good works; in thy doctrine showing uncorruptness, gravity, sound speech, that cannot be condemned; that he that is of the contrary part may be ashamed, having no evil thing to say of us." (Tit. 2:1-8.) Sound doctrine here covers the whole range of human conduct, including our duties in our every-day affairs at home. Some otherwise good preachers fail to be sober-minded, grave, etc. We are to be sound in faith, love and patience. Has not many a man boasted of his soundness, when, as a matter of fact, he was very unsound? Study those verses carefully, and see if you feel like saying, "I am a perfectly sound Christian." Can any man or church afford to boast about being sound? We should strive to be sound, even though we do not attain to perfect soundness. Let us not forget that the word *sound* is a descriptive adjective, not a part of a party name.

How is soundness promoted? Much attention these days is given to the development and maintenance of bodily health. Let us notice three essentials to health:

1. Wholesome food. A person cannot eat or drink just anything and keep a sound body; neither can a Christian feed on just any kind of doctrine, and remain sound. Filthy jokes are poison; and the most of the moral and spiritual food you get out of the movies is destructive to Christian health. The Christian's food is the word of God. (Matt. 4:4.) Cultivate a taste for the word of God, till you can say with David that it is sweeter than honey. (Ps. 19:10; 119:103.)

2. Love for God. If we do not love God we will not feed upon his word. "He that loveth me not, keepeth not my words." Such people refuse to have God in their knowledge. (Rom. 1:28.) "If a man love me he will keep my word." "He that hath my commandments, and keepeth them, he it is that loveth me." (See John 14:21-24.) Without this love there is no soundness in us—"The whole head is sick, and the whole heart faint. From the sole of the foot even unto the head there is no soundness in it; but wounds, and bruises, and fresh stripes: they have not been closed, neither bound up, neither mollified with oil." (Isa. 1:5,6.)

3. Proper exercise. Not all exercise is healthful. Even the right kind of exercise may be carried to a hurtful extreme. And not all religious exercise promotes soundness. Some of it is hurtful. It does not prove a man's worth and soundness to say that he is a great worker, for the devil is a great worker. Many in the last day will claim a right to heaven on the grounds that they were great workers, and meet bitter disappointment. (See Matt. 7:22,23.) A man may do the works the Lord approves, and yet be not sound. Such was the case with the church at Ephesus, Rev. 2:1-7. They opposed, and even hated false teaching—the Lord approved that; but they were at the point of being rejected, for they had left their first love. It was a working church, had no fellowship with false pretenders, and held fast to the name of the Lord; but it seems that they did all this as party measures, not out of love to God. They were unsound at heart.

4. Pure air to breathe. No man can develop or

maintain a sound body if the air he breathes is heavily charged with poisonous gasses, poisonous dust, or smoke. The company you keep makes up your moral and spiritual atmosphere. "Be not deceived: Evil companions corrupt good morals." But one says, "What am I to do, for I am constantly in contact with people of corrupt speech?" You do not have to listen to such speech—you do not have to breathe such atmosphere. The deep sea-divers do not breathe the briny substance surrounding them: by a mechanical device they breathe the pure air above. And so can the Christian do. He can associate with the patriarchs and prophets of old, and with the Lord's apostles; yea, with the Lord himself as he walked among men.

With reference to work, there are three classes of horses: the runaway, the steady puller and the balky one. There are just three classes of professed Christians. The progressives and other sectarians have run away with everything, and some have balked because others have run away. There is no use to run away or balk, either; let us have a good, steady, faithful pull.

Progress

Recently I heard a man, a Baptist preacher, make a short talk over the radio on progress. He spoke of what some people called progress—always going on, advancing. But he said that to make real progress we sometimes had to go back; and he used the prodigal son as an illustration. He did not say so, but he could have said that all the time the boy was away from home he was slipping—losing his money, worse than wasting his time, and destroying his self-respect and his manhood. Yes, to make any progress he had to go back.

Some years ago some brethren decided to be "progressive." When they went out from us they soon spent what Christianity they started off with in riotous indulgences in all sorts of innovations. Now some no longer believe that Jesus is the Christ, the Son of God. With them the religion of Christ is just one of the religions of the world. They are now in the condition of the prodigal son when he hired himself out to feed hogs; but they are not as wise as that boy—they are feeding on husks and think it is good eating. Progressive? They will never make any real progress till they return to the Father's house.

Jeremiah Seeking A Man

Jerusalem and all Judah had fallen very low; the cup of their iniquity was full. This command came to Jeremiah: "Run ye to and fro through the streets of Jerusalem, and see now, and know, and seek in the broad places thereof, if ye can find a man, if there be any that doth justly, that seeketh truth; and I will pardon her." (Jer. 5:1.) Male inhabitants were plentiful in Jerusalem, but Jehovah told Jeremiah to find a *man—one man*, as in the Jewish translation. Neither among the poor nor among the great did Jeremiah find *one man*. According to the description a *man* deals justly and seeks truth. Many people have grown up in stature, but are dwarfs in mind and heart, unable to think intelligently, or form correct judgments, and are without emotional balance. They have not learned the first principles of justice, honesty, and truth. In the essentials of manhood they are babes. That was what brought Jerusalem and all Judah so low in Jeremiah's day. Neither among the poor nor among the great did Jeremiah find a *man*, and so Jerusalem was not pardoned. Their treatment of Jeremiah shows that they were immature—they had not grown up.

The world needs men and women. There are males and females of the human species in plenty; but the turmoil and confusion in the world today show that few people have really grown up. A man may be wise in mechanics or chemistry, and yet be undeveloped in his knowledge of the fundamentals of human relationships, undeveloped morally and spiritually. He is just a smart babe. If people were reasonably mature in their ideas of right and wrong, crackpots like Hitler or gorillas like Stalin and his crowd could not create such confusion and cause such destruction. The people would tell them to go back and sit down, for such men are so immature that they do not know the first principles of decent behavior. They have not grown up except in body and in a certain kind of twisted intellect. If all men behaved as sane men should there would be no wars or rumors of wars, nor would there be any stealing, nor family fusses. But a few man-sized brats can make an awful lot of trouble for those who would like to be at peace with all men. And that is true even in the church.

Babes in Christ should grow up. Read 1 Cor. 3:1-5. God's children at Corinth, at least, a majority of them, had not grown out of babyhood, when Paul wrote this first Epistle. They were still carnal, still babes, unable to stand solid food. What evidence did he give that they were still carnal, still babes? There was among them jealousy and strife. People who are full of jealousy and stir up strife are babes. It is a pity that even now, as at Corinth, there are such people in some churches. Even some preachers are full of jealousy and a spirit of strife. No matter how intellectual such people are, in the essentials of Christian character, they are babes, they have not grown up.

"Putting away therefore all wickedness, and all guile, and hypocrisies, and envies, and all evil speakings, as newborn babes, long for the spiritual milk which is without guile, that ye may grow thereby unto salvation; if ye have tasted that the Lord is gracious:" (1 Pet. 2:1-3.) So long as a proposed Christian does not put away "all wickedness, and all guile, and hypocrisies, and envies, and all evil speakings," he will not "long for the spiritual milk," and therefore cannot grow unto salvation. The word of God is the food for a child of God. A child of God in good spiritual health will long for spiritual milk just as a healthy babe longs for the milk of its mother's breast. Do you delight in the law of Jehovah? Can you say with David, "Oh how love I thy law!"? If not, there is something wrong with you. What is it? Have you put away "all wickedness"? For *wickedness* the marginal reading has *malice*. The same Greek word is translated malice in 1 Cor. 14:20. Malice results from continued anger, and desires or does harm to its object, and so we have in the law the expression "malice afore-thought." If you have that feeling or purpose you are a babe, and cannot grow unto salvation, unless you put it away. And then you must put away *guile*—the practice of deceit for personal advantage, and hypocrisies—pretending to be what you are not, and envies—resentful begrudging the good fortune of others, and all evil speakings—talk that may result in harm to another. These things must be put away, or you can never grow unto salvation. Put these away and be men. Too many are pretending to be men, but are yet babes.

Finally—"Brethren, be not children in mind: yet in malice be ye babes, but in mind be men." (1 Cor. 14:20.) It seems that the Corinthians had been wrangling over the relative merits of spiritual gifts. Some prized the speaking with tongues above other gifts—that gift was more spectacular than others.

Their wrangling about things was childish. So, while discussing these matters, Paul inserted the exhortation just quoted. A babe cannot have the mind of a man; neither does a child have malice in its heart. And a man should not have the mind of a child. "Watch ye, stand fast in the faith, quit you like men, be strong." (1 Cor. 16:13.) My fellow-christian soldier, you are in the fight of your life, and you are fighting for life. Be alert; let no evil slip up on you. You have espoused the faith, the gospel. Stand fast; do not retreat, do not even waver. "Quit you like men." Do not act like children—play the part of men. Fight the good fight of faith. Let nothing hinder you; do not give up. "Be ye steadfast, unmovable, always abounding in the work of the Lord." "Be strong." There is no place for cowards, and no need for weaklings, in the Lord's army. And you will be neither a coward nor a weakling, if you have a living faith in the living God. "Finally, be strong in the Lord, and in the strength of his might. Put on the whole armor of God, that ye may be able to stand against the wiles of the devil." "Quit you like men." "Ye therefore, beloved, knowing these things beforehand, beware lest, being carried away with the error of the wicked, ye fall from your own steadfastness. But grow in the grace and knowledge of our Lord and Savior Jesus Christ." (2 Pet. 3:17,18.)

God Reigns Within

Jesus said, "The kingdom of God cometh not with observation: neither shall they say, Lo, here, or, there! for lo, the kingdom of God is within you." (Luke 17:20,21.) You do not see the reign of God, for he reigns within the heart. That reign in the heart leads to right living; but even so, a man's self-interests may lead him to so live that outwardly he seems to be a fine character, but God does not reign in his heart. To such characters Jesus says, "Woe unto you, scribes and Pharisees, Hypocrites! for ye are like unto whited sepulchres, which outwardly appear beautiful, but inwardly are full of dead men's bones, and of all uncleanness. Even so ye also outwardly appear righteous unto men, but inwardly ye are full of hypocrisy and iniquity." (Matt. 23:27,28.) Jesus says also, "From within, out of the heart of men, evil thoughts proceed . . ." These evil thoughts proceed into evil deeds. (Mk. 7:21-23.) Again Jesus tells us that "out of the abundance of the heart the mouth speaketh," and that "the evil man out of his evil treasure bringeth forth evil things." (Matt. 12:34,-35.) One pity is, that a man with an evil heart may cause others to be "evil affected against the brethren." (Acts 14:2.)

But what is the remedy for evil hearts? The remedy is within the reach of every one so afflicted, but he must take the remedy voluntarily, in a spirit of humility and reverence. In view of calamities that were about to come upon Jerusalem, Jehovah gave this exhortatory command: "O Jerusalem, wash thy heart from wickedness, that thou mayest be saved. How long shall thine evil thoughts lodge within thee?" (Jer. 4:14.) God makes the inner-man responsible for what the body does. "Let no sin therefore reign in your mortal body, that ye should obey the lusts thereof:" (Rom. 6:12.) If the inner-man allows the body to sin it disobeys God. Peter says that God cleansed the hearts of the Gentiles by faith. (Acts 15:9.) In the Greek it is "the faith." And that means the gospel—purified their hearts by their obedience to the gospel. "Seeing ye have purified your souls in your obedience to the truth unto unfeigned love of the brethren, love one another from the heart fervently:" (1 Pet. 1:22.) If a man harbors evil thoughts in his heart, he is not living in obedience to the gospel. So therefore, "Let the word of Christ dwell in you richly." (Col. 3:16.) A man cannot improve his ways on the same old stock of ideas that he has always had; for a man lives out in his life the thoughts he cherishes in his heart. But one's selfish plans and purposes may be polished up, or covered up, till some one begins to interfere with his selfish plans; then he blows up. One sure proof that a man's plans and purposes are selfish is, that he becomes angry and abusive when some one begins to teach things that interfere with his plans. He has not let the word of Christ dwell in him richly. If you want to live as Christ lived let his thoughts be the moving power in your life. In that way God works in you to will and to do his good pleasure.

"The love of Christ constraineth us." Read 2 Cor. 5:14,15. Christ was not moved by selfish impulses and desires. He died for all, and that love constrains, or restrains, men from living unto themselves, or for themselves.

"Finally, brethren, whatsoever things are true, whatsoever things are honorable, whatsoever things are just, whatsoever things are pure, whatsoever things are lovely, whatsoever things are of good report; if there be any virtue, and if there be any praise, think on these things." (Phil. 4:8.) It seems to me that the exegetes I have examined miss the point in the last clause. Certainly Paul did not raise the question as to whether there was any virtue or anything worthy of praise in the things he had mentioned. What then? In as much as he tells the brethren to think on these things, he must have meant, if there were any virtue and praise in their hearts they were to think on the excellent things he had mentioned; for it is a fact that people can become so corrupt and selfish and so devoid of all goodness of heart and mind that they cannot meditate on good qualities or have any praise for any goodness, or good person. If you still have any liking for virtue or any praise for goodness, think on these things Paul mentioned. It will do you good, and that will have a transforming effect on your own character. Character comes from within. And Paul also tells us to be transformed by renewing the mind. (Rom. 12.2.)

The heart determines the character, and Paul shows plainly that God counts as nothing the person who has not love, no matter what display of powers he may make. (1 Cor. 13.) Notice what love does and what it does not do. "Love suffereth long, and is kind; love envieth not; love vaunteth not itself, is not puffed up, doth not behave itself unseemly, seek-

eth not its own, is not provoked, taketh not account
of evil; rejoiceth not in unrighteousness, but rejoiceth
with the truth; beareth all things, believeth all things,
hopeth all things, endureth all things. Love never
faileth." Love is not a mere sentiment; it is practical. Love for others is right conduct toward them.
It is not arrogant and selfish, but helpful and considerate. If the traits Paul mentions do not abound
in you, then no matter what great things you do or
what claims you make you are nothing in God's
sight. So the condition of the heart is made manifest in thoughts and action. Had Simon's heart been
right he would not have offered money for the gift
of God.

If a disciple will be what he ought to be, he will
do what he ought to do. Here should be placed the
main emphasis, but is it done? Too often emphasis
is placed on doing something, instead of being something. Yes, it is do, do, do; and people get into such
a whirl of "working for the Lord," or doing "church
work," that they have no time to think of the Lord.
Faithful work, faithful obedience to God, is essential; but all service to God must spring from the
right attitude of mind and heart. I fear that pride
has much to do with building fine meeting houses.
Some reports seem to reflect pride in achievements.
We do not want the denominations to make a bigger
show than we do! When pride comes in, the Lord
goes out. "Keep thy heart with all diligence for
out of it are the issues of life." (Prov. 4:23.) "The
good man out of the good treasure of his heart bringeth forth that which is good." (Luke 6:45.) All improvement, all reformation, all growth in grace, all

worship, all gracious conduct toward others, must come from within; out of the heart. Is your heart right? We have had striking demonstrations that some hearts are not right. Of course what you do has a reflex influence on the heart, but the condition of the heart has a direct influence on what you do.

There can be no foundation for a good character without a deep feeling of personal responsibility to God. There must be a feeling of entire dependence on him. There can be no development of Christian character without a living faith in God and in Jesus the Christ, and the Bible as a revelation from God. Read, study, meditate, pray. Take God into account in all you do. Some people become so busy serving the Lord, that they have no time to think of him. Try to be what the Lord requires you to be, then you will want to do his bidding.

Anvil Sparks:

Truth is universal — that is the reason a person sometimes thinks the speaker is aiming every thing he says at him.

There is no real intelligence where there is no real thinking.

Sometimes there isn't anything in a name, but there ought to be.

The more monkey business we have in our seats of learning, the less civilization we have.

People are already drunk on something when they imagine that liquor will bring prosperity.

Imagine how things would be, if everybody in this country would get drunk at the same time.

Optimism is ambition on a spree; pessimism is next morning's headache.

A Permanent Building

Character is the only permanent thing we build in this world. We talk about making permanent roads, building permanent houses, erecting permanent monuments; but no material structure can be permanent. However, if we go to put up a great building, which we, in a relative sense, call a permanent structure, we want the builders to follow faithfully the blueprints of an architect who knows his business. That sort of building cannot go up by accident, nor in a haphazard way. But if you are building a shack or temporary shed, you need neither blueprints nor skilled workmen. And yet there is some difference when it comes to building a character.

You are building a character, a permanent character, even though you do not so much as think about it. You go blindly on your way, but all the while you are building up a permanent structure—you are building for eternity foolishly. As character is the only really permanent thing we can build it does seem that sensible people would be interested in putting up such a structure as would be approved by the Great Architect when we meet him in the judgment. How shall we build?

We have, so to speak, the blueprints prepared and laid down in the Bible by the Master Architect, and he will judge our work by his blueprints. The builder must carefully study the blueprints as he builds. He must give diligence to show himself approved by the Master Architect, a workman that needeth not to be ashamed, handling aright the blueprints. A mistake can be corrected, but a deliberate departure from the plans and specifications is presumption, and cannot be tolerated.

But building a good character requires more than a mere outward compliance with the plans and specifications of our Architect. There must be sincerity, devotion, trust, reverence, love. Put heart into your work. Paul says, "Think on these things"—meditate on them. Jehovah said to Joshua: "This book of the law shall not depart out of thy mouth, but thou shalt meditate thereon day and night, that thou mayest observe to do according to all that is written therein: for then shalt thou make thy way prosperous, and then shalt thou have good success." "Blessed is the man that walketh not in the counsel of the wicked, nor standeth in the way of sinners, nor sitteth in the seat of scoffers: but his delight is in the law of Jehovah; and in his law doth he meditate day and night." (Ps. 1:1,2.)

In the first Psalm we have outlined the development and results of both kinds of character—the bad and the good. Read the entire Psalm carefully, thoughtfully. If you begin to take the counsel or advice of sinners, you will soon find yourself taking your stand with them; and you may become so hardened in sin, that you scoff at the Bible and those who seek to follow it, and in the end perish. There is a better way—delight in God's word and meditate on it day and night. "I will meditate on thy precepts, and have respect unto thy ways." "O how love I thy law!" "It is my meditation all the day." (Ps. 119:15,97.) "I remember the days of old; I meditate on all thy doings; I muse on the work of thy

hands." (Ps. 143:5.)   But knowledge comes before
meditation; for how can one meditate on that concerning which he knows nothing?   Learn the word
of God, and meditate on what you learn.   In this way
you make it a part of your very being—God's
thoughts become your thoughts, and his ways your
ways.   "Take time to be Holy."—Take time to meditate; it will help you to be what you ought to be.

It is easy to develop a wrong ambition, and thus
work injury to your character.   To do things to be
seen of men, hurts your character and brings you no
reward from your father in heaven.   You cannot
build a christian character by trying to build a reputation.   There is a lot of difference between growing
up and swelling up.   You cannot blow up a character
like you blow up a toy balloon.   Love the Lord and
serve him, with no thought of your reputation, and
you will build a good character.   "If ye love me, ye
will keep my commandments."   "He that hath my
commandments, and keepeth them, he it is that loveth
me: and he that loveth me shall be loved of my Father, and I will love him, and will manifest myself unto
him."   (John 14:15,21.)   And what more do you
want?

Let us follow another Bible figure.   Character
grows, whether for the worse or the better.   Jesus
said, "This people's heart is waxed gross."   "And
because iniquity shall be multiplied, the love of the
many shall wax cold."   Their love would grow cold.
"But shun profane babblings: for they will proceed
further in ungodliness."   (2 Tim. 2:16.)   "But evil
men and imposters shall wax worse and worse, de-
ceiving and being deceived."   (2 Tim. 3:13.)   The

worst criminal was once an innocent babe. Most likely his first crime was of a minor nature, but his criminal course increased till he became a hardened, heartless criminal. And so there is growth in wickedness, growth in criminal character.

A new-born babe may be perfect physically, but it needs to grow, and it will grow, if properly cared for. And the babe in Christ needs to grow, and it will grow with proper food and care. But there is a difference; the babe in Christ is not so helpless as the natural babe. His mind is already developed, and he has a sense of responsibility. He is capable of receiving and following instructions. "Putting away therefore all wickedness, and all guile, and hypocrisies, and envies, and all evil speakings as newborn babes, long for the spiritual milk which is without guile, that ye may grow thereby unto salvation;" (1 Pet. 2:1,2.) Here the Lord puts the responsibility for growth on the individual. He has given us the food, and expects us to make proper use of it. On the phrase, "that ye may grow thereby," MacKnight says, "In the former chapter the apostle told the Christians of Pontus, that they were born again of the incorruptible seed of the word. Here he told them, that the word is also the milk by which the new-born grow to maturity. The word, therefore, is both the principle by which the divine life is produced, and the food by which it is nourished." The Common Version has, "desire the sincere milk of the word." The Greek word which they here translate by the phrase *of the word*, they translate by the word *reasonable* in Rom. 12:1. In both passages the American Standard Version has *spiritual*. And for the word translated *sincere* in the Common Version, the American Version has *"which is without guile."* "Sincere milk," "milk which is without guile." Can you think of milk as sincere, or as being without guile? The word so translated may apply to people, but not to things. Thayer defines the word thus: "guileless, of things, *unadulterated, pure."* Liddell and Scott; "of liquids, *unmixed, pure."* Now read the passage with these Lexical definitions incorporated—"long for the spiritual unadulterated milk," or "long for the spiritual unmixed (or pure) milk." I lay no claim to Greek scholarship; but I can read definitions, and I know which definitions make sense in this passage.

And we are to feed on spiritual milk; that, of course, is the word of God, for that is our food. (Matt. 4:4.) But it must not be adulterated; it must be pure. To mix human opinions and inventions with the word adulterates it; to feed on such adulterated food prevents one from growing unto salvation. Food must be wholesome to promote growth.

And ponder this: "But grow in the grace and knowledge of our Lord and Savior Jesus Christ." (2 Pet. 3:18.) The knowledge of our Lord and Saviour Jesus Christ is the knowledge revealed in the Bible. Too few people realize that we are commanded to learn the Bible more and more. And in view of what some people say about grace, it would be hard for them to explain how we can obey the command to grow in grace. We are told that the performance of any condition makes void the grace of God. How then can we obey the command to grow in grace? for that command means for us to grow more and more in the favor of God.

Questions About the Destruction of the Temple

The questions the disciples asked Jesus about the destruction of the temple and the answer Jesus gave them have been the source of an endless amount of speculation and bad exegesis. Some try to make almost everything Jesus said in answering their questions refer to his second coming; and yet his second coming was not the topic of his speech. Read the three records of what led to his speech, and carefully compare them, keeping in mind that the destruction of the temple implied the destruction of Jerusalem.

Matt. 24:1-3: "And Jesus went out from the temple, and was going on his way; and his disciples came to him to show him the buildings of the temple. But he answered and said unto them, See ye not all these things? Verily I say unto you, There shall not be left here one stone upon another, that shall not be thrown down. And as he sat on the mount of Olives, the disciples came unto him privately, saying, Tell us, when shall these things be? and what shall be the sign of thy coming and of the end of the world?"

Mark 13:1-4: "And as he went forth out of the temple, one of his disciples saith unto him, Teacher, behold, what manner of stones and what manner of buildings! And Jesus said unto him, Seest thou these great buildings? there shall not be left here one stone upon another, which shall not be thrown down. And as he sat on the mount of Olives over against the temple, Peter and James and John and Andrew asked him privately, Tell us, when shall these things be? and what shall be the sign when these things are all about to be accomplished?"

Luke 21:5-7: "And as some spake of the temple, how it was adorned with goodly stones and offerings, he said, As for these things which ye behold, the days will come, in which there shall not be left here one stone upon another, that shall not be thrown down. And they asked him, saying, Teacher, when therefore shall these things be? and what shall be the sign when these things are about to come to pass?"

The questions the disciples asked must have related to what Jesus said about the destruction of the temple; but many authorities take it for granted that the disciples asked about the second coming of Christ, as well as about the destruction of the temple. But how could the disciples have asked about his second coming when they did not believe he would be killed? When Jesus, a few days before the events of this lesson told them that he would be killed during this visit to Jerusalem, and would rise again, "They understood none of these things; and this saying was hid from them, and they perceived not the things that were said." (Luke 18:31-34.) They evidently held the Jewish idea that the Messiah would not be killed, but would abide here for ever. (John 12:32-34.) So firmly rooted in their minds was this idea, that when Jesus was killed, their hopes died. They still thought of him as a great prophet, but no longer as the Messiah. "But we hoped that it was he who should redeem Israel." (Luke 24:19-21.) No; they did not think the Messiah would be killed; and when Jesus was killed, they no longer believed him to be the Messiah, till he rose again. With their idea that the Messiah would not be killed, but would remain on earth forever, how could they have asked about his second coming? But what was the import of their question? Compare the reports. Where Matthew has, "What shall be the sign of thy coming, and of the end of the world?" Mark has, "What shall be the sign when these things are all about to be accomplished?" And Luke has, "What shall be the sign when these things are about to come to pass?" For "the end of the world," the marginal reading has, "Or, the consummation of the age," that is the Jewish age. The three reports of the question begin with the words, "what shall be the sign?" Is it not reasonable, even necessary, to conclude that all that is in the question as reported by Matthew is in the question as reported by Mark and Luke? As the disciples believed that Jesus as Messiah would be a universal Monarch with his throne in Jerusalem, it would be natural for them to think that he, at the proper time, would return with his armies, and do what he had just told them would be done to the temple, destroy his enemies, and bring to an end that Jewish age.

Read the parable of the vineyard as recorded in Matt. 21:33-46; Mark 12:1-2; Luke 20:9-19. The Pharisees, scribes and priests were the ones who had charge of the vineyard. They had killed the prophets whom God had sent to them, and they were then plotting to kill the Son. What then was to be done with these wicked husbandmen? The verdict: The Lord of the vineyard "will come and destroy these husbandmen, and will give the vineyard unto others." The disciples heard this parable. Even the Jewish leaders knew it was aimed at them. And it seems that this parable was spoken the same day Jesus foretold the destruction of the temple. It was therefore fresh in the minds of the disciples, though they evidently did not see that the son was Jesus himself.

Jesus did not give a definite answer as to when these things would come to pass, but he gave several signs that would presage the near approach of this awful destruction, the greatest tribulation ever experienced or ever to be experienced by mankind. After giving the illustration of the fig tree, Jesus added, "Even ye also, when ye see these things, know ye that he is nigh, even at the doors." That is, they should know that his coming in destructive judgment on Jerusalem was nigh. But some, ignoring what was the topic of discussion, try to make the signs refer to events preceding the second coming of Christ. To them wars and rumors of wars are sure signs that the second coming of Christ is near; they will not see that Jesus gave them as signs of the near approach of the destruction of Jerusalem. Yet after mentioning these and other signs, presaging the near approach of the destruction of Jerusalem, Jesus said, "Verily I say unto you, this generation shall not pass away, till all these things shall be accomplished." But some will have it that *generation* here means *race*—that the Jewish *race* would not pass away till all these things were accomplished; but that would have Jesus making the absurd statement that the Jewish race would not cease to be till all things that were going to happen to them had happened! But the plain meaning is, that the generation then living would not pass away till all the things foretold about the destruction of Jerusalem had been accomplished. It was in part the answer to the question, "When shall these things be?" Jesus did not reveal to them the exact day nor hour when all these things would be accomplished. "But of that day and hour knoweth no one, not even the angels of heaven, neither the Son, but the Father only." And that is frequently quoted as referring to the second coming of Christ, though Jesus had just said that the generation then living would not pass away till all the things he had foretold had been accomplished. But no one, not even the angels knew when these things would be accomplished. The verse says nothing about the second coming of Christ, and it is astonishing that even casual Bible readers should so apply it. The phrase, "neither the Son," is not in the common version; and the American Standard Version has this foot-note: "Many authorities, some ancient, omit, *neither the Son.*" No one should put emphasis on a phrase that has so much against it. But even if it belongs in the text, the verse does not apply to the second coming. If it could be proved that the verse applies to his second coming and that Jesus while in the flesh was ignorant of the time it would occur, it does not prove that the glorified Christ is now ignorant of that time. Let us be far from charging the glorified Christ with ignorance—"in whom are all the treasures of wisdom and knowledge hidden." (Col. 2:3.)

I Learn By Listening

I was well acquainted with Brother R. A. McCurry who lived here, and passed away some time ago. He went to school very little, and had to work for a living all his long life. He did not call himself a preacher, though he preached some. He read much and was a good thinker. In combatting the idea that a sinner can do nothing to be saved, he quoted Luke 13:24: "Strive to enter in by the narrow door." He then asked, "Does not striving require an effort? Can a person strive without doing something?" The question that gave rise to the command to *strive* to enter in by the narrow door shows that Jesus was talking about entering by the narrow door into salvation. Think about it.

In a conversation with a Baptist preacher, this passage was quoted as it is in the King James version: "For what shall it profit a man, if he shall gain the whole world, and lose his own soul." (Mk. 8:36.) Said Brother McCurry, "A man—what man? Not the unregenerate man, for he is lost whether he gains the world or gains nothing. And not the regenerate man for you say he can do nothing to cause his soul to be lost. Now, what man?" That question has not been answered.

Yes, I learn by listening.

Some Scriptures Discussed

Read Gen. 4:1-9.

Some people profess to see a type in about every incident and person in the Old Testament. I cannot enumerate the many foolish notions I have heard advanced, along these lines. Some represent Abel as a type of Christ, and yet I have never seen even a supporting hint for that notion in all the Bible. Abel did not die for any body, and I cannot see that his death benefited any one. Do not advocate any notion that you cannot prove, and no one can prove that Abel was a type of Christ.

Gen. 6:14-16.

And some would have us believe that Noah's ark was a type, the three stories representing the world, the church, and heaven. But it will not fit. In caring for the animals Noah and his sons would have to pass daily from one story to the others, up and down, up and down. Can you make that fit. And there were more animals, fowls, and birds in the ark than people; can you make that fit? Some one said everybody in the ark were Noahs. Not so, there were no family names, no surnames, then—only individual names. But there is a type, image, or figure connected with the flood. Peter says that "eight souls were saved through water: which also after a true likeness doth now save you, even baptism." (1 Pet. 3:-20,21.) It has been foolishly remarked that they were saved from drowning by staying out of the water, but it is extremely foolish to say that any one was saved by water from drowning in water. But wherein is the figure—the true likeness of their being saved by water and our being saved by baptism? The water transported them from a world of corruption into a world made pure by water; and so baptism takes us out of a life of sin and corruption into a state of righteousness—out of the kingdom of darkness into the kingdom of Christ. Their being saved from drowning was not the type at all; if so, it could not be said that they were saved by water.

Read Gen. 11:1-9.

When I was young I heard it said that the people in the land of Shinar after the flood decided to build a tower so high that they could climb up it into heaven. I had an idea that that foolish notion was dead; but recently I read an article that advocated the notion that these people were trying to go to heaven on their own plan. Well, will curious notions never cease? Their proposed plan is plainly stated in Genesis 11:4. They said, "Come let us build us a city, and a tower, whose top may reach unto heaven." Now if they wanted to climb up that tower into heaven, why would they want to build a city to leave behind? Their proposed plan is plainly stated. Read this verse: "And they said, Come let us build us a city, and a tower, whose top may reach unto heaven, and let us make us a name; lest we be scattered abroad upon the face of the earth." It was their plan for unity. They wanted a centralized rallying point. God had commanded, "Be fruitful, and multiply, and replenish the earth;" but they did not want to "be scattered abroad upon the face of the whole earth." But here is what the Lord said of their efforts: "Behold, they are one people, and they have all one language; and this is what they begin to do: and nothing will be withholden from them, which they purpose to do. Come, let us go down, and there confound their language, that they may not understand one another's speech." And because their plan ran counter to God's plan, he confounded their language so they could not understand one another's speech. "So Jehovah scattered them abroad from thence upon the face of all the earth." All man-made schemes for unity fail. If people would study what to say instead of just studying something to say, it would help. Gen. 12:1-3.

A man may make a false argument and pervert some scriptures in support of the truth; but if he tries to argue for a false proposition he is bound to make false arguments and pervert the scriptures. About the longest, if not the longest, false argument I know of is the one in favor of infant sprinkling, based on the supposition that the church was organized in the family of Abraham. It is argued that circumcision was then the door of entrance into that supposed church, and that now baptism takes the place of circumcision. In his debate with Mr. Campbell, N. L. Rice put in most of his time in twelve speeches on that line of argument in an effort to prove that infants of believing parents should be "baptized." I mention this merely to show what importance the pedo-baptists attach to this line of argument, but I will not follow him in his rambling efforts to establish his proposition. It will be enough for the purpose of this article to show that the whole theory is wrong.

1. If the church began when God called him out

of Ur, and gave him the promises, as related in Gen. 12:1-3, then circumcision was not the door into the church, for Abraham was not circumcised till many years later.

2. Circumcision did not bring the descendants of Abraham into the covenant—they were born into it, and were cut off, if not circumcised. "And the uncircumcised male who is not circumcised in the flesh of his foreskin, that same shall be cut off from his people; he hath broken my covenant." (Gen. 17:14.) Unless the infant was in the covenant he could not break the covenant, nor be cut off from it. Yes, the infants of the chosen family of Abraham were born into the covenant. Abraham's men-servants—those bought with money—were circumcised. No faith on the part of these slaves was required. But if a foreigner joined Israel, it seems that he did so because he believed in Jehovah. (Ex. 12:48,49.) Pedo-baptists, at least some of them, assert that no mature males were ever circumcised except on the basis of faith, and they call on us *to prove* that their assertion is not true, though they give no proof of their assertion, which they cannot do. A man had to circumcise every man he bought, and not one word about making a believer of him first.

3. If the supposed Abrahamic church continued on in the Christian dispensation, even till now, there should have been some hold-over members; but so far as the record shows no Jew became a member of the church under the preaching of the apostles without baptism. Who were the hold-over members? Pedobaptists answer that no one can prove that the apostles were baptized. But the challenge does not meet

the issue. If we could not prove that the apostles were baptized, does that prove that they were not baptized? Pedo-baptists put the apostles forward as hold-over members; let them prove that they were not baptized. To make such proof they would have to show first that the apostles were sinless, and therefore did not need to make confession of sins and to be baptized. Could the apostles fulfill all righteousness by refusing to do what Jesus did? Those who refused to be baptized rejected the counsel of God against themselves (Luke 7:30,31.) Jesus would not make apostles out of men who rejected the counsel of God. Now read carefully Matt. 3:11,12: "I indeed baptize you in water unto repentance; but he that cometh after me is mightier than I, whose shoes I am not worthy to bear; he shall baptize you in the Holy Spirit and fire: whose fan is in his hand, and he will thoroughly cleanse his threshing-floor; and he will gather his wheat into the garner, but the chaff he will burn with unquenchable fire." The apostles were baptized in the Holy Spirit; the language shows plainly that they were among those whom John baptized in water.

4. Sometimes people take a position that involves more than they think. If the supposed Abrahamic church is identical with the church of Christ, then every living member before the cross continued to be a member after the cross. If not, then there is no identity. They tell us that circumcision was the door into the "Abrahamic church." If that were true, every Jew was a member of it. Whether Nicodemus was a good man or a bad man, what Jesus said to him is illuminating. "Except one"—Greek, *tis*, any

one—"be born anew he cannot see the Kingdom of God." "Any one" includes every one. Again, "Except one (any one) be born of water and the Spirit, he cannot enter into the Kingdom of God." And then Jesus uses the plural pronoun "ye"—"Ye must be born anew." That certainly included all the Jews. And it proves two things: (1) the Jews were not in the kingdom, or church, and (2) they would have to undergo radical change in order to enter.

5. Pedo-baptists seek support for their identity argument from Paul's olive tree illustration. (Rom. 11:17-24.) They assume that the olive tree represents the "Abrahamic church;" but if their assumption were correct, the infants of Jews were born into it, and still are. Read Rom. 11:11-22, and notice how Paul expresses the plight of the Jews—they fell, were cast away, broken off, cut off. From what did they fall, or were cast away, or were broken off? Read verse 22: "Behold then the goodness and severity of God: toward them that fell, severity; but toward thee, God's goodness, if thou continue in his goodness: otherwise thou also shalt be cut off." It was therefore God's goodness—his kindness to them —from which the Jews fell, or were cut off. Paul was not discussing the identity of things before the cross and after it.

6. If circumcision and baptism both answered the same purpose, why were both practiced on the same persons, as in the case of all Jews who were baptized? There is not an intimation that baptism took the place of circumcision. When the matter of circumcising the Gentile Christians was under consideration, why did not some one remind the Judaizers that

baptism took the place of circumcision? **Silence on** this point is conclusive evidence against the claim. And if baptism took the place of circumcision and served the same purpose, why did not Paul tell Gentiles that in being baptized they put themselves under the whole law of Moses? (See Gal. 5:3.)

7. The Messiah and his gospel were foretold in promise and prophecy, and revealed to us in the New Testament. We have a new and living way. (Heb. 10:20.) We have a new church. "But now in Christ Jesus ye that once were far off are made nigh in the blood of Christ. For he is our peace, who made both one, and brake down the middle wall of partition, having abolished in his flesh the enmity, even the law of commandments contained in ordinances; that he might create in himself of the two one new man, so making peace; and might reconcile them both in one body unto God through the cross, having slain the enmity thereby:" (Eph. 2:13-16.) This "new man" is the new church, and Christ is its foundation, builder, and Savior. The religion of Christ was ushered in as a new religion—a new covenant, a new priesthood, a new foundation, a new church, a new way. It is not the old way resurfaced, having new sign boards along the way; it is not the old church remodeled and moved onto a new foundation. The Judaizers tried to make the church a mere extension of Judaism. And Pedo-baptists have tried to do a similar thing.

Gen. 15:6.

One of the strangest and most inexcusable false arguments is based upon a perversion of Gen. 15:6: "And he believed in Jehovah; and he reckoned it to him for righteousness." This is connected with Paul's quotation of it Rom. 4:3. It seems to be taken for granted that both passages refer to the justification of an alien sinner, but notice Abraham's standing before God before this language was used. See the promise made to Abraham in Gen. 12:1-3: "Now Jehovah said to Abram, Get thee out of thy country and from thy kindred, and from thy father's house, unto the land that I will show thee: and I will make of thee a great nation, and I will bless thee, and make thy name great; and be thou a blessing: and I will bless them that bless thee, and him that curseth thee will I curse: and in thee shall all the families of the earth be blessed." Do you think that God made such promises to an unbelieving alien sinner? Then read this: "By faith Abraham, when he was called, obeyed to go out unto a place which he was to receive for an inheritance; and he went out, not knowing whither he went." (Heb. 11:8.) When he reached the land of Canaan, "Jehovah appeared unto Abram, and said, unto thy seed will I give this land: and there builded he an altar unto Jehovah, who appeared unto him." (Gen. 12:7.) Then he moved over near Bethel, "and there he builded an altar unto Jehovah, and called upon the name of Jehovah." (Gen. 12:8.) When he returned from Egypt, he went to the place of this altar; "and there Abram called on the name of Jehovah." (Gen. 13:4.) Again Jehovah appeared to Abram and renewed his promises of a numberless posterity and the land possession. (Gen. 13:14-18.) When Abram returned from rescuing Lot, Melchizedek, "priest of God Most High;" "blessed him, and said, Blessed be Abram of

God most High." Could that be said of an unbelieving alien? "After these things the word of Jehovah
came unto Abram in a vision, saying, Fear not,
Abram: I am thy shield, and thy exceeding great
reward." (Gen. 15:1.)   Such talk would not be made
to an unbelieving alien sinner. But Abraham's faith
in Jehovah's ability to overcome a defect of nature
was to be put to the test. Sarai was barren, and
God promised for Abram a son. Both were too old
according to nature to become parents; yet Abram
believed in Jehovah's power to fulfill his promise.

Notice Paul's language concerning Abram, "Who
in hope believed against hope, to the end that he
might become a father of many nations, according
to that which had been spoken, so shall thy seed be.
And without being weakened in faith he considered
his own body now as good as dead . . . ." (Rom.
4:18,19.)   "Wherefore also it was reckoned unto him
for righteousness." (v. 22.)   And so neither Gen.
15:5 nor Paul's argument in Rom. 4:3 has reference
to making an alien sinner into a righteous man. What
was the purpose of Paul's argument?

Peter's defence of his carrying the gospel to the
Gentiles convinced Jewish Christians that Gentiles
had a right to become children of God; but some said
that Gentile Christians must be circumcised and keep
the law of Moses, or they could not be saved. The
decrees that went out from Jerusalem should have
stopped that contention; but some fanatical perverts
kept up that contention. With them there could be
no righteousness aside from keeping the law of Moses. Paul had declared the gospel to be God's power
for salvation, for in it was revealed God's plan for

making men righteous. Paul was not arguing for justification by faith only as opposed to justification by an obedient faith, but for justification by gospel faith as opposed to justification by keeping the law. As the Judaizers contended that baptized believers, even if Gentiles, had to keep the law in order to be justified, it is plain that Paul was contending that baptized believers are justified by gospel faith, but as Christians could not be justified by the law, neither could aliens be justified by law.

Failing to see that Paul was not discussing justification by faith only as opposed to justification by the obedience of faith, but was discussing justification by the gospel as opposed to justification by the law, some have built a false and hurtful argument on verses 4 and 5: "Now to him that worketh, the reward is not reckoned as of grace, but as of debt. But to him that worketh not, but believeth on him that justifieth the ungodly, his faith is reckoned for righteousness." Denominational preachers, and some others tinctured with denominational ideas, have used these verses in trying to show that baptism is not a condition of salvation from alien sins; but as we have already seen, that was not the point in Paul's argument. The one who works, as Paul contemplates, receives the reward as a matter of debt. If baptism is the work Paul had in mind, then let us read it into the text: "Now to him that is baptized, the reward is not reckoned as of grace, but as of debt"—to him that is baptized the reward is reckoned as of debt. Again, if being baptized is the work Paul had in mind, then the only one whose faith is reckoned for righteousness is the one who is not baptized—the one who refuses to be baptized! But their contention is seen to be the more absurd in the fact that being baptized is not working—the one being baptized is not working at all: the Lord is doing the baptizing through the agency of the administrator. (John 4:1,2.) It seems that preachers and agitators cannot, or else will not, learn that the one who is being baptized is not working, but is passive; he is not operating, but is being operated upon. In no other act of obedience is the obedient person passive. It is true that he goes, or is taken, to the place of baptism, but in being baptized he is passive; just as a person goes, or is taken, to the hospital for an operation, but in the operation he is entirely passive. If preachers would realize these facts, they would quit using Rom. 4:4,5 in an effort to prove that baptism is a work which the one baptized does. When the matter is understood such attempted argument is so weak that any intelligent man will be ashamed to so argue.

If a Jew had kept the law perfectly, he would have been justified on the grounds of his works; yet sometime ago a writer in the Gospel Advocate denied that self-evident truth, and brought forth the case of Paul as proof.

"Impute—Reckon." In some Confessions of Faith and Church Manuals, as also in many sermons and theological writings, the claim is made that righteousness of Christ is imputed—transferred—to the believer, also the obedience and sanctification of Christ is imputed, or credited, to the believer. In this view the believer is credited with something that he does not have, something that really belongs to another. And so a peculiar twist was given the word "impute," a meaning that originated in the brains of theologians; and with this supposed meaning of the word in mind, they find their doctrine in Rom. 4, though the doctrine is not in that chapter nor any other chapter. In that chapter is a Greek verb (logidzomai) which is translated in the Common Version by three different verbs, namely, count - reckon - impute; but the American Standard Version does not have "impute" in the entire chapter. "Impute" in Rom. 5:13, is from a different verb. To impute something to a person does not mean that you charge, or credit, him with something that he does not have.

It seems that Albert Barnes, a Presbyterian Commentator, made a close study of this matter. He says, "In the Old Testament the verb—(hashab), which is translated by the word "logidzomai" means literally, "to think, to intend, or purpose; to imagine, invent or devise; to reckon, or account; to esteem; to impute" i.e., to impute to a man what belongs to himself, or what 'ought' to be imputed to him." He then gives a list of the many places where the word occurs in the Old Testament, and then gives this observation: "I have examined 'all' the passages; and as the result of my examination have come to the conclusion that there is not 'one' in which the word is used in the sense of 'reckoning' or 'imputing' to a man that which does not strictly 'belong' to him; or of charging on him that which 'ought' not to be charged on him as a matter of personal right. The word is never used to denote 'imputing' in the sense of 'transferring,' or of charging that on one which does not properly belong to him. The same is the case in the New Testament. The word occurs about forty times (see Schmidius'

Concord.), and in a similar signification. No doctrine of 'transferring,' or setting over to a man what does not properly belong to him, be it sin or holiness, can be derived, therefore, from the word." And James MacKnight says, "As it is nowhere said in scripture, that Christ's righteousness is imputed to believers." Honest scholarship compelled these men to go contrary to their Confession of Faith.

Abraham's faith was not reckoned to him as righteousness, or as equal to righteousness, or as a substitute for righteousness; but it was reckoned to him (eis) in order to righteousness—(Eis) into, unto, or in order to, righteousness. Paul quoted from Gen. 15:6. Abraham had been a believer in Jehovah for many years, but his faith had not been perfect, though he all this time had been a worshipper of God. He had not perfectly obeyed the command to get out from his kindred and his father's house; and it does not seem that it was in God's plan that he should go down into Egypt, and he certainly did wrong in having Sarai to make a false statement to Pharaoh; but when he believed God's promise that he should be the father of a son, when all nature indicated otherwise, God recognized the greatness of his faith, and reckoned it to him as the basis for the forgiveness of his sins, thus making him a righteous man. Righteousness was then reckoned to him. No sin was then reckoned to him, for his sins had been forgiven.

It seems to me that those who advocate the doctrine of imputing, or transferring the personal righteousness of Christ to the credit of the believer fail to understand the purpose and power of the gospel. Paul says that the gospel is God's power to save believers, for in it is revealed God's plan for making men righteous, a plan by which sinners may be made righteous. He does not "play like" a man is righteous when he is not, but he takes him through a process of cleansing that makes him clean, free from sin, just as a washer-woman takes a soiled garment through a process of cleansing that makes it clean. It may become soiled again, and so also may a cleansed man become polluted again by sin; "but if we walk in the light, as he is in the light, we have fellowship one with another, and the blood of Jesus his Son cleanseth us from all sin. . . . If we confess our sins, he is faithful and righteous to forgive our sins, and cleanse us from all unrighteousness." (1 John 1:7-9.) That makes a man righteous, and God reckons righteousness to him, for he is righteous. It is a righteousness to which we attain. (Rom. 9:30.)

JUSTIFIED BY LAW: Any law justifies the one who keeps it perfectly. If a Jew had kept the law of Moses perfectly, he would have been justified by the law; he would have merited justification. I have enlarged on this point, both in sermons and in print. But several months ago a staff writer for the Gospel Advocate took issue with the idea, though he did not call any name and may not have had my writing in mind. Anyway he pronounced the idea a mistake. Well, if a man under the law kept it perfectly, and was not justified but was still a sinner, why was he not justified? And why was he still a sinner? I can see how an advocate of the doctrine of inherited sin could contend that a Jew was still a sinner, even if he kept the law perfectly, and was guilty of no sin of his; but how can any man who repudiates that doc-

trine argue that a Jew was still unjustified, still a
sinner, even though he kept the law perfectly. What
proof did the brother give? That Paul said that as
touching the law he was blameless. (Phil. 3:6.) And
yet he considered himself a great sinner. That is all
true; and it is also true that Ananias told him to be
baptized, and wash away his sins. But what does
all that prove against what I said? Nothing, absolutely nothing. The law ended at the cross, and ceased
to be God's law. No one could then be justified by it
in God's sight, even though he kept it perfectly. And
between the cross and his conversion, Saul became a
great sinner in persecuting Christians. The brother's
argument therefore has no point to it, and it is strange
that he himself did not see the fallacy of his argument. If a man is not justified by a law when he
keeps it perfectly, then there is no such thing as justice: "For Moses writeth that the man that doeth the
righteousness which is of the law shall live thereby,"
(Rom. 10:5; Lev. 18:5), that is, he shall not be condemned. Such a man would have been righteous, and
to be righteous is to be in a state of justification;
". . . for not the hearers of the law are just before
God, but the doers of the law shall be justified." (Rom.
2:13.) Paul's statement is too plain to be misunderstood—"the doers of the law shall be justified." Again
the writer said: "Some think that a man would have
been justified had he obeyed the law perfectly, but
that is not correct; for Paul says that 'by the works
of the law shall no flesh be justified.' (Gal. 2:16)."
Such was the brother's reasoning.

Several things are wrong with the brother's reasoning. Remember he was arguing that perfect obe-

dience to the law justified no one. To use Gal. 2:16 to mean, as the brother evidently did, that no one could be justified by perfect obedience to the law, makes Paul plainly contradict himself, when he said that "the doers of the law shall be justified." (Rom. 2:13.) With his idea he cannot show the harmony between the two passages. If you will read with understanding Gal. 3:10 you will see this matter clearly as to why people could be justified by the law and why they could not be justified by the law: "For as many as are of the works of the law are under a curse: for it is written, Cursed is every one who continueth not in all things that are written in the book of the law, to do them." To be under the curse of the law is opposite of being justified by the law; and people were under the curse of the law because they failed to do all that the law required. Had they done *all* the law required they would not have been under a curse, and would therefore have been justified. But what about Paul's statement, that, "as touching the righteousness which is of the law blameless," and yet his confession that he was the chief of sinners. It seems incredible that the brother did not know that Paul's relation to the law had nothing to do with his confessing himself to be chief of sinners. It seems that Paul tells us why he considered himself such a sinner. (1 Tim. 1:13-15.) The law was not binding after the cross. Certainly Paul was not "a blasphemer, and a persecutor, and injurious" while the law was in force, for a blasphemer under the law was not blameless. Paul became the chief of sinners when he became the leader of others in blaspheming the name of Christ and in persecuting the church, and making havoc of it. If a man had kept the law perfectly after the cross, he would not have been justified in the sight of God. It is astonishing that the brother used the case of Paul to prove that no one could have been justified by the law, for the sins he charges against himself were committed after the law ended.

According to the brother's argument God gave a law, which a man might keep perfectly, and yet be the chief of sinners. That makes God a whimsical tyrant. If a man kept the law perfectly, wherein was he a sinner? He was not a sinner by transgression, if he kept the law perfectly. What made him a sinner? Was he a sinner by inheritance?

The brother put an undue stress on the word "blameless" in Paul's statement, that, "as touching the righteousness which is of the law, blameless." If he did not use that to prove that Paul had never violated any provision of the Old Covenant, then there was no point in bringing it up. Apply that meaning to a man under the New Covenant, we could have no elders or deacons, for both must be blameless! (1 Tim. 3:10; Tit. 1:6,7.) And no member of the church could be blameless, for, "If we say that we have no sin, we deceive ourselves, and the truth is not in us." (1 John 1:8.) Yet we are taught to be blameless. (Phil. 2:15; 2 Pet. 3:14.)

If a man under the law violated any requirement, and then made the required offerings and sacrifices he was then blameless. If a church member violates any New Covenant requirement, and then makes the required confession, he is then blameless.

Exodus 14:

Two commands in Exodus 14 have been mistakenly

contrasted to show a difference between man's command and God's command. Moses said, "Stand still; and see the salvation of Jehovah." Jehovah said to Moses, "Speak unto the children of Israel, that they go forward." Sometimes we get so anxious to make a point that we use a passage of scripture without noticing its connection or why the words were spoken or written. That should never be done. Moses was not setting forth a do-nothing doctrine—he said just what needed to be said, as you will see by reading carefully the preceding verses, "And Jehovah spake unto Moses, saying, Speak unto the children of Israel, that they turn back and encamp before Pihahiroth, between Migdol and the sea, before Baal-zephon: over against it shall ye encamp by the sea. And Pharaoh will say of the children of Israel, They are entangled in the land, the wilderness hath shut them in. And I will harden Pharaoh's heart, and he shall follow after them; and I will get me honor upon Pharaoh, and upon all his host; and the Egyptians shall know that I am Jehovah. And they did so." (Ex. 14:1-4.) So Moses knew that disaster would come upon the Egyptians, though it does not seem that Jehovah directed Moses. So when they saw the Egyptians closing in on them and they saw no way of escape, they raised a howl. To quiet them and keep down a panic, Moses said, with good reason, "Fear ye not, stand still, and see the salvation of Jehovah, which he will work for you today: for the Egyptians whom ye have seen today, ye shall see them again no more forever. Jehovah will fight for you, and ye shall hold your peace." This language shows Moses' faith and confidence in Jehovah.

Why did he say, "Stand still?" That should be plain to any thoughtful reader who has faith in Jehovah. They had gone as far as they had directions to go; they had encamped where Jehovah told them to camp. When the Egyptians came in sight, if Moses and the people had moved without further directions from Jehovah, they would have done as many religious people do today.

It is a great lesson to us, if we heed it. Do not move in any direction without divine guidance. And when you shall have done all that God has commanded you to do, as Moses and the people had done up to that encampment, then and only then will you have the right to stand still and see the salvation of Jehovah. But as the gospel has marked out your duty for life, you will not reach the end of the way marked out until you reach the point where you cannot do more. There is this however: if at any time in life you reach the point where you do not know what to do next, wait—do not do anything—till by study you find God's will in the matter. Then act promptly.

When the people saw the Egyptians, they began to murmur, and to blame Moses for the fate they felt sure was about to come upon them. Moses had led them as far as God had commanded him to go. It would be natural for him to pray God's protection and guidance. Jehovah said to him, "Why criest thou unto me? speak unto the children of Israel, that they go forward." But how could they go forward, for the Red Sea was before them? How they crossed the Red Sea, and how the Egyptian army was destroyed is plainly told. Jehovah opened up the way, but the people had to do the crossing. "Thus Jehovah saved

Israel that day out of the hand of the Egyptians."
(Ex. 14:30.) In this manner—by opening a way for
them and by doing as Jehovah directed—Jehovah
saved them from the Egyptians.

Ex. 27:20; Lev. 24:2:

Basing their contention on the word *continually*
as used in such passages as Ex. 27:20; Lev. 24:2
some have argued that the lamps in the Holy Place
were never allowed to go out, and they suppose this
is a type of the word of God in the church. It makes
a pretty little theory, but has no foundation in fact.
The lamps could not burn while being moved from
camp to camp; neither could there have been fire on
the altar of burnt-offerings. (See Num. 4:9-14.) For
a thing to be done continually or perpetually, does
not mean that there are no regular intermissions. David said to Mephibosheth, "Thou shalt eat bread at my
table continually . . . " (2 Sam 9:7-13) " . . . he did
eat *continually* at the king's table." The priests were
to offer "The tenth part of an ephah of fine flour
for a meal offering perpetually, half of it in the
morning, and half thereof in the evening." (Lev.
6:10,20.) That offering was to be made perpetually,
yet only of mornings and evenings. Notice this:
"Now this is that which thou shalt offer upon the
altar: two lambs a year old day by day continually.
The one lamb thou shalt offer in the morning; and
the other lamb thou shalt offer at evening." (Ex.
29:38,39.) There was several hours intermission between these offerings, yet they were to be made morning and evening continually. And so the lamps did
not burn without any interruption. Of the altar of
incense and the lamps it is said, "And Aaron shall

burn thereof incense of sweet spices: every morning when he dresseth the lamps, he shall burn it. And when Aaron lighteth the lamps at even, he shall burn it, a perpetual incense before Jehovah throughout your generations." (Ex. 30:7,8.) The lamps were dressed of mornings and lighted at evening. The following incident shows that the lights burned into the night till the oil in them was consumed, and then went out. "And it came to pass at that time, when Eli was laid down in his place (now his eyes had begun to wax dim, so that he could not see), and the lamp of God was not yet gone out, and Samuel was laid down to sleep, in the temple of Jehovah, where the ark of God was; . . ." (1 Sam. 3:2,3).

I would not deny that the lamps of the candlestick were a type of the word of God, but there are difficulties in such an idea. The lamps did not burn while Israel was on the march from camp to camp. It seems that the lamps were lighted at evening and burned into the night so long as the oil lasted, then went out. Besides, these lamps gave light only to those who went into the Holy Place—the light shined only in the Holy Place, and only for the priests. That would fit fairly well the Calvinists' idea that the word of God benefited only those within the circle of the regenerate. I used to hear the Primitive Baptists argue long and loud, that the word of God did not do the unregenerate person any good—it was not a light to him. I do not think the Primitive Baptists ever thought of using the candlestick as a type of the word of God, and from that idea argue that, as the candlestick gave light in the Holy Place only, so the word gives light to them who are in the fold, and to no one else. I leave you to wrestle with them on that point.

1 Samuel 21:1-10:

Sometimes writers and speakers, to stir people to greater action, make a stagger at quoting David's language, making him say: "The king's business demands haste." But even to quote that correctly in an effort to stir people to action is to show little respect for truthfulness. Read 1 Samuel 21:1-10. When David knew that King Saul was fully determined to kill him, he fled into hiding. "Then came David to Nob to Abimelech the priest: And Abimelech came to meet David trembling, and said unto him, Why art thou alone, and no man with thee? And David said unto Abimelech the priest, The king hath commanded me a business, and hath said unto me, Let no man know anything of the business whereabout I send thee, and what I have commanded thee: and I have appointed the young men to such and such a place." There was no truth in these words of David. David then asked for bread, and the priest gave him the holy bread. Then David asked for sword or spear —"for I have neither brought my sword nor my weapons with me, because the king's business required haste."

That statement is as false as can be; he was not on the king's business at all, but was fleeing from the king to save his life. Yet people will quote these words as if they are gospel truth. It is a shame to do so. We need to know the difference between an inspired statement and a false statement recorded by inspiration.

Jer. 6:16:

Brethren sometimes preach sermons and write articles on Jer. 6:16: "Thus saith Jehovah, Stand ye in the ways and see, and ask for the old paths, where is the good way: and walk therein, and ye shall find rest for your souls: but they said, We will not walk therein." Now, when you preach on that text, do you urge people to seek "the old paths" that Jehovah was urging the Jews to seek? I heard one brother preach a sermon on that text, urging brethren to seek the old paths, but before he finished, he said we now have a new and living way! No, I have never preached a sermon nor written an article on Jeremiah 6:16; I prefer to urge people to seek the new and living way, and to walk in it. This new and living way is "the way which he dedicated for us." (Heb. 10:19,20.)

A New Twist—John 4:1-3:

Recently I heard one of Frank Norris' preachers say over the radio, "If baptism is essential to salvation, Jesus did not save any one, for he baptized no one." Read the passage he was talking about: "When therefore the Lord knew that the Pharisees had heard that Jesus was making and baptizing more disciples than John (although Jesus himself baptized not, but his disciples), he left Judea, and departed again into Galilee." (John 4:1-3.) It is plainly stated that Jesus made and baptized more disciples than John. How did he baptize them? Through his authorized agents. A merchant sells goods even when he is a thousand miles from his store; he does it through his authorized salesmen. People are saved by faith, though Jesus does not now in person cause any one to believe; people are made believers by his disciples. The Baptists might as well say that, if faith is essential to salvation, then Jesus has not saved any one since he ascended from the earth, for he has not in that time in person made any believers. Let us put it this way:

> If baptism is essential to salvation,
> then he saved no one;
> for he in person baptized no one.

Now this:

> If faith is essential to salvation,
> then Jesus now saves no one;
> for he in person produces faith in no one.

Absurd? Worse; it is concentrated foolishness.

Luke 2:7—No Room for Jesus.

Do you take a text when you preach? It is a useless habit. Sometimes a preacher will take a word or two out of a verse, and use them as a basis when the sermon has no reference to the verse out of which he extracted the word or two. Is that treating the word of God right? Sometimes a passage is perverted or an incident distorted to get a basis for a fanciful sermon. You have heard sermons on "No Room for Jesus." The subject of the sermon is drawn from a perversion of the scriptures and a misstatement of facts concerning the birth of Jesus. It seems to be assumed that the innkeeper was very much opposed to the unborn Jesus, so much so that he would not let him be born in his inn! If that is not the assumption, then there is no point in saying there was no room for him in the inn. But I heard one preacher say that the Bible says that there was no room for him in the inn, but the Bible says no such thing. What

Luke says about the birth of Jesus and the circumstances connected with it is a beautiful and touching narrative, if we read it just as it is without trying to read into it some false ideas.

We cannot know how many of those who came to be enrolled had been born in Bethlehem, nor how many whose forefathers were from Bethlehem, but sufficient number had come from other places to take up all the rooms in the inn before Joseph and Mary arrived. So far as we know many others besides Joseph and Mary found no room in the inn. Nor do we know how long Joseph and Mary were there before Jesus was born. Notice the language: "And it came to pass while they were there, that the days were fulfilled that she should be delivered. And she brought forth her firstborn son; and she wrapped him in swaddling clothes, and laid him in a manger, because there was no room for them in the inn." Custom has much to do with the way people feel about things. Even now in some places animals and people are sheltered under the same roof. Besides there is no indication that Joseph and Mary were in the same stable with animals. But it was a lowly beginning for the earth life of Jesus. However it seems certain that he never mentioned it in his whole public life—he made no effort to gain fame by referring to his lowly beginning. And yet his mission was not to the proud and haughty, but to the meek and lowly.

John 12:32:

A preacher once told me of a great sermon he had heard on "Lifting Up Christ" from the text, "And I, if I be lifted up from the earth, will draw all men unto myself." In the sermon it was argued that we may "lift up Christ" in our walk, conversation, worship, and preaching. But the text has no such thought in it. Jesus had reference to being lifted up on the cross, as the next verse plainly declares: "But this he said signifying by what manner of death he should die." (John 12:33.) I so informed the brother, and he astonished me further by saying, "Could it not be made to refer to these other things also?" To make the statement of Jesus refer to any one of a dozen things is to convict him of talking to no purpose. In each statement of scripture the Holy Spirit sought to convey certain information to our minds. When that information is gleaned from a passage you have all there is in it. Trying to make more out of it is not "handling aright the word of truth." It is hard for some folks to realize that a passage of scripture means now just what it meant when written. If a passage means one thing, then it does not mean another.

Acts 2:

It has been argued that the apostles did not speak different languages on Pentecost, but that some kind of a miracle was wrought on the air waves so that each one present heard his own language; but if that were true, then the apostles did not speak in different tongues. And yet the record plainly says, "And they were all filled with the Holy Spirit, and began to speak with other tongues, as the Spirit gave them utterance." All the apostles spoke. Peter evidently spoke to the Jews of Jerusalem and Judea. Notice his first words: "Ye men of Judea, and all ye that dwell at Jerusalem . . . ." And he reminds them that they knew of the mighty works which God did by Jesus in their midst. Evidently the others were speaking to different groups, but only Peter's speech was recorded, and that I judge in a very condensed form. They spake in other tongues as the Spirit gave them utterance. That is stated in language too plain to be misunderstood. Why should any one espouse a theory that flatly contradicts Luke's plain statement?

Several months ago I read an article in one of "our" papers, in which the writer told how people were saved. Then he made the strange statement, that after a person is saved, the Lord adds him to the church, and the saved person has nothing to do with being added, the Lord does that. That is a false argument. Think a little. The Lord saves, too, does he not? If the brother is correct in his reasoning, then a man has nothing to do in being saved, for the Lord saves. Besides, the church is the family of God; and being born again adds one to this family, and there is no subsequent adding to be done.

1 Cor. 2:9:

Perhaps no verse of Scripture has been so often thoughtlessly misused as 1 Cor. 2:9, the quotation is usually made from the King James Version, and applied to the glories of heaven. Likely you have heard it quoted in exhortation and funeral talks. It is argued that the verse teaches that we do not know the glories of heaven. I suppose we do not fully know the glories of heaven, but that is not what Paul is saying. It is strange that so many preachers can accurately quote verse nine but seem never to have seen verse ten. Concerning what is said in verse nine Paul immediately adds, "But unto us God revealed them

through the Spirit." The Spirit knows the things
of God. The apostles received the Spirit that they
might know the things that God freely gives—"which
things also we speak." If you really want to get the
force of Paul's line of reasoning here, you should begin with chapter 1, verse 17. He was sent to preach
the gospel, but not in words of wisdom, "lest the cross
of Christ should be made void."

From chapter 1 verse 18 through chapter 2 Paul
delivers a powerful argument on the absolute necessity of a revelation from God. Verses 19 and 20 apply to the Jews, as shown by the quotation from Isaiah and Paul's mentioning the scribes. Their wise
men, their scribes and disputers—what had they concluded as to the blessings the Messiah, the promised
Redeemer, would bring? Paul pronounced their rea-
sonings foolishness. You who tell us the Jews had
a correct understanding of the nature of the Messiah's kingdom and its blessings, think on what Paul
says. Or just what do they think Paul meant by saying that God made their wisdom foolishness?

"The world through its wisdom knew not God."
The wisdom of the world includes all that man knows,
aside from what God has revealed. God has never
been discovered by scientific or philosophic research.
And yet any one is bound to know that back of every
made thing, there is a maker or makers; but no one
studying nature can know whether all things were
made by one God or by a thousand Gods. The idea
of one God is due to revelation. The heathen nations
who had no revelation had a god for about every
force and phenomenon of nature. And the sad thing
is that people who believe in one God attribute to him

characteristics to suit themselves. And until God revealed the blessings he had in store in the redemption that is in Christ Jesus, no eye had seen, and no ear had heard, nor man's heart conceived, the riches of the blessings in Christ. Paul tells how we came to know these things. "But unto us God revealed them through the Spirit, . . . that we might know the things that were freely given to us of God. Which things also we speak." And so we may know what man's natural powers, without revelation, could never see nor hear nor know. So let us not ignorantly try to make it appear that we are still in the condition mentioned in verse nine.

1 Cor. 10:1,2:

"For I would not, brethren, have you ignorant, that our fathers were all under the cloud, and all passed through the sea; and were all baptized unto Moses in the cloud and in the sea." (1 Cor. 10:1,2.) Let us get some of the facts about this baptism; if you will notice that there were two elements in their baptism, cloud and sea, it will help you to see the folly of some theories, for some foolish statements have been made about it in an effort to make this baptism sprinkling. Jehovah divided the waters of the sea and dried the passageway: "And the children of Israel went into the midst of the sea and upon dry ground: and the waters were a wall unto them on their right hand, and on their left." (Ex. 14:22.) The cloud that had gone before them moved back behind them, and was darkness to the Egyptians, so the children of Israel were buried out of the sight of the Egyptians, baptized in the cloud and in the sea.

The theory has been advanced, that the wind blew a mist or spray from the walls of water; but that leaves entirely out one element of their baptism. If they were baptized by a mist or spray, the cloud had no part in their baptism. Besides in their song of deliverance, they sang, "And with the blast of thy nostrils the waters were piled up, the floods stood upright as a heap; the deeps were congealed in the heart of the sea." (Ex. 15:8.) So the walls of water were frozen ise.

Another theory is, that it rained on them as they marched across; but the record plainly says they marched on dry land. Besides, if they were baptized in the rain, they were not baptized in the cloud and in the sea. Both of these theories contradict the plain word of God, which says plainly that they were baptized in the cloud and in the sea. "Thus Jehovah saved Israel that day out of the hand of the Egyptians." (Ex. 14:30.) The passage in Psalms 68:7-9 refers to what occurred at Sinai.

"By faith they passed through the Red Sea as by dry land: which the Egyptians assaying to do were swallowed up." (Heb. 11:29.) You have often heard it said that if a person has to do anything to be saved, that leaves the Lord out and makes the person his own savior. They crossed "by faith," but any one knows they did not cross by faith only. They did not simply trust God, and were immediately transported to the other side. Here the term "by faith" spans the Red Sea from shore to shore, and therefore includes every step they took, and all that was done in crossing. It therefore includes their baptism unto Moses in the cloud and in the sea. Or, according to the marginal reading in the American Standard Version, they were baptized into Moses—into the complete leadership of Moses. Previous to their baptism they were in Egyptian territory, and were unwilling subjects of Pharaoh; but by crossing the Red Sea by faith, being baptized into Moses, they became entirely free from the dominion of Pharaoh. And as "faith" included baptism in the case of Israel, so does "faith" include baptism when it refers to becoming children of God. Notice carefully Gal. 3:26,27: "For ye are all sons of God, through faith, in Christ Jesus. For as many of you as were baptized into Christ did put on Christ." They were children of God by faith, because they had been baptized into Christ. So then their faith included baptism. But it is argued that Israel were the Lord's people before they crossed the Red Sea. Certainly, and they were the Lord's people when they went down into Egypt. But it seems that Paul was using their salvation from the Egyptian bondage as a type of our deliverance from the bondage of sin. It is argued that they were saved by the blood on the lintels and doorposts. Now, were they? The blood saved only the first born in each family from death by the destroying angel, the others were safe. It had nothing to do with salvation from sin; and yet Christians sing, "When I see the blood," so ignorant are we! The blood saved the firstborn from physical death—no one else; the baptism in the cloud and sea saved the whole nation from Egyptian bondage. Baptized into, or unto Moses—into his leadership, guidance, and care, and freed from their former bondage.

1 Cor. 11:1:

"Be ye imitators of me, even as also I am of Christ."
I have heard it argued this way: you follow me only
in so far as I follow Christ. But that implies that
these Corinthians were so familiar with the way
Christ lived that they could know just how he lived.
With that view Paul was not an example to them at
all. If that had been what Paul meant he would have
said, "Be ye imitators of Christ," for Paul was not
given to the use of unnecessary words. No, Paul was
putting himself forward as an example for them to
imitate. Notice 1 Cor. 4:16: "I beseech you therefore
be ye imitators of me." Again Phil. 3:17: "Brethren,
be imitators together of me, and mark them that so
walk even as ye have us for an ensample." Also Phil.
4:9: "The things which ye both learned and received,
and heard and saw in me, these things do." Paul did
not mean that Christians should follow him as if he
were their Lord, but because his life was an example
of what a Christian should be.

1 Cor. 12, 13, 14:

There has been some loose talk about things in the
twelfth, thirteenth and fourteenth chapters of First
Corinthians. Spiritual gifts and miraculous powers
are discussed in these chapters. Even chapter thirteen is not primarily a lesson of love, but Paul is there
showing the superiority of love over the spiritual
gifts coveted by the Corinthians. And chapter twelve
verse 28, is often misapplied: "And God hath set some
in the church, first apostles, secondly prophets, third-
ly teachers, then miracles, then gifts of healings,
helps, governments, divers kinds of tongues." From
this some have argued that the apostles become mem-

bers of the church before any one else did; but that
misses the point entirely. Paul was not talking
about putting members in the church. Does any one
think God made "miracles, then gifts of healings,
helps, governments, divers kinds of tongues," members of the church? In the church the apostles were
first in rank, and not in point of time.

"These three:" And now abideth faith, hope, love,
these three; and the greatest of these is love. (1 Cor.
13:13.) Many times it has been said that love is
the greatest because it will continue on in eternity
when faith and hope have ceased. That has been said
by the people who do more talking than thinking.
These three abide, and there is not a hint that either
will ever cease. Yet you perhaps have often heard
some preacher say something like this: "When we
get to heaven faith will be lost in sight, hope will
end in a richer fruition than hope had ever dared to
envision, but love will continue on into eternity—it
will never end." Considering only the language, it
makes a rather beautiful conception, if it were wholly
true, but that statement has no support in reason
or revelation. Who originated the notion that faith
is lost in sight? Perhaps it grew out of 2 Cor. 5:7:
"We walk by faith, and not by sight." But if you
will notice this marginal reading in the American
Standard Version, you will find that the Greek means
"not by appearance." And so, according to the marginal reading the verse should read, "We walk by
faith, not by appearance." And that opens up a
field for some very profitable thinking.

Faith in a person always has in it an element of
trust or confidence, and the more you see and the

better you know people the more faith you have in them. Sight has sometimes restored faith. You who think faith is lost in sight, did you ever read what Jesus said to Thomas? Then read it: "Because thou hast seen me thou hast believed." And what was true of Thomas was true of all who believed in Jesus before he was crucified. Why single out Thomas and call him "doubting Thomas?" They all doubted till they saw the Lord alive. Sight revived faith in all of them. No, faith is not lost in sight.

What of hope? Hope is made up of desire and expectation. When you obtain the thing you desire and expect, you do not hope for that particular thing any more, though you may hope to remain in possession of it. Now, does any one think that desire and expectation will end when we get to heaven? I would not be dogmatic, but surely heaven is not a place of stagnation—nothing like that. "Therefore are they before the throne of God; and they serve him day and night in his temple." (Rev. 7:15.) "And his servants shall serve him." (Rev. 22:3.) We know not what shall be the nature of that service, but it seems to me that in all agreeable service there is bound to be desire and expectation. We would certainly hope that our service would be pleasing to the Lord, and that we would not suffer the fate of some angels. (2 Pet. 2:4.)

Some who think faith and hope will cease when we get to heaven but love will continue, on that false notion, conclude that love is the greatest; but is any thing great because of its continuity? Love is greatest here and now. Verse 13 is a conclusion of the preceding part of the chapter. No matter how great the faith is, it is as nothing without love, and without love it profits nothing. Love gives vitality to faith and makes hope possible. Faith and hope are both necessary, but neither, nor both together, can do what love does. Love is the great moulder of character. "Love suffereth long, and is kind; love envieth not; love vaunteth not itself, is not puffed up, doth not behave unseemly, seeketh not its own, is not provoked, taketh not account of evil; rejoiceth not in unrighteousness, but rejoiceth with the truth; beareth all things, believeth all things, love never faileth." That is character, Christian character; it is what love does for us in our relations with our fellow beings.

"But now abideth faith, hope, love, these three: and the greatest of these is love." All three *abide*.

"Ambassadors—Earthen Vessels:" 2 Cor. 5:20, "We are ambassadors therefore on behalf of Christ." Paul speaks of himself as "an ambassador in chains." (Eph. 6:20.) These two are the only passages in the New Testament where the Greek word occurs. It will do you good to look up the definition of the English word "ambassador," for it fairly represents the Greek word. And yet we sometimes hear a preacher refer to himself as an ambassador for Christ. He is either ignorant or presumptuous. The apostles were ambassadors; none others were.

A mistake, similar to that made concerning ambassadors, is made concerning "This treasure in earthen vessels." "But we have this treasure in earthen vessels, that the exceeding greatness of the power may be of God, and not from ourselves." (2 Cor. 4:7.) A fair study of the context will show that Paul had reference to the apostles. In the third chapter he says, "And such confidence have we through Christ to God-ward: not that we are sufficient of ourselves, to account anything as from ourselves; but our sufficiency is from God; who also made us sufficient as ministers of a new covenant." (2 Cor. 3:4-6.) In and of themselves the apostles would not have been sufficient to minister, or reveal the new covenant, but God, by the baptism of the Holy Spirit, made them sufficient. Then Paul makes some comments on the superiority of the new over the old, and then says, "Therefore seeing we have this ministry . . . " this ministry of the new covenant, "even as we obtained mercy we faint not." (4:1.) In verse 3 he calls it "our gospel," meaning the gospel which they preached, the gospel for which they were ministers. Notice how the light of the gospel goes out: "Seeing it is God, that said, Light shall shine out of darkness, who shined in our hearts, to give the light of the knowledge of the glory of God in the face of Jesus Christ" (v. 6.) How can light shine out of darkness? In and of himself a man cannot give out any spiritual light—in him is only darkness, but by the Holy Spirit light shined out of these apostles— out of these men who of themselves were darkness, but out of them shone forth the glorious light of the knowledge of God. And then Paul calls this knowledge of the glory of God a "treasure." "But we have this treasure in earthen vessels, that the exceeding greatness of the power may be of God, and not from ourselves."

The whole connection shows that they were the earthen vessels in whom and by whom the treasure was conveyed to the world; and it was conveyed to the world by men—"earthen vessels"—that it might be known that the exceeding greatness of the power of that message was not in the messenger. Do you see the significance of this? Use your imagination, and you will see. Suppose, on Pentecost, a group of angels had poised in the air over Jerusalem, and had preached the gospel to the astonished people as they gazed toward the heavens—well why was it not done that way? And why was it not so done in other cities? Why put the task on men, thus subjecting them to all sorts of persecution and even death in taking that message to a lost and hostile world, when angels could have announced the gospel out of any danger of harm? But suppose this had been done till it became safe for men to preach. But what then? People would have said, the gospel is powerful when an angel preaches it, but what good will it do when preached by a mere man? They would have thought the power was in the vessel and not in what was brought in the vessel. As it is, I used to hear some good old simple minded Primitive Baptists put stress on a supposed audible sound. They loved to quote John 5:25, and never failed to stress voice— " . . . the dead shall hear the VOICE of the Son of God; and they that hear shall live." Had they read such passages as Gen. 4:10; Acts 13:27 they would have known that *voice* did not always mean an audible sound. With them, what had been said and recorded was "a dead letter" to the unregenerate till he heard that mystic *voice*. For that reason many turned away their ears from hearing the truth. Instead of Pilate's question,

"What is truth?" they posed another question, "What account is truth to the unregenerate?

Eph. 6:10-20:

Armor of God: "And take the helmet of salvation, and the sword of the Spirit, which is the word of God." Read about the armor of God in Ephesians 6:10-20. It is well to keep in mind that the armor of God is not the armor that God puts on, but the armor he furnishes his soldiers. And yet often you hear some one say that the word is the sword which the Spirit uses. Often I have heard it argued that the word is effective if the Spirit uses it, but not at all effective when man uses it—the sword of the Spirit must be used by the Spirit! Such arguers do not notice that Paul commands the brethren to take "the sword of the Spirit, which is the word of God." Why take it if they cannot use it effectively? The phrase "sword of the Spirit" does not mean the sword which the Spirit uses any more than "armor of God" means the armor which God uses, or puts on. It is the armor God furnishes his soldiers just as the armor of Rome was the armor the Roman government furnished its soldiers. The sword of the Spirit, the word of God, is the sword which the Spirit forged for us and gave to us to be used in our warfare. Yes, God's soldiers are to use that sword. "Preach the word." The word of God is a sharp sword, "sharper than any two-edged sword." And if a professed-Christian will not use that weapon, he is not a soldier in God's army. "Fight the good fight of the Faith." The Holy Spirit furnished the sword; God's soldiers are commanded to use it.

COMMENTS ON JAMES 5:14-16: "Is any among

you sick? let him call for the elders of the church; and let them pray over him, anointing him with oil in the name of the Lord: and the prayer of faith shall save him that is sick, and the Lord shall raise him up; and if he have committed sins, it shall be forgiven him. Confess your sins one to another, and pray one for another that ye may be healed. The supplication of a righteous man availeth much in its working."

Others besides the apostles had spiritual gifts, enabling different ones to do different things. When many churches were established, the apostles could not be present at all of them. So they needed inspired men in these many churches, for the New Testament had not then been written; and those inspired men needed miracle working powers to convince the people that they were God's representatives. As the elders were to feed the flock, we conclude that some of them were endowed with spiritual gifts. James MacKnight thought James here referred to miraculous healing. A discussion of that point does not belong in this essay; but there is a clause in verse 15 that must be noted. That is the statement that the healed person, if he had committed any sins, "it shall be forgiven him." But there is no record that God ever forgave sins without repentance. Verse 16 comes in as a part of this healing. The word "therefore" shows this. "Confess therefore your sins one to another, and pray one for another, that ye may be healed." And therefore as a condition of healing the sick he was required to confess his sins—to whom? The elders? Not unless he had sinned against an elder, and then only to the one he had sinned against.

God did not appoint elders to be priests to whom confessions were to be made, and no elders should assume the role of Roman Catholic priests. It is therefore certain that the confession here commanded was not to be made to the elders as such, but to the person who had been sinned against; and when things are made right with the injured brother, then pray for one another, "that ye may be healed." If the healing of verse 16 means spiritual healing, so must the sickness of verses 14, 15 refer to spiritual sickness! But we must stick to our subject, and not be sidetracked.

An evil practice by some preachers has grown out of a wrong application of a part of James 5:16. A part of verse 16 is quoted and then, in a rousing exhortation, brethren are exhorted to come forward and confess their sins before the whole congregation, though the verse does not even hint at such practice. They quote the statement, "confess therefore your sins one to another," and make it mean, confess your sins before everybody. That is a hurtful practice, because the scriptures are perverted to sustain it, and also because it leaves some of the best people in the church under suspicion. Others do not know what these people, hitherto regarded as upright men and women, have done; and many will wonder what secret meanness they have done. Do they confess any sins? Oh, no; likely each one says, "I have not been living right"; or, "I have not been living as a Christian should," etc. A blanket confession is really no confession of sins. But such confessionals help the preacher get a movement started and swells his report to the papers. And you will notice that the

preacher who calls for such confessions never does
any confessing himelf. Did you ever try to figure
out why he does not practice his own preaching on
that point?

Did you ever note the action of a denominational
preacher in a revival meeting, or the performances
of a union meeting preacher? They know the value
of getting a movement started, and so they try various schemes to get people to move. A long time
ago I saw that worked in getting people to make some
move. They knew if they could get the "Christians"
to come to the altar to pray for the unconverted,
such a movement would be contagious and would
spread to some they wanted to influence to come to
the mourners' bench. It worked. But now, since the
mourners' bench has been practically abandoned by
the more conservative denominations, some of "our
brethren" have instituted a sort of mourners' bench
for Christians! Yes, "Come forward, confess your
sins, and pray for forgiveness, and be prayed for."
Great is the denominational garbage can!

In the Old Testament confession of sins to Jehovah
is mentioned a number of times. David said, in Ps.
32:5: "I acknowledge my sin unto thee, And mine
iniquity did I not hide: I said, I will confess my
transgressions unto Jehovah; And thou forgavest the
iniquity of my sin."

It seems plain enough that the servant of God,
when he sins, must confess that sin to God and pray
for forgiveness. Of course, that implies repentance.
If only you and the person who sinned with you know
of that sin, the public need not know anything about
it. In fact, it is far better that they never know.

Repent of it, make confession unto God, and pray for his forgiveness, and let that end the matter. Don't parade your sins before people that otherwise would not know anything about them. But if you have maligned, slandered, and persecuted your brother before the world through every available avenue, you can't make that right with God by sitting in your home crying about it. The mischief of your deed was aimed at your brother, but the sin of it reached to High Heaven. A public wrong must be publicly corrected, or it is not corrected at all. Of course, to graciously make public amends would be considered very humiliating, but to do so would be such an outstanding example of Christian manhood at its best that every right-thinking person would applaud the deed; and such a deed would ease the conscience and make the one feel more content with himself. "Too much pride for that," do you say? Remember, "Pride goeth before destruction, and a haughty spirit before a fall." (Prov. 16:18.)

And sometimes there are other cases that seem to demand a public confession, though I know of no scripture that requires that a public confession be made. When a member of the church indulges in drunkenness, immoral practices openly, so that people know about it, or if he has engaged in contention and strife, or in any other sin, so that he brings shame upon himself and injury to the church, and then wishes to reform, how can he clear himself without publicly confessing his sins, and praying God for forgiveness, and asking the church to pray for him and to help him?

1 Pet. 1:1-2:

"Peter, an apostle of Jesus Christ, to the elect who are sojourners of the Dispersion in Pontus, Galatia, Cappadocia, Asia, and Bithynia, according to the foreknowledge of God the Father, in sanctification of the Spirit, unto obedience and sprinkling of the blood of Jesus Christ; Grace to you and peace be multiplied." Peter never lays any claim to superiority over the other apostles. He speaks of himself as an apostle of Jesus Christ; in giving elders a charge, he refers to himself as "a fellow elder, and a witness of the sufferings of Christ;" (1 Pet. 5:1), and "a servant and apostle of Jesus Christ" (2 Pet. 1:1.) And notice how he makes the words of all the apostles equal in authority by referring to "the commandment of the Lord and Savior through your apostles." (2 Pet. 3:2.) Our Lord and Savior selected the apostles to be his ambassadors, and gave them the Holy Spirit to guide them into all truth. They spake as the Spirit gave them utterance. It is absurd to think that the words of the Holy Spirit spoken through one apostle would be more authoritative than his words spoken through the other apostles. Peter made no claims of superiority over the other apostles. Had he done so, he would have contradicted these words of Paul: "For I reckon that I am not a whit behind the very chiefest apostles." (2 Cor. 11:5) "For in nothing was I behind the very chiefest apostles," (2 Cor. 12:11.) Peter therefore had no priority over the other apostles. Hence the language of Jesus in Matt. 16:18,19 ("And I also say unto thee, that thou art Peter, and upon this rock I will build my church; and the gates of Hades shall not prevail against it. I will give unto thee the keys of the kingdom of heaven: and whatsoever thou shalt bind on earth shall be bound in heaven; and whatsoever thou shalt loose on earth shall be loosed in heaven.") Jesus also said to all the apostles, "Verily I say unto you, What things soever ye shall bind on earth shall be bound in heaven; and what things soever ye shall loose on earth shall be loosed in heaven" (Matt. 18:18); Luke 10:16, "He that heareth you heareth me; and he that rejecteth you rejecteth me; and he that rejecteth me rejecteth him that sent me"; John 20:22,23, "And when he had said this, he breathed on them, and saith unto them, Receive ye the Holy Spirit: whose soever sins ye forgive, they are forgiven unto them; whose soever sins ye retain, they are retained." And so the Holy Spirit spoke through each of the apostles with equal authority. "And they were all filled with the Holy Spirit, and began to speak with other tongues, as the Spirit gave them utterance." (Acts 2:4.)

A sojourner is a temporary resident in a place, or a stranger. He is not a permanent resident of the place where he is. Commentators have wasted time and space in advancing probable reasons as to why Peter referred to the people he addressed as "sojourners of the dispersion." The scattering of the Jews was called the Dispersion, and as the translators spelled the word with a capital "D" they evidently thought Peter was writing to the dispersed Jews. However, it is plain from the contents of both letters that he was writing to Christians, and not to Jews as such; and that is the thing that matters to us.

I shall take up no space in discussing the geography and the people of the districts Peter mentions. If the reader is curious about them, he can consult a good Bible Dictionary or Encyclopedia.

The phrase "according to the foreknowledge of God the Father," connects back with "the elect—" "the elect according to the foreknowledge of God the Father." The *elect* are Christians, those who have obeyed the gospel of Jesus Christ. People have not been unconditionally elected, but by obeying the truth, as is clearly shown in this first chapter, verses 22, 23. In the ark Noah was saved from the corrupt world by water, but he certainly was not saved unconditionally; and by like figure we are saved by baptism. If we are saved unconditionally there is no likeness between Noah's salvation and ours.

What is meant by "foreknowledge of God?" It will give us light to learn what the phrase "knowledge of God" means. It is not what God knows, but what we know, or may know, about him—but things he has revealed. "'Jehovah hath a controversy with the inhabitants of the land, because there is no truth, nor goodness, nor knowledge of God in the land." (Hosea 4:1.) "Some have no knowledge of God: I speak this to move you to shame." (1 Cor. 15:34.) It was a shame that some had no knowledge of what God had revealed. Christians should be "increasing in the knowledge of God." (Col. 1:10.) We cannot increase in what God knows, but we can increase in the knowledge he has revealed to us. The knowledge of God is therefore the knowledge he has revealed to us. And so the foreknowledge of God is what God had formerly revealed in the promises and prophecies concerning Christ and his plan of salvation. How could these Christians have become God's elect according to the foreknowledge of God if no promise of prophecy referred to the plan by which they became God's elect? This one statement made by Peter completely overthrows the contention of those who claim that no promise or prophecy referred to the plan of salvation preached by the apostles, but all referred to a supposed time when the Jews would all be restored to Palestine with Christ ruling over them on David's throne in Jerusalem. And yet all admit that only one scheme of human redemption was foretold in promise and prophecy. This proposition can be easily maintained by any Bible student: THE SCHEME OF REDEMPTION PREACHED BY THE APOSTLES BY WHICH PEOPLE BECAME GOD'S ELECT IS THE SCHEME FORETOLD IN PROMISE AND PROPHECY.

"In sanctification of the Spirit." The mere fact that the translators used capital "S" in the word "spirit," only shows that they thought the Holy Spirit was meant. The fact is, when the New Testament was written the Greek alphabet had only capital letters. Hence, every word from beginning to end was spelled with capital letters. The small letters were a later development. Even the Greek here does not determine whether the Spirit is the source of sanctification or the spirit is the object of sanctification—does not determine whether it is the Holy Spirit that sanctifies or the human spirit that is sanctified. But if this expression means that the spirit of man is sanctified, the passage does not mean that the person is saved. It is done in order to obedience and the sprinkling of the blood of Christ. It is almost parallel to John 1:11,12: "He came unto his own, and they that were his own received him not. But as many as received him, to them gave he the right to become children of God, even to them that believe on his name." The believer is sanctified, or set apart from the unbeliever, and given the right to become a child of God—given the right to obedience and the sprinkling of the blood of Christ. Sanctification here cannot mean the same as salvation; for this sanctification was unto, or in order to, obedience and the sprinkling of the blood of Christ. Certainly no one will claim that a person is saved without the blood of Christ.

But if the phrase means that the Holy Spirit sanctifies, what then? Jesus prayed "Sanctify them in the truth: thy word is truth." (John 17:17.) And Jesus said to the apostles, "Howbeit when he, the Spirit of truth is come, he shall guide you into all the truth." (John 16:13.) The truth revealed by the Spirit through the apostles sanctifies. By this truth people are made believers, and are set apart unto obedience and the sprinkling of the blood of Christ.

The imagery of the sprinkling of the blood of Christ is drawn from the sprinkling of the law of Moses. "Wherefore even the first covenant hath not been dedicated without blood. For when every commandment had been spoken by Moses unto all the people according to the law, he took the blood of the calves and the goats, with water and scarlet wool and hyssop, and sprinkled both the book itself and all the people, saying, This is the blood of the covenant which God commanded to you-ward." (Heb. 9:18-20.) Only by keeping the covenant could the people receive the benefits of the typical blood. But the new and living way, the new covenant, has been dedicated with better blood, the precious blood of Christ; and we get the benefits of that blood by keeping that covenant. We purify our souls by obedience to this covenant, this truth, and not by some mystical application of the blood of Christ, as if the literal blood of Christ has been preserved. A brother asked me, "When do we come into actual contact with the blood of Christ?" And we sing "Let thy precious blood be applied——." And I have heard brethren make this argument: "The blood of Christ was shed in his death, and to come into contact with his blood we must be baptized into his death." Christ died for us, we are redeemed by his blood, saved by the merits of his blood, but not by coming into literal contact with it; and to talk about coming into contact with it is folly.

"Grace to you and peace be multiplied," is both a prayer and a salutation. The words express a desire that God's grace continue to be upon them and that peace among them be multiplied.

Verses 3-5: "Blessed be the God and Father of our Lord Jesus Christ, who according to his great mercy begat us again unto a living hope by the resurrection of Jesus Christ from the dead, unto an inheritance incorruptible, and undefiled, and that fadeth not away, reserved in heaven for you, who by the power of God are guarded through faith unto a salvation ready to be revealed in the last time."

"Blessed——" Revere, praise, thank, and glorify God. Instead of "The God and Father" the marginal reading has "God and the Father." This seems preferable. In a general sense God is the Father of all men; in a peculiar sense, he is the Father of all who have been born again—all Christians; but in a special sense he is the Father of the Lord Jesus Christ. Jesus Christ is the son of God in a sense in which no mere man is, ever was, or ever can be. He is now on the throne of his glory, the King of Kings and Lord of Lords. But we cannot imagine the misery and gloom that engulfed the woebegone disciples while the body of Jesus lay in the tomb. Darkness was upon them— hope was gone. But God in his great mercy gave them a living hope by the resurrection of Jesus from the dead. There is a difference in grace and mercy, yet both may merge in one operation of helpfulness. Grace is help to the needy, no matter what the need may be. Mercy is for the guilty, the condemned, and also for the distressed, the miserable, the hopeless. Mercy manifested in the resurrection of Christ relieved the disciples of their distress and hopelessness. Grace, or favor, of God brought merciful relief to the depressed and hopeless disciples by the resurrection of Christ Jesus, reviving in them a living hope, a hope that continued to live.

2 Pet. 1:20,21. ". . . . knowing this first, that no prophecy of scripture is of private interpretation. For no prophecy came by the will of man; but men spoke from God, being moved by the Holy Spirit."

The foregoing passage, especially verse twenty, gives commentators a lot of trouble; and that is partly because they do not consider Peter's explanation in verse 21. I do not know how many theories have been advanced about the words "private interpretation." One theory is, that one person by his own individual study could not interpret prophecy, for that would be "private interpretation." But Paul exhorted Timothy to study and to give himself to reading, and Peter exhorted the brethren to add knowledge. That theory would do away with individual, or private, study, and make Paul's and Peter's exhortation out of place. Another theory is, that Peter meant that a construction should not be placed on one verse without considering what other passages say on the subject. It is true that other passages on the same subject must be considered, but Peter here does not even hint at that idea. In his comments on verse 20 Thayer, in his Lexicon, says, "No one can explain prophecy by his own mental power (it is not a matter of subjective interpretation), but to explain it one needs the illumination of the Holy Spirit in which it originated." (Page 116, Corrected Edition.) According to this, a man must have the same degree of inspiration to interpret a prophecy that the prophet had to make the prophecy. If Thayer is correct, he completely upsets these future kingdom folks who are so busy telling us what the prophecies mean. But if Thayer is correct in what he says, he does not teach what Peter says. You will notice that Peter does not say that no prophecy is *for* private interpretation, but that no prophecy of scripture is, or comes, of private interpretation. There is a difference between prophecy and mere prediction. Sometimes a man on his own private thinking can predict what a certain trend or course of actions will terminate in; but the prophets did not make predictions based upon their private opinion as to what the outcome would be—"For no prophecy ever came by the will of man: but men spake from God, being moved by the Holy Spirit." And so these verses have to do with the way prophecies came and not what we should do, or not do, with them.

The correctness of the view presented is made more sure by what Peter had said in verses 12-19. He would have the brethren, after his death to keep in memory what he had taught them; "For we did not follow cunningly devised fables, when we made known unto you the power and coming of our Lord Jesus Christ, but we were eye-witnesses of his majesty." The prophecies that foretold the coming of the Messiah, the Son of God, were not cunningly devised fables, did not come by the will of man, nor by man's own private interpretations, but from God's inspired men. And Peter's faith in what the prophets said concerning the Messiah, the Son of God, was confirmed by the demonstrations on the mount of transfiguration and by the voice from heaven, saying, "This is my beloved Son." So he said, "And we have the word of prophecy made more sure." I quote the American Standard Version, which is much better here than the King James Version. "Whereunto ye do well that ye take heed . . . Knowing this first"— know it as of first or prime importance—that no prophecy came by man's private invention—not by man's will, "but men spake from God, being moved by the Holy Spirit.

Anvil Sparks:

It may be possible to refute a fallacious argument, but who among mortals can refute a gust of wind?

And, brother preacher, did you ever think what might happen to that discourse, if the Holy Spirit should suddenly take possession of you as he did the apostles, and cause you to speak as he gave you utterances?

Booze-befuddled brains bring brawls, bumps, and bruises.

Discussion of Some Words and Phrases

"Now make us a king to judge us like all the nations." (1 Sam. 8:5.) So spoke the elders of Israel to Samuel. These men did not say to Samuel: "Make us a king so that we may be like God wants us to be." God had never demanded that they have a king. They wanted to follow the pattern that other nations set; they wanted to take their place among the nations of the world. Before this they had been only an aggregation of loosely connected tribes and were not reckoned among the nations. When nations were enumerated, they were left out. They wanted that changed—wanted to take their place among the nations of the earth. And when people want a thing that they know is not exactly the right thing, they can always find an excuse. An excuse is usually a thing we use as a covering with which to hide our motive.

Yes, these elders had excuses in plenty—enough to satisfy any one who was more anxious to be like the nations than he was to follow God's way. To Samuel they said: "Behold, thou art old, and thy sons walk not in thy ways." Samuel had been an upright judge, as the people themselves testified: "Thou hast not defrauded us, nor oppressed us, neither hast thou taken aught of any man's hand." (1 Sam. 12:4.) But when Samuel was old, he made his sons judges over Israel. "And his sons walked not in his ways, but turned aside after lucre, and took bribes, and perverted justice." He loved· his sons and wanted to give them a chance, and most likely did not know of their corruption. But the elders of Israel knew, and had a right to complain about their conduct. However, they did not have any right to try to correct the evil by resorting to another wrong course. They were proposing to correct one wrong with another wrong, but the conduct of these sons gave them a good talking point. It is often so. Even in church troubles those who are really contending for the right are often open to criticism, and that sort of thing gives an unruly faction a talking point. With such a talking point, the real issue is frequently covered up. But when people want to go wrong, they can always find excuses. It is hard for people to be satisfied with God's way.

The besetting sin of the human family is a lack of confidence in God, manifested in every kind of a departure from the word of God. If our confidence in God were what it should be, we would never want to turn aside from his way. Eve lacked confidence in God, and so she followed the devil; Adam lacked confidence in God, and so he followed his wife. Why did Abel do what God said, and why did Cain not do what God said? Abel had confidence enough in God to follow his commands; Cain did not. No man today would depart from the plain word of God, if he had full confidence in God; and the elders of Israel would not have asked for a king, had they not lacked confidence in God's way.

Some people contend that a man is entirely a creature of circumstances; that his surroundings make him what he is. If that were so, a man would not be responsible for what he is nor for what he does. Yet it is true that our surroundings will mold and shape our character, if we make no effort to fight against them; and herein is our responsibility. God demands that we do not allow our surroundings to control us. "Be not fashioned according to this world." This world is not the Christian's pattern. I used to read this admonition by Paul, and thought it was a mere prohibition against our making an effort to be like the world. Of course, it does prohibit our making an effort to be like the world, but there is more in it than that. We are so easily influenced by our surroundings that we have to make a fight to keep from slipping into the habits and speech of those about us; otherwise we will find ourselves speaking "half in the speech of Ashdod." It is true that there are some restless spirits among us who look longingly on the way others do in religion and long to be like them. Lacking confidence in God, they are not satisfied with God's way. Not so many, however, are really active in trying to be like others. The chief danger with most of us is that we allow ourselves unconsciously to drift into the speech and habits of the denominational world. Often we are not as wide-awake and alert as we should be, and imitate others without knowing it. It is easy to borrow or absorb expressions from others; and we have done too much of that sort of thing. One often hears brethren using expressions that were heard a few years ago only among the denominations. I do not want to be fussy, but I call attention to a few expressions to stimulate thought along these lines.

1. "Bring us a message." Often a good brother prays that the speaker of the day "may bring us a great message." You frequently hear, "I'll bring you

a message on . . . ;" "You brought us a great message" and so on; ad nauseam. Till a few years ago that sort of talk was confined, so far as I know, to the denominations. When the denominations thought their preachers had some sort of communications from the Lord, they could consistently expect their preacher to "bring a message;" but I cannot understand how plain New Testament Christians can get the consent of their minds to use such expressions. Now, *message* and *messenger* are correlative terms. If a man brings a message, then he is a messenger. If he is a messenger, then some one has sent him with a message. In religious matters a message is "a divinely inspired or revealed communication, as of a prophet." God is not now sending messages through inspired men, and it is impossible for an uninspired man to bring a message from God.

2. "Going to church," "before church," "at church," "after church." These are expressions not found in the New Testament, nor is the idea found there. And yet we read long articles on "Why I go to Church." In such expressions, what does the word "church" mean? The meeting house is not the church. As used in the New Testament, the word "church" refers to God's people, to those who have been called out of sin into his service. If a person has been called out of sin, he is a member of the church, a part of the church. If a person is a part of the church, where does he go when he goes to church? Paul did not advise people to "go to church," but he did exhort church members not to forsake the assembling of themselves together. (See Heb. 10:25.) And he uses this expression: "If therefore the whole church

be assembled together." (1 Cor. 14:23.) It would have sounded queer if he had said: "If therefore the whole church goes to church." It is the duty of the church to assemble on the first day of the week, but I do not read anything about "going to church." One writer said that going to meeting and going to church mean the same thing, but do they? It seems that some people think the church does not exist except when the members are gathered together. These are small matters, you say. Certainly; and so is an acorn a small thing, but it may grow into a great tree, and may in time produce a great forest. The deadly cancer is small at its beginning, and is not noticed for a time. A disease begins before any symptoms appear. A loose and careless use of words is the result of loose and careless thinking.

3. "Sacrament." "Sacrament" is derived from the Latin word *sacramentum,* which signifies an oath, particularly the oath taken by soldiers to be true to their country and general." The word is not found in the Bible; yet brethren sometimes apply it to the Lord's Supper. It has no fitness when applied to anything pertaining to Christianity. It is a word of frequent occurrence among the denominations. The Romanists have seven "sacraments"—namely: *Baptism, the Lord's Supper, confirmation, penance, extreme unction, ordination,* and *marriage.* Christianity has no sacraments.

4. "Baptize—Immerse—Mode of baptism." Ever since I first heard brethren discuss baptism, I have heard them say that the Greek words *baptizo* and *baptisma* mean immerse and immersion. And they have correctly argued that if the Greek words had

been translated, instead of giving them an English spelling, we would have "immerse" and "immersion" where the Greek words occur, and the words *baptize* and *baptism* would not be in the New Testament at all. But one of the strangest and most senseless things is, that some brethren have attached a mystic significance to *baptize* and *baptism* that they do not attach to *immerse* and *immersion*. And so you sometimes hear this expression: "He may have been immersed, but he was not baptized." That is the same thing as saying, "He may have been immersed, but he was not immersed." Or, "He may have been baptized, but he was not baptized." When Paul found these disciples at Ephesus who had been baptized into John's baptism, though their baptism was wrong, he did not say, "You have not been baptized at all." He gave them some needed teaching, and they were then rebaptized. Why try to shun the word rebaptize or rebaptism? If a man did not obey the Lord the first time he was baptized, he should be rebaptized after proper preparation of mind and heart. Yes, baptism is immersion and immersion is baptism, and you talk foolishly when you try to make it otherwise. I can see how an affusionist can refer to immersion as a mode of baptism; but if a person believes that immersion is baptism, how can he call immersion a *mode* of baptism? "Mode" means the manner or method of doing a thing: and if immersion is a mode of baptism, that implies that there are other modes of baptism. To my way of thinking, the mode of baptism is of no consequence, just so you really baptize. You might baptize a person by leaning him forward or backward; you might carry him into the water in your arms or on a stretcher and lower him beneath the water. You can adopt any of these modes that the exigencies of the case demand. I would not argue a minute about the mode of immersion.

5. "Reconsecrations." Where do you read of such performances? In some reports of meetings. I do not think that such an expression could be found in any report sent in by brethren ten years ago. That word has been borrowed by some brethren from high-powered revivalists among the denominations. If a person comes forward and says he wants to be baptized or wants to confess his sins and be restored to the fellowship of the church, I know what to do; but if one should come forward and tell me that he wanted to be "reconsecrated," I would not know how to carry out his wishes.

Do you say these are small matters? Well, falling chaff will show which way the wind blows, when a large stone would not. But staying with the Bible is not a small matter, and adopting ideas and expressions not found in the Bible is not a small matter. "Be not fashioned according to this world." "If any one speak, let him speak as the oracles of God require." (1 Pet. 4:11, MacKnight's Translation.)

"Authorized Version." As the English language is a living language, it is constantly acquiring new words. For this reason many changes have taken place in the English language since the so-called "Authorized Version," which never was, in fact, authorized by anybody; was first published in A. D. 1611. *To let* then meant *to hinder,* and *to prevent* meant *to precede,* or *to go before;* and the expression, *do you to wit,* has entirely passed out of use. So for the translation in the King James, or Common Version of Paul's language: "Moreover, brethren, we do you to wit," the American Standard Version has: "Moreover, brethren, we make known to you." The King James Version represents Paul as saying that he had often purposed to visit Rome, "but was let hitherto." The American Standard has hindered instead of let. In the King James David prevented the dawning of the morning—got up before dawn; Paul said the living saints would not prevent those who were asleep—they would not ascend before the dead saints would ascend—all would go up together. Webster tells us that the spelling *shew* is especially British, but they pronounce it *sho*. The American spelling is *draft* and the word draught should be so pronounced.

But a word that needs special attention is the word *peculiar*. The word *peculiar* occurs seven times in the Authorized Version. It seems that some never have an idea that this word means anything but *singular* and *queer*.

Theories are propagated, sermons are preached, and articles are written on the assumption that the word has that meaning in the Authorized Version. It is argued that we must differ from other people in order to be peculiar, and a few items are usually mentioned wherein we must differ from others. It is argued that if we have human societies and instrumental music we will not be peculiar for other folks have such things. But why stop with these? Well, some do not stop with these items. Some have argued that if we have classes and literature we are not pe-

culiar, for others have such things. But why stop
even with these? If the argument is sound, it will
hold good all the way down the line. Others sing,
too, do they not? Sectarians have Bibles, carry their
Bibles to meeting, read their Bibles, build meeting-
houses, use songbooks, and wear clothing. Now, if
you do any of these things, or all of them, you certainly are not *peculiar!* "But that's foolishness," you say.
And so it is, and that is what I wanted you to see;
the whole thing is foolishness.

Webster's Collegiate Dictionary defines "peculiar"
as follows: "One's own; belonging to an individual;
particular; special; as, of *peculiar* interest. 2. Singular; queer." A little reflection will show that the
meanings *queer* and *singular* do not belong to the
word in the Authorized Version. Ex. 19:5: "Then
ye shall be a peculiar treasure unto me"—that is, peculiar to him and to no one else. And so in the other
places where the word occurs. In common usage the
word has departed somewhat from its original meaning, so much so that the American Standard Version
left it out. Compare the Authorized Version and the
American Standard Version in the following verses:
Ex. 19:5; Deut. 14:2; 26:18; Ps. 135:4; Eccles. 2:8;
Tit. 2:14; 1 Pet. 2:9. "Mine own possession from
among all peoples"—"a people for his own possession"
—"a people for God's own possession." How much
richer in meaning these passages are when we get
over the idea that the Lord was merely reminding
us that we were to be queer or odd!

But are we to take sectarians as our patterns? Certainly not. The Lord never did put them up as a
pattern for us to go by; neither did he set them up

as scarecrows to frighten us into a lot of foolish antics. It is strange how many people are influenced by the practices of other religious groups. The man who tries to be like them and the man who tries to be different from them are both being influenced by them. But an intelligent Christian, free from all sectarian influence, seeks to know what the will of the Lord is that he may do it. What others do or do not is not a determining factor with him. A horse that shies at every bush, chunk, or piece of paper along the road is as unsatisfactory as a saddle horse as the one that wants to turn aside to pick every bunch of grass he sees. But there are professed Christians just like that.

"Atonement—Reconciliation." It does not seem to me that a valid argument can be made on English words if the same argument can not be made on the Greek words for which these English words are used in translation. For example: the King James translators give us the word *atonement* as a translation of a word Paul used (Rom. 5:11.) Many preachers have pronounced that word at-one-ment, and gave it a sort of mystical meaning. The English word does yield itself to that analysis, but the word Paul used —katallage—cannot be so divided with any such significance. And thus the one who makes such a play on the English word does something that Paul could not have done with the Greek word he used. The American Standard Version of the New Testament does not have the word atonement, but the word reconciliation instead. The word atonement does occur a number of times in the American Standard Version of the Old Testament; but I do not see how an argument could be made on the at-one-ment theory when it speaks of making "atonement for the altar," "atonement for the house," "atonement for the sanctuary," etc. While the King James Version gives us "atonement" in Rom. 5:11, it gives "reconciliation" as the translation of the same word in 2 Cor. 5:18,19. We can understand the word reconciliation without any theological splitting of the word.

"Back-to-the-Bible." Some raise the cry, "Back-to-the-Bible." What do they mean? Ever since I obeyed the gospel, I have been trying to catch up with the Bible. In many things it is still ahead of me. How about you? No, you have not outstripped the Bible.

"Christian" — The name Christian signifies a follower of Christ. A long time ago I made the argument so often heard; that is, that being married to Christ we should wear his name, just as a woman takes the surname of her husband, but I learned better. When a woman marries a Smith, you do not call her Smithian, but Mrs. Smith. If the argument was worth a fig, and if you make a faithful application of your line of talk, what would you call one who is married to Christ? It would border on to blasphemy to say, would it not? The name Christian has no connection with the marriage relation in any sense. As a matter of fact, surnames, in the sense of family names, were not used for more than a thousand years after Christ. The Normans began the custom to some extent before the Norman conquest. In that conquest, they carried the custom to England. Before that a surname was a name given to some one because of some exploit or characteristic, but such surnames did not pass to the children, nor was it worn by the wife. It was an individual name, not a family name. Yes, the name Christian indicates a follower of Christ, and when a man ceases to follow Christ he ceases to be a Christian. That does not mean that he ceases to be a child of God.

"Charge of the Church." Once I asked a young preacher where he lived. He named a town in another state, and added, "I have charge of the church there." I have an idea he was telling the truth, and that's the pity of it. Such talk revealed how little he and the church knew about the Bible order—about the New Testament church. But that was many years ago. He and the church have both had time to learn much.

"Dedications." Some time ago I read that some people of a certain church were going to have a rally and then assist in dedicating a church—perhaps they meant a meeting house. But I have read no such reports in the Bible. What do people do to a meeting house when they dedicate it? All I know about the religion of Christ is what I read in the Bible.

"The Dictionary." A dictionary may be useful, or not, depending on the use you make of it. It may be useful when you use it to learn the meaning of some of the words you find in reading. However, if I have to go to the dictionary often to see what the writer is trying to say, I lay it aside. I like to read an author whose meaning is so clear that I am scarcely conscious of the words he uses. You should use the dictionary to see that a word you are about to use means what you want to say, but never to hunt up unusual words to dazzle the hearer or reader. This is like loading a gun with blank cartridges when you start hunting; the blank cartridge may make a big noise and startle the game, but you bring home no meat. To be effective use short, simple words. Do you think it better to use unusual and high-sounding words? If so, try this: A concrete mass in rotative progression accretes no bryoprytic organisms. Would it not be better to say, a rolling stone gathers no moss?

"Doctrine." Doctrine is teaching. If there is any teaching in a speech or an article it is a doctrinal speech or article. More than once I have seen the absurd expression, "doctrinal teaching," as if there could be any teaching that was not doctrinal. But to me there is an interesting thing about doctrine and practice. Some doctrines cannot be practiced. Do you doubt that? How can one practice universalism, or the Calvinistic doctrine of unconditional election and irresistible grace, the direct operation of the Holy Spirit, or the future kingdom theory? The Christian Scientist says "all matter is a delusion of the mortal mind"—the brick wall is not there, you just think it is. How practice that? A doctrine may be kept alive by agitation or by practice, or by both methods; if it cannot be practiced, it can be kept alive only by agitation. If a doctrine cannot be practiced, then without agitation it will fade out of your thinking. I think the advocates of these doctrines that cannot be practiced unconsciously realize the truth of what I say; hence the abundance of agitation these days. They will not cease their agitation so as to prove that these doctrines can live and thrive in silence! Think on these things.

"Custom to whom custom is due." It is surprising how many blunders even preachers make in their misuse of familiar words and scriptures. Some years ago a preacher of some ability and experience was telling me about preaching the Sunday before in a small town. The brethren were discussing the propriety of changing their order of worship from time to time, lest some might think their custom was the scriptural order. This preacher gave this advice, as he related it to me: "No brethren, if it is your custom to do things in a certain order, I would not change the custom; you know Paul says, 'custom to whom custom is due'."

"Forsake—Neglect." A good rule, though likely none of us adheres to it perfectly, is never to write or preach something that cannot be proved. Another good rule is, never be so anxious to make a point that you will see things in a passage that are not there. Both of these rules, if you will allow me to call them rules, are often violated in the pulpit and in the press. And when a person sees a thing in a passage that is not there, he fails to see what is in it. Take Heb. 10:25—Read so carefully and attentively that you really see what is in it: ". . . not forsaking our own assembling together, as the custom of some is, but exhorting one another; and so much the more, as ye see the day drawing nigh." I do not recall that I ever read an article or heard a sermon in which this verse was brought forward for discussion that the writer or speaker did not begin at once to talk about "neglecting the assembly." Now why is this? Do writers and preachers pay attention to the meaning of words? Or do some think they can make a word mean anything they want it to mean. *Neglect* and *forsake* do not at all mean the same thing. To forsake is to abandon, to quit or leave entirely, to desert. A man may on occasions neglect the assembly without forsaking—abandoning—it, just as a man may neglect to provide for his wife and children as he should without forsaking them. Certainly no one should neglect the Lord's day worship; for frequent neglect, with the attendance growing further apart, may cause a person to become so indifferent that he will forsake the assembly. But when the letter to the Hebrews was written, the Hebrew Christians were subjected to great pressure and persecutions. They could escape such bitter persecutions by forsaking the assembling of themselves together. That meant that they had given up their faith in Christ, and it seems that many did so. Do not neglect the Lord's day worship, and do not pervert Hebrews 10:25. Both are bad.

"Keys." Another strange doctrine is that Peter is the gatekeeper of heaven. Many Protestants hold this doctrine. They talk about "meeting Saint Peter at the gate up there." Matt. 16:19 furnishes no more evidence that Peter will be gatekeeper in heaven than it does that he was supreme head of the church and the generalissimo of the apostles. One is as false as the other. The gates of heaven stand wide open to all those who love and do the Lord's commandments (Rev. 22:14.)

It would be rather amusing if it were not so serious to listen to some as they seek to count the number of "keys of the kingdom of heaven." Some say that Peter used one on the day of Pentecost and another one at the house of Cornelius, and still another one when he gave the Christians (?) grace. Others count the number of keys in this fashion: Hearing equals one; faith equals two; repentance equals three; confession equals four; and baptism equals five. "If" Peter had been appointed special doorkeeper and carried all the keys that have been "counted," he would have needed a ring larger than we have yet seen. Poor Peter would have been weighted down with the keys.

What is meant by "keys" in Matt. 16:19? We all know that a key serves to lock and unlock, to close and to open. In our text "keys of the kingdom" are associated with "binding and loosing." A key has been and still is a symbol of responsibility, power, and authority. Listen to this: "And the key to the house of David will I lay upon his shoulder; so he shall open, and none shall shut; and he shall shut and none shall open." (Isa. 22:22.) See the fulfillment in Christ according to Rev. 3:7. Jesus charged that the "expounders of the law" had taken away the key of knowledge. (Luke 11:52.) To them belonged the responsibility, and the authority to expound and make known the law to the people. When Jesus used the term "keys" in the plural, he did not intend to convey a certain number of keys. He was telling them that into their hands he was intrusting the affairs of the kingdom, and that they were to make known the terms of admission and the rights and privileges of the kingdom, and the solemn obligations imposed upon its citizens. Jesus assured them that whatever they bound on men on earth would be ratified and bound in heaven. A proper recognition of the nature of the kingdom of Christ will aid greatly in solving the "keys" question. Let us preach, respect and exalt the authority that the apostles were empowered with, and the "keys" will retain rightful "key positions."

"Leadership." Some time ago the editor of Collier's Weekly mentioned the hatred a great newspaper (the London Times, I think) had for the word *personnel,* and then mentioned some words that he himself would like to murder. I have in mind some words and expressions that I would like to see crippled so they would not show up so often, and a few that I would like to see murdered. The word *leadership* is too prominent in reports and articles, and should be crippled. Some brother makes a report like this: "Under the leadership of Brother Heza Whopper the church here has progressed by leaps and bounds." (Can you imagine a church of God performing such acrobatic stunts. "Under the leadership of Heza Whopper," indeed. What were the elders doing while Heza Whopper was leading the church by "leaps and bounds?" "Leaps and bounds" is an expression that I would like to see murdered. I like to see churches grow, but I do not want to be around when one begins leaping and bounding. A church should not progress like a kangaroo or a jack rabbit. And a preacher who starts a church to so acting should be sent away "by leaps and bounds."

"More convenient." There is a kind of man-made scripture that is harmful. It consists in inserting a word or phrase in a passage, so as to change the meaning, and the same result may be obtained by leaving out a word or phrase. Often brethren have quoted Felix as saying to Paul, "Go thy way for this time;

and when I have a more convenient season I will call thee unto me." And they usually comment that the more convenient season never did come. Of course Felix was not inspired, but his language should be correctly quoted. "More" is not in what he said. The use of this word makes a wrong impression— makes the impression that there is a convenient, and then a more convenient, season to become a Christian; but that is wrong. No one ever finds it convenient to become a Christian. To become a Christian requires that one deny himself, and self-denial is not convenient. It is not convenient to take up one's cross, nor is it convenient to follow Christ. It is never convenient to make such a radical change.

"Our Fallen Nature." In recent months I have heard more than one brother use the expression *Our fallen nature*. I do not know what they mean by that expression, and I doubt that they know; but it sounds as if they were tinctured with the doctrine of inherited depravity.

"Religion." There are many religions—the Jew's religion, Mohammedan religion, Heathen religion, Vain religion, Pure religion, etc. For a time I heard repeatedly that the word religion was derived from "re," again and "ligio," a latin word that meant "to bind;" and the compound word was said to signify the rebinding, or binding back, to God. I did not feel able to refute the idea, and yet I could not see how a false religion could rebind people to God, and so I refrained from saying so. I think linguists have given up that idea. Webster does not set forth that idea in his definition of religion; he tells us that the word religion is derived from the Latin word religio, properly, taboo, restraint. To me that makes sense, for that can be true of all religions; for every religion has its taboos, or restraints.

"Resigned." That word should be so crippled that it would not be able to crawl into the reports of gospel preachers. It is not a gospel word and expresses no Bible idea. And yet you *resigned*. For a time you labor with a church as its evangelist; and then you announce that you have resigned, or have offered your resignation, to take effect at a certain date. You say you were not a pastor or any other sort of an officer, but just an evangelist working under the direction of the elders, and yet you resigned. Resigned from what? Now did you really and freely resign, or did you become resigned to the inevitable and announce your resignation as a sort of "cover-up"? There is, you know, quite a difference between resigning and becoming resigned. You say you are an evangelist for the church. If you were conducting a series of meetings for a church, would you not be an evangelist for that church during the meeting? After the meeting had gone on for some days, would you turn in your resignation to take effect next Tuesday night? Why the difference? Quit talking about resigning—that sounds like a Baptist or a Presbyterian pastor. A man's words betray him. We should use "sound words that cannot be condemned." (Tit. 2:8.) If a man puts himself forward as a leader he should be especially careful to speak the things that befit the sound doctrine. (Tit. 2:1.) Paul gave this charge to Timothy: "Hold the pattern of sound words, which thou hast heard from me, in faith and love which is in Christ Jesus." (2 Tim. 1:12.) When a preacher or elder talks about resigning he is not holding the pattern of sound words.

"Responses." A good friend of mine, a man of much experience as elder, Bible teacher, and business man, writes: "You could appropriately say something on our abuse or misuse of *respond,* when one is asked to obey the Lord, and the word response is used. I believe the king's translators of the last will overlooked this word wholly." There is a better reason for the absence of that word from Luke's reports. In reporting conversions he did not use a Greek word that could be translated respond or response. I would like to see some reports patterned after Luke's reports. Do I get an amen on that? Do we speak as the Oracles of God speak?

"Save—Salvation—Perish." Sometimes the words *save* and *salvation* refer to deliverance from physical harm, more often in the New Testament they refer to deliverance from sin and its consequences. It has been said that Noah and family were saved by faith, by the ark, and by water, but that is mixing things up. A Methodist preacher said they were saved by water by staying out of the water. That sounded as if he were making fun of what Peter said. His remarks were silly, but not more so than to think Heb. 11:7 and 1 Pet. 3:20 refer to the same salvation. They were saved in the ark from being destroyed by the flood; they were saved by water in being transferred from the corrupt world into a new and clean world, the corruption having been destroyed by water. "The world that then was, being overflowed with water perished." (2 Pet. 3:6.) It is a striking and impressive figure of our salvation by baptism. When the disciples on the storm tossed sea said, "Save, Lord; we perish," they were praying to be saved from physical death. And so, in the last two quotations, *perish* refers to physical death, as it also does in Luke 13:1-5, and some other passages. In such passages as John 3:16; Rom. 2:12; 2 Pet. 3:9 perish evidently refers to future punishment; but a close examination of Luke 13:1-5 will show that perish in that place does not refer to punishment in the world to come. Read it carefully. "Now there were some present at that very season who told him of the Galileans, whose blood Pilate mingled with their sacrifices, and he answered and said unto them Think ye that these Galileans were sinners above all the Galileans because they have suffered these things? I tell you, nay; but except ye repent, ye shall all in like manner perish. Or those eighteen, upon whom the tower in Siloam fell, and killed them, think ye that they were offenders above all the men that dwell in Jerusalem? I tell you, nay: but, except ye repent, ye shall all likewise perish." (Luke 13:1-5.) Jesus was talking to Jews, not aliens, and he was telling them that they would perish in the same manner or way, that the men mentioned perished, that is by violence, unless they repented. He was warning them of the doom awaiting them, which did come upon them when the Roman armies overran Judea and destroyed Jerusalem, more than a million Jews perished by violent means. Luke 13:1-5 was then fulfilled. The language of that scripture said nothing about what would be the fate of these impenitent Jews after death. A long time ago I repented of applying that scripture to those we now term alien sinners.

"Sermon Outline Books." For many years after I began to preach no gospel preacher, so far as I know, put out a book of sermon outlines; but now "the woods is full of 'em." It is a bad thing for any preacher to get into the habit of using sermon outlines prepared by some one else, and he should not become a slave to outlines he prepares for himself. The slave to sermon outlines will never learn the Bible as he should. Sermon outlines, especially those written by others, are mental crutches. The command, "Let the word of Christ dwell in you richly," cannot be obeyed by studying sermon outline books. A preacher may look over a sermon outline book, and then "say a speech," after the school boy fashion, but he will not preach a sermon. Real sermons grow out of prayerful, conscientious study of the Bible. Giving the people little sermons in capsules may become such a habit that the preacher may be found giving empty capsules. Besides the preacher needs to study the Bible for the development of his own character. Do I hear a second?

"Service." About a generation ago the pious and scholarly O. A. Carr, in an article, lamented the growing wrong use of the word *service*—"the song service," "the praise service," "the communion service," etc. He wondered how long it would be before brethren would be talking about the "prayer service." Ah, Brother Carr, had you lived but a few years longer you would have often heard that absurd combination of words; and you would have heard the brethren using the equally absurd expression, "the worship service." Do brethren know what worship is, or what service is? "Song service," "praise service," "prayer service," "worship service"—will some one find for me such expressions in the Bible? We are picking too many things out of denominational garbage cans.

"Sponsor." Words spread out in their uses. About fifty years ago sponsor was defined as follows in Webster's International Dictionary: "1. One who binds himself to answer for another, and is responsible for his default; a surety. 2. One who at the baptism of an infant professes the Christian faith in his name, and guarantees its religious obligation; a godfather or godmother." It has a wider application now, but its meaning has not changed. Only in late years has this noun been used as a verb. If a church sends a preacher to do a certain work and assumes all obligations for his support and for all necessary expenses, it can be said that it sponsors that preacher. But even so, we do not read in the New Testament that any church was a sponsor for a preacher in a certain meeting or mission. We sometimes speak where the Bible does not speak.

"Suggest." No one should say in print or in oral speech anything that might have a tendency to lessen in the minds of people the importance of anything God says or commands. Sometimes it is unwittingly done. I used to hear a faithful preacher on the radio frequently say, "May I suggest to you." He used the word *suggest* till its use became such a habit that he said, "Paul suggests." Then I heard another say "Jesus suggests." It sounds bad when preachers soften God's commands to mere suggestions, or were these brethren using words without knowing what they were saying? When God commands, do not say he suggests, lest some one suggest that a suggestion is binding on no one.

"Truth—Fact." We have used the word "fact" so loosely that it now is made to apply to everything that is real; but in reality it applies to what has been done or what has occurred. "Truth is, in general, conformity to fact or reality." That God is, is a truth but not a fact. The death, burial, and resurrection of Christ are facts, and also truths. Truth is the broader term, covering all facts and all realities. We used to hear something like this; The gospel of Christ consists in truths to be believed, facts to be received, commands to be obeyed, and promises to be enjoyed.

"Two three-letter words." The devil completely changed the meaning of what God said to Adam and Eve by inserting a little three-letter word; and by inserting another little three-letter word some have represented Peter as saying to Simon, "Thou art *yet* in the gall of bitterness and in the bond of iniquity." Some heard it quoted that way so much they thought the word "yet" belonged there. The word "yet" was added in the interest of the doctrine of the impossibility of apostasy, to show that Simon had not really been saved. Adding a word to support a doctrine is sinful. And another statement is made up to support this same doctrine. You have heard this: "Judas was a devil from the beginning." And that statement has been so often repeated, that some brethren think it is in the Bible.

And there is the *unto-into* argument. You have heard that "unto" indicates the direction of the act, and "into" puts one into that toward which "unto" was directed. And so you have perhaps seen this outline on chart and blackboard: "Believe unto righteousness"—"Repentance unto life"—"Baptized into Christ." It is a pretty argument; but an apostle could not have made it, because unto and into are translations of the same Greek preposition. It is *eis* righteousness, *eis* life, *eis* Christ. Now if you still want to make an argument on into-unto, and argue that unto tends toward a goal, but does not reach, then read Acts 2:38—American Standard Version: "Repent ye, and be baptized every one of you in the name of Jesus Christ unto the remission of your sins." How will you make the unto idea work there. And remember we have the same Greek preposition here. Another defect in this *into-unto* argument is the thoughtless perversion of Acts 11:18. Some days— possibly some weeks—after Peter baptized Cornelius and those with him, he returned to Jerusalem. The brethren there brought a charge against him, which he answered to their satisfaction. "And when they heard these things, they held their peace, and glorified God, saying, Then to the Gentiles also hath God granted repentance unto life." Now, life is in Christ; and Cornelius and his people had already been baptized into Christ. These brethren did not therefore mean that Cornelius and those with him were just on the way to life. Sometimes one condition of salvation is mentioned as including all the conditions. That is true of repentance here and also in Acts 17:30,31: "The times of this ignorance therefore God overlooked; but now he commandeth men that they should all everywhere repent: inasmuch as he hath appointed a day in which he will judge the world in righteousness by the man whom he hath ordained; whereof he hath given assurance unto all men, in that he hath raised him from the dead." Repentance here includes all that is necessary to prepare one to be judged in righteousness. The same thing is true of some other words. The word turn sometimes includes all that is included in becoming a Christian, and sometimes it does not. Compare Acts 3:19; 11:21; 14:15; 15:19; 25:18. And so does the word believe, and the word faith sometimes includes the whole process of becoming a Christian.

The brethren at Jerusalem did not refer exclusively to Cornelius and his people, but to Gentiles in general. God had now granted to them the right to become Christians, and enjoy the life of Christ. Surely no one will contend that God had merely granted the Gentiles the right to repent in the direction of life!

"Vision." Some years ago some people of the denominations claimed to see visions, or to have visions. They would tell about them in giving their experiences. But brethren then knew the Bible meanings of visions. But now some of "our preachers" not knowing the Bible meaning of visions, urge churches to have visions, and ignorantly pervert Prov. 29:18. The common version reads, "Where there is no vision the people perish." The American Standard Version reads, "Where there is no vision, the people cast off restraint." Lesser, a Jew gives this translation: "Without a prophetic vision, a people become unruly." I remember the first time I heard a brother preacher quote that verse, and apply it to our own plans and purposes; his making such use of the verse astonished me. Now the verse is perverted by many preachers who condemn sectarians for perverting the Scriptures. Am I right, or am I seeing visions?

"Want—Need." Many times of late I have read in the papers such expressions, as, "God wants us to do" thus and so; "Christ wants us to do" so and so. Now does the word *want*, used as a verb, suggest any authority on the part of him who wants a thing to be done. I have often wanted certain things done, but there is no authority in what I want. Take your concordance and you will find that the noun *want* is used a number of times in the sense of *need* or a lack of something; but I do not recall any place that says God wants anything. Let us not soften God's commands as if he merely wants or suggests certain things. To me such softening of God's commands is abominable. Besides, *want* implies a need. I recommend that some writers consult the Dictionary to see the meaning of some every day words.

Anvil Sparks:

Prejudice is a robber which many of us entertain in our hearts. It robs us of generous feelings which we should have for others, and leaves us the tormentings of hate; by shutting our eyes and stopping our ears it robs us of many precious truths, and leaves us the dross of our distorted opinions; it robs us of light, and shuts us up in the darkness of our own ignorance. No other robber can leave us so poor.

The scarcity of serious thinking is a serious thought.

Building up a party spirit is not edifying the church.

The intellect directs, the emotions generate heart, and the will turns on the steam.

Sometimes you can know which way you are headed by looking at the crowd with you.

Credit the monkey with this: He has not become upish over being exalted to such close kinship with man.

Index

(379)